Learning CSS3 Animations Transitions

Addison-Wesley Learning Series

▲ Addison-Wesley

Visit informit.com/learningseries for a complete list of available publications.

The Addison-Wesley Learning Series is a collection of hands-on programming guides that help you quickly learn a new technology or language so you can apply what you've learned right away.

Each title comes with sample code for the application or applications built in the text. This code is fully annotated and can be reused in your own projects with no strings attached. Many chapters end with a series of exercises to encourage you to reexamine what you have just learned, and to tweak or adjust the code as a way of learning.

Titles in this series take a simple approach: they get you going right away and leave you with the ability to walk off and build your own application and apply the language or technology to whatever you are working on.

▲ Addison-Wesley   **informIT.com** | Safari" Books Online

ALWAYS LEARNING   PEARSO

Learning CSS3 Animations and Transitions:

A Hands-on Guide to Animating in CSS3
with Transforms, Transitions,
Keyframe Animations, and JavaScript

Alexis Goldstein

✦✦Addison-Wesley

Upper Saddle River, NJ • Boston • Indianapolis • San Francisco
New York • Toronto • Montreal • London • Munich • Paris • Madrid
Cape Town • Sydney • Tokyo • Singapore • Mexico City

Many of the designations used by manufacturers and sellers to distinguish their products are claimed as trademarks. Where those designations appear in this book, and the publisher was aware of a trademark claim, the designations have been printed with initial capital letters or in all capitals.

The author and publisher have taken care in the preparation of this book, but make no expressed or implied warranty of any kind and assume no responsibility for errors or omissions. No liability is assumed for incidental or consequential damages in connection with or arising out of the use of the information or programs contained herein.

The publisher offers excellent discounts on this book when ordered in quantity for bulk purchases or special sales, which may include electronic versions and/or custom covers and content particular to your business, training goals, marketing focus, and branding interests. For more information, please contact:

U.S. Corporate and Government Sales

(800) 382-3419

corpsales@pearsontechgroup.com

For sales outside the United States, please contact:

International Sales

international@pearsoned.com

Visit us on the Web: informit.com/aw

Library of Congress Cataloging-in-Publication Data is on file.

Adobe and Flash are either registered trademarks or trademarks of Adobe Systems Incorporated in the United States and/or other countries.

ISBN-13: 978-0-321-83960-2

ISBN-10: 0-321-83960-9

Text printed in the United States on recycled paper at Edward Brothers Malloy in Ann Arbor, MI.

First printing: December 2012

Editor-in-Chief:
Mark Taub

Acquisitions Editor:
Trina MacDonald

Development Editor:
Michael Thurston

Managing Editor:
Kristy Hart

Project Editor:
Elaine Wiley

Copy Editor:
Kitty Wilson

Indexer: WordWise Publishing Services

Proofreader:
Deborah Williams

Technical Reviewers:
Joseph Annuzzi, Jr.
Louis Lazaris

Editorial Assistant:
Olivia Basegio

Cover Designer:
Chuti Prasertsith

Senior Compositor:
Gloria Schurick

❖

To my family

❖

Contents at a Glance

Table of Contents

Preface

Welcome aboard *Learning CSS3 Animations*! We're so glad you've joined us for a journey through all the fun that CSS animations can bring. This practical, example-driven text explains the basics of CSS animations and how you can use them, and it provides you with plenty of examples both simple and complex in order to give you many jumping-off points for your own code. You will explore examples that are purely HTML and CSS driven, as well as examples that make use of JavaScript and jQuery to serve as animation triggers or to add interactivity to the page.

CSS3 has brought with it a wave of new ways to add life, movement, and neat effects to your sites. These can be simple enhancements to existing pages, or they can be rich, complex animations that add new content to your sites.

The cornerstone of this book is simple code examples and detailed explanations of the techniques used in the code. The book presents a series of examples that highlight a given CSS animation technique and gives you a starting point to customize your own sites and projects.

Where it is practical to do so, the examples use CSS itself in order to craft CSS-created graphics rather than relying on images. The idea behind this approach is that it gives you more practice using the inherent drawing and visual effect-creating abilities of CSS3. But, one can just as easily take the animation concepts learned in such examples, and use with custom tailored images.

Who This Book Is For

This book is aimed at beginning and intermediate-level web developers and designers who have a solid foundation in HTML and CSS, as well as a basic grasp of HTML5 and CSS3. While you need not have expert-level knowledge of all topics in CSS3 (if you did, you wouldn't need this book), you should have an overall grasp of things like vendor prefixes and how they are used in CSS3, as well as popular new properties in CSS3, such as `text-shadow` and `border-radius`.

Who This Book Isn't For

This book is not for absolute beginners who have never used HTML or CSS. This book is also not for those with basic HTML or CSS skills and no experience at all in CSS3 who are looking to get up to speed. This book presumes a solid foundation in HTML/CSS and at least a passing familiarity with the new CSS3 properties (those that don't have to do with animations, that is!).

If you are not familiar with basic CSS concepts such as what a selector is, the kinds of selectors you have to choose from, and how you use them, you'll need to acquire that knowledge before this book is of use to you. This book does not devote any time to reviewing the basics of CSS, how it interacts with HTML, and the most common CSS properties.

How This Book Is Organized

This book consists of 11 chapters, each of which contains detailed code examples to demonstrate the concepts discussed. Nearly all chapters build on content presented in previous chapters. It is suggested that you read them continuously rather than skip around.

Chapter 1, "Working with CSS3 Animations"

Chapter 1 discusses the approach this book takes to browser support, including a review of the Modernizr JavaScript library, which you can use to detect which HTML5 features are supported in the user's browser, as well as other tools and resources that are recommended for use throughout this book in order to make development easier.

Chapter 2, "Building a Foundation with Transforms"

Much of this book leverages the power of CSS3 transforms. Chapter 2 introduces the various kinds of two-dimensional transforms that can be accomplished with CSS3, in order to get you familiar with the effects it can achieve. In this chapter, you use transforms to draw a bicycle using only CSS.

Chapter 3, "Animating Elements with Transitions"

Chapter 3 discusses how you can combine transforms with transitions in order to animate changes over a period of time. It discusses how other CSS properties can be animated through transitions. In this chapter you enhance the bicycle example from Chapter 2 to spin the bike wheels and move the bike itself in response to user actions.

Chapter 4, "Keyframe Animations"

Keyframe animations give you more fine-grained control over the various stages of an animation than transitions do. In Chapter 4 you learn about the many properties available for use with keyframe animations by applying them to a simple animation. You also create a bouncing spring and a floating balloon in order to see the effects you can achieve through the use of keyframe animations.

Chapter 5, "Creating 3D Effects with Parallax Scrolling"

Chapter 5 combines keyframe animations and transforms with the concept of parallax scrolling, which allow you to build content that has a 3D feel without actually doing any 3D manipulation. This chapter outlines two sample projects, both of which use the concept of parallax scrolling to create a sense of depth in a 2D space.

Chapter 6, "Adding Depth with 3D Transforms"

Chapter 6 reviews how to change the depth of elements through the use of 3D transform properties. It explores the various transform functions that can be applied to the `transform` property, as well as how to effectively use the `perspective` property in order to view the results of your transforms.

Chapter 7, "Animating 2D and 3D Transforms"

Chapter 7 demonstrates how you can combine 2D and 3D transforms with CSS3 transitions and keyframe animations in order to create interesting effects. In this chapter, you enhance the 3D cube you built in Chapter 6 with transitions, a few HTML5 range input type elements, and a bit of JavaScript in order to allow the cube to be rotated about each of the three axes.

Chapter 8, "Using Transitions and Transforms to Animate Text"

In Chapter 8 you combine keyframe animations, transitions, transforms, and a bit of jQuery to create a text-driven animation. You use CSS3 to do some basic styling on elements to make them look like a part of a typewriter, and then you animate the text the typewriter types to give life to a much-loved quote by Virginia Woolf.

Chapter 9, "Building Flash-Style Animations with Keyframe Animations"

In Chapter 9 you create a cartoon-style animation of a cat that combines the approaches discussed in previous chapters. The animation includes two characters across a few different scenes, animated through the use of keyframe animations, that are triggered by JavaScript timers.

Chapter 10, "Creating Animated Infographics"

Chapter 10 covers the basics of infographics and how you can enhance them by adding CSS animations. Combining the techniques used previously in this book, Chapter 10 outlines the steps to build a simple data visualization of the ratios of different ingredients in six kinds of mixed drinks. CSS animations are used as an enhancement that improves on the base infographic.

Chapter 11, "Building Interactive Infographics"

A natural enhancement to infographics on the web is the addition of interactivity to the diagrams through a language such as JavaScript or a library such as jQuery. In Chapter 11, you make some simple additions to the infographic from Chapter 10, enriching it with the details of the drink recipes using a combination of CSS animations and jQuery.

About the Sample Code

The sample code for this book is all compiled on GitHub. The code is available at https://github.com/alexisgo/LearningCSSAnimations for easy forking. If you find any issues with the sample code, I encourage you to file an issue at the GitHub project page for the book.

If you have never worked with GitHub or git before, not to worry! You can also download a zip archive containing all the code from the GitHub site. The specific link to the zip file is https://github.com/alexisgo/LearningCSSAnimations/zipball/master.

In addition, a website outlines all the examples in all the chapters and provides links to demos of the examples. This page is http://alexisgo.github.com/LearningCSSAnimations/, and I encourage you to have it open as you read through the book so you can test the examples you build throughout the text.

Acknowledgments

Thank you to Chuck Toporek, who first encouraged me to take on this project.

Thank you to my technical editors, Anthony Calzadilla, Joseph Annuzzi, Jr., and, of course, Louis Lazaris. Anthony is a wizard of CSS3-driven animations, having created stunning projects such as Madmanimation (http://animatable.com/demos/madmanimation/) and the adorable Rofox CSS3 animation for Mozilla's Demo Studios (https://developer.mozilla.org/en-US/demos/detail/rofox-css3-animation-by-anthony-calzadilla), and it was an honor to have his feedback for this text. I am indebted to Joseph for his testing of my code and his discovery of those errant code samples I wrote, abandoned, and then forgot to remove. And I have now had the pleasure of working with Louis Lazaris and gaining from his expertise across two book projects, and I am ever grateful for his wide expertise, attention to detail, and tremendous help in the course of this project. Louis's eyes on this text have made it immensely better than it would have been without him.

Thank you to Kitty Wilson for a heroic effort and invaluable help with copyedits. Thank you to Elaine Wiley for help during the Production phase.

A very big thank you to my editor Trina MacDonald, for her invaluable help and assistance throughout this process.

Thank you to Tab, who tolerated many, many evenings of me coding and writing late into the night in the course of this project.

Thank you to my family, who have been a very solid source of support over a very difficult summer.

Finally, thank you to my late father. You always believed in me, and you were such a wonderful, wonderful dad. I will carry the lessons that you taught me, the pride that you had in me, and the tremendous pride that I have in you, with me always. I miss you, more than I could ever hope to express in words. Thank you for everything.

About the Author

Alexis Goldstein first taught herself HTML while a high school student in the mid-1990s and went on to get a bachelor's degree in computer science from Columbia University. Alexis previously co-authored the book *HTML5 & CSS3 for the Real World* with Louis Lazaris and Estelle Weyl. Alexis began her career with a seven-year stint in technology on Wall Street, where she worked in both the cash equity and equity derivative spaces at three major firms and learned to love daily code reviews. Alexis now runs a software development and training company, aut faciam LLC. She also teaches with Girl Develop It in New York, a group that conducts low-cost programming classes for women, and is a member of NYC Resistor in Brooklyn. In her spare time, you can find Alexis organizing with affinity groups of Occupy Wall Street in New York City.

1

Working with CSS3 Animations

CSS3 animations have gained enormous interest and popularity, in part due to the lack of support for traditional Flash animations in mobile devices such as the iPhone. This chapter introduces the tools this book uses to deal with browser support. It reviews how to use the Modernizr JavaScript library to ensure that older browsers are notified of missing content and nudge users toward a newer browser. This chapter also reviews other tools and resources that make development easier.

Intro to CSS3 Animations

The effects available with CSS3-driven animations can typically be achieved through other means, such as JavaScript-based animations and Flash®. So why use CSS3 animations?

Like much of HTML5, the CSS3 animations and related specs bring techniques commonly accomplished through plugins or external libraries and make them part of the core standard. CSS3 also simplifies the process of creating animations, allowing us to leverage web standards to create dynamic effects rather than use plugins such as Flash® that do not work on all devices.

> **Note**
>
> When I use the term "CSS3 Animations" in this book, I am using to refer to both transitions (which will be discussed in Chapter 3, "Animating Elements with Transitions"), and keyframe animations (discussed in Chapter 4, "Keyframe Animations").

This book explores the new features of CSS3 animations, explaining how to use them through basic examples that demonstrate the key concepts. More than focusing on what is safe or conservative or universal, this book digs into what's possible with a little imagination. As you work with CSS3 animations in this book, you won't be bending over backward to accommodate older browsers. While it is certainly possible to re-create every animation you will build in this book in a JavaScript library such as jQuery or MooTools in order to achieve universal support, this isn't a book about animating with JavaScript libraries. This book instead focuses on creating animations for modern browsers and mobile devices, and it avoids re-creating the animations for older, unsupported browsers. And while this book doesn't specify exhaustive fallback code and explanations in absolutely every chapter, it does provide you with fallbacks often enough that you will have the knowledge and practice you need to write your own custom fallbacks, as needed.

The source code for this and all subsequent chapters can be found on this book's GitHub site: https://github.com/alexisgo/LearningCSSAnimations. I have also supplied a demo site, alexisgo.github.com/LearningCSSAnimations/, where you can find demos of all examples, so that you can follow along with the code and see the results as you make your way through this book.

Summary of CSS3 Animation Tools

Web developers, designers and animators can use a number of tools in order to make our lives easier and leverage the expertise of the web development community. These tools range from templates like the HTML5 Boilerplate, to online tools like css3please and Animation Fill Code, to libraries like -prefix-free.

HTML5 Boilerplate

The HTML5 Boilerplate (http://html5boilerplate.com), or "H5BP" for short, is a wonderful template started by Paul Irish and Divya Manian and maintained by a number of talented contributors, including Shi Chuan, Mathias Bynens, and Nicholas Gallagher. The H5BP allows you to leverage the collective wisdom of the web community and quickly get going with HTML5. Rather than learn through painful firsthand experience, the must-have Internet Explorer directives, or the really-should-have-added-that CSS reset, the H5BP gives you a starting point with all of that code already provided.

The H5BP includes a large collection of files in its basic template, including a 404.html page and a default favicon. For our purposes, the most important resource that comes with the H5BP is its stylesheet. Rather than rewrite custom reset styles yourself or set up your own @media queries to adjust your styles for mobile browsers as needed, why not use the tools that a panel of experts have already compiled? Throughout this book, you will see the sample code include a CSS file called base.css. This file is based on conventions in the H5BP's stylesheets, which you can explore on their GitHub page at https://github.com/h5bp/html5-boilerplate.

Tools for Generating Vendor Prefixes

One of the biggest headaches of writing CSS3 animations—particularly keyframe animations, which are covered in Chapter 4—is generating all the appropriate vendor prefixes. Two tools can help you do this: Prefixr and css3please.

Prefixr

One tool that I strongly recommend to assist you with the generation of the vendor-specific code is Prefixr (http://prefixr.com) by Jeffrey Way. This tool allows you to write all your CSS using just the standard syntax. When you are finished and happy with your page, you paste your code into the tool, and it generates all the vendor prefixes for you. This is an invaluable resource that will save you lots of time, allowing you to take the basic code you've written and extend it to work across all browsers.

css3please.com

Another tool that can assist with the generation of the vendor-specific code is css3please (http://css3please.com). You can use this online editor to specify a given property, and then it automatically updates the other vendor prefixes with the values you have specified. There is a link to copy the code generated to the clipboard, as well as a simple element that will generate a preview of the styles you have specified. Figure 1.1 shows an example of using css3please to generate the necessary code for the `border-radius` property.

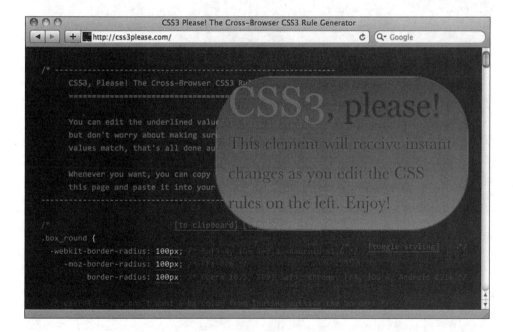

Figure 1.1   Dynamically generating all `border-radius` vendor prefixes with css3please

In terms of best practices, it is always a good idea to pick which browser you will use for testing and then code only to that specific vendor prefix as you develop your page. It is not a good idea to try to insert all of the vendor prefixes right from the beginning, as you will inevitably need to change your code after some testing, and that means regenerating all the vendor prefixes. Thus, I recommend coding just to one browser, and when your code is complete, use Prefixr or css3please to generate the other vendor prefixes, and then test your code in all of the browsers.

Animation Fill Code

Another tool that is specific to keyframe animations is a tool by Louis Lazaris called Animation Fill Code (http://animationfillcode.com). With this online tool, you write keyframe at-rules (more on this in Chapter 4) in one vendor prefix, select which prefix you're using from a set of radio buttons, and paste in your code. The tool generates the other needed keyframe at-rules for you. You can see this tool in action in Figure 1.2.

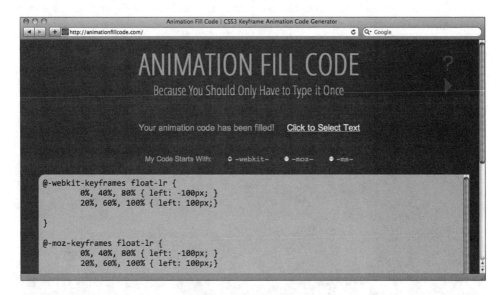

Figure 1.2   Dynamically generating all keyframe at-rule vendor prefixes with Animation Fill Code

-prefix-free

Another tool for generating vendor prefixes is Lea Verou's JavaScript library -prefix-free. -prefix-free is a JavaScript CSS processor that adds the required vendor prefixes automatically, based on the browser the visitor is using. You can download the library from http://leaverou.github.com/prefixfree/. You can read Verou's article describing the library at http://coding.smashingmagazine.com/2011/10/12/prefixfree-break-free-from-css-prefix-hell/.

Tools for Reviewing Browser Support

This book provides detailed information about specific browser support for each feature discussed. For more information on browser support, the best resource is the website http://caniuse.com, which allows you to search or browse by feature and see a matrix of how various features are supported by different browsers and versions. The site is constantly updated and also provides links to relevant articles about the features.

Another worthy site is http://html5please.com. It provides suggestions about whether to use a given feature, and provides information on how fallbacks should be provided. It covers CSS3 features as well as other new HTML5 features that are outside the scope of this book.

The Modernizr Library

If you have used HTML5 at all, you have undoubtedly heard of the Modernizr JavaScript library (http://modernizr.com). The Modernizr library allows you to test, on a feature-by-feature basis, what is supported by a visitor's browser. You can use the dynamically generated classes for styling hooks in CSS, you can query a global Modernizr object that it creates, or you can do both, and then you can customize your pages to fall back when certain features are not supported.

Modernizr also includes a key feature called html5shiv, which solves a problem that exists in Internet Explorer version 8 and earlier. In Internet Explorer 8 and earlier, if you try to style an element that Internet Explorer does not recognize—for example, some of the new HTML5 elements, such as `section` or `article`—the element will not be styled. This problem prevented many designers and developers from using the new HTML5 semantic elements. In response, the web development community quickly came up with a solution. In January 2009, Remy Sharp created the HTML5 enabling script, which uses a technique first discovered by Sjoerd Visscher to get around the problem with Internet Explorer by simply creating the unknown elements programmatically via JavaScript. Modernizr leverages this same technique in its html5shiv to ensure that older browsers that don't recognize the new elements are still able to apply styles to them.

But the real power of Modernizr is its ability to check for the presence of specific features. When you download Modernizr, you must specify which features you want to check for, as you can see in Figure 1.3.

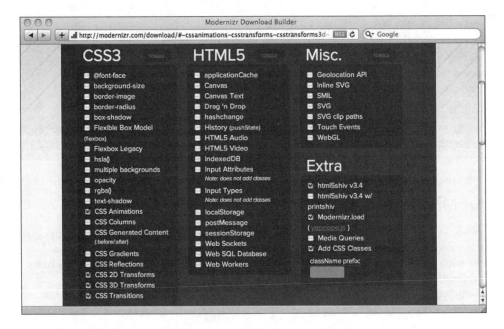

Figure 1.3   Customizing a Modernizr build

As you read this book, you need a copy of Modernizr that can check for the following features:

- CSS animations (also known as keyframe animations)
- CSS 2D transforms
- CSS 3D transforms
- CSS transitions
- html5shiv

The sample code for this book includes a production copy of Modernizr that is configured to check for all of these features. Instead of using the copy of Modernizr that comes with this book, you could customize your own build of Modernizr, selecting the features you plan on using in your website. Or, you could download the development version of Modernizr, which includes checks for all features and also consists of non-minified JavaScript code, so you can learn from the library and how it works. But for live websites, you will always want to use a production version that only checks for the features you will be using.

Leveraging the Modernizr Library

When you use a customized build for Modernizr, you need to reference it from the head element of your HTML page because the html5shiv enables HTML5 elements in Internet Explorer and so must execute before the body. HTML5 documentation also suggests that the

Modernizr script be placed after the style sheet references. In Listing 1.1, we include the link to Modernizr in the head section, as well as a link to the two stylesheets we'll be using, base.css and error.css (which will be defined later, in Listing 1.3).

Listing 1.1   **Preparing a Page for Modernizr to Run (warning.html)**

```
<html class="no-js" lang="en">
  <head>
    <link rel="stylesheet" href="css/base.css">
    <link rel="stylesheet" href="css/error.css">
    <script src="js/modernizr.custom.57498.js"></script>
  </head>
```

Modernizr is particularly useful because it gives you a choice of how to use it. You can use it by writing conditional CSS or by querying the global Modernizr object that the library creates. This chapter focuses on using Modernizr to create styling hooks via CSS.

CSS Fallbacks via Modernizr

The first thing that Modernizr does when it runs is loop through all the features you've asked it to check for and make note of which ones are supported and which ones are unsupported by adding entries to the class attribute of the opening html element.

But before Modernizr can do its job, you need to set up one last thing with your page. You need to add the class no-js to the html element:

```
<html class="no-js">
```

When Modernizr runs, if your browser has JavaScript enabled, it will replace that class with the class "js":

```
<html class="js">
```

This gives you a styling hook that reflects whether JavaScript is enabled. Modernizr then adds classes for *every* feature it detects, prefixing them with no- if the browser doesn't support it. For the custom build of Modernizr you use in this book, the latest version of Chrome generates the following:

```
<html class="js cssanimations csstransforms csstransforms3d csstransitions" lang="en">
```

The Default Message for Unsupported Browsers

For each animation you create in this book, you will leverage Modernizr to perform a check to see if the browser supports the features you need to run the animation. In the browsers that don't have the proper support, you could provide, if you like, a default message that informs the visitor of the problem and provide links to download one of the new browsers with the appropriate support.

This message will consist of a simple div element, some text and links, and the most basic of styling. By default, this div will be styled to display: none. But if any of the required features you rely on for your animations are not present, a selector will follow the default styling to update this div to display and to add additional styles to it.

Listing 1.2 outlines the code for this fallback message, which is contained in the file `warning.html`. In addition to the fallback message, which includes an unordered list with links to the modern browsers, the listing includes a small div called `#dismiss` that can be used to close this message. Toward the end of Listing 1.2 you can find the JavaScript that hooks the `#dismiss` element up to a click event and then applies the style hide to the `#unsupportedBrowser` element upon click. You can find the complete `warning.html` file in the ch1code/ folder of this book's GitHub project, available at: https://github.com/alexisgo/LearningCSSAnimations.

Listing 1.2   HTML and JavaScript for a Warning Message (warning.html)

```
<body>
  <div id="unsupportedBrowser">
    <div id="dismiss">
      <span>x</span>
    </div>
    <div id="warningText">
      Oh no! Your browser doesn't support CSS3 animations! Please download one of
      the following modern browsers in order to see what you're missing!

      <ul>
        <li><a href="http://www.mozilla.org/en-US/firefox/new/">Firefox</a></li>
        <li><a href="http://www.google.com/chrome">Chrome</a></li>
        <li><a href="http://www.apple.com/safari/download/">Safari</a></li>
        <li><a href="http://www.opera.com/">Opera</a></li>
        <li><a href="http://ie.microsoft.com/testdrive/">IE 10</a></li>
      </ul>
    </div>
  </div>

  <h1>YOYOYOYOYOYOYO</h1>

  <script type="text/javascript">
  window.onload = setup;

  function setup() {
    var dismiss = document.getElementById("dismiss");
    dismiss.onclick = hide;
  }
  function hide() {
    document.getElementById("unsupportedBrowser").className = "hide";
  }
  </script>
</body>
```

Listing 1.3 first styles the `#unsupportedBrowser` div to not display by default. Next, the code applies some basic styles to the unordered list. The fun kicks in after that, when you leverage Modernizr's additions to the opening `html` tag in order to define a grouped selector. This grouped selector will be applied if even one of the key features is missing.

The grouped selector used will vary slightly based on each specific example used in the book, as not all examples use all the features checked for in Listing 1.1. Typically, the examples reviewed in subsequent chapters check for a subset of the list in Listing 1.3.

After the large grouped selector, let's add some additional styles for the links, as well as the `#dismiss` div. Figure 1.4 shows what the warning looks like.

Listing 1.3 **Custom Style for an "Unsupported Browser" Message Added to H5BP Base CSS File (error.css)**

```css
#unsupportedBrowser, #unsupportedBrowser.hide { display:none; }

#unsupportedBrowser ul li {
  display: inline;
  list-style-type: none;
  padding: 0 10px;
}

#unsupportedBrowser ul  { margin:5px; }

.no-keyframes #unsupportedBrowser,
.no-cssanimations #unsupportedBrowser,
.no-csstransforms #unsupportedBrowser,
.no-csstransitions #unsupportedBrowser
{
  display: block;
  text-align: center;
  width: 100%;
  font-size: 0.8em;
  padding: 10px;
  background-color: rgb(15,70,131);
  color: white;

  -webkit-box-shadow: 0px 2px 2px rgba(0,0,0,0.2);
     -moz-box-shadow: 0px 2px 2px rgba(0,0,0,0.2);
          box-shadow: 0px 2px 2px rgba(0,0,0,0.2);
}

#unsupportedBrowser a { color:white; font-weight:bold; }

#unsupportedBrowser #dismiss {
  background-color: rgb(242,242,242);
```

```
    width: 25px;
    height: 25px;
    color: red;
    -webkit-border-radius: 13px;
    -moz-border-radius: 13px;
    border-radius: 13px;

    -webkit-box-shadow: 1px 1px 2px rgba(0,0,0,0.2);
        -moz-box-shadow: 1px 1px 2px rgba(0,0,0,0.2);
            box-shadow: 1px 1px 2px rgba(0,0,0,0.2);

    position:absolute;
    right: 3%;
    top: 2%;
    margin-left: 100px;
    font-size: 1.2em;
}

#warningText { margin:0 10%; }
```

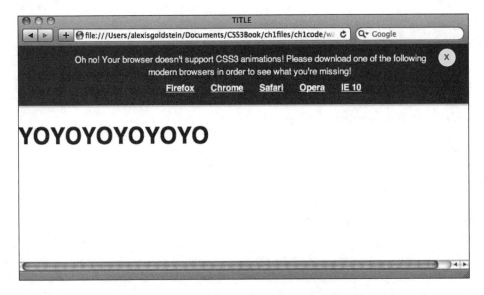

Figure 1.4   A default warning message that appears if the required properties for the CSS3 animation examples are not present.

While there are certainly more graceful and labor-intensive means to falling back when a visitor is using an older browser—namely, rewriting your animation with a library jQuery—the aim of this book is to focus on what you can do with the new technologies, not how to use old ones.

Thus, rather than waste space reviewing old techniques, this book focuses on the new properties and how to use them most effectively.

One approach you might take when dealing with CSS3 animations is to fall back to a plain static object that doesn't animate. That way, the animation is a bonus for modern browsers. In a real world project, it's often best to allow the animation to degrade to a static object or group of objects.

Repeated CSS Property Definitions

There are times in this book when you will make use of another new CSS3 property, rgba, which allows you to add an alpha value to colors in order to make them semi-transparent. While Modernizr does support checking for this property, you can use a simple method to accommodate noncompliant browsers: Use repeated CSS property definitions.

Anytime you use the new rgba property, you preface that line with a simple background-color property. That way, if the browser does not support rgba, it simply ignores that line and applies the background-color property from the line before. For example, see the code in Listing 1.4.

Listing 1.4   **Repeated CSS to Allow for Older Browsers**

```
#someSelector {
  background-color: black;
  background-color: rgba(0,0,0,0.4);
}
```

Hardware Acceleration

Later in this book, when you understand the basics and begin to tackle more complex animations, the question of performance becomes very important. In order to optimize the ways your CSS3 animations run, you will use hardware-accelerated properties as much as possible. Hardware acceleration is the ability of certain devices to offload work from the CPU to the GPU (the graphics processing unit, more commonly referred to as simply "the graphics card"). In order to view hardware acceleration, you can take advantage of some features in Chrome and Safari.

In CSS3 there are a few properties that can take advantage of hardware acceleration:

- CSS3 transitions

- translate3d

- translateZ

Chapter 3 discusses CSS3 transitions, and Chapters 6 and 7 explore translate3d and translateZ. The best way to see if using these properties is having an effect is to color any hardware-accelerated layers in a distinctive way so you can easily see them. You can achieve this in both Chrome and Safari by setting certain browser options.

Viewing Hardware-Accelerated Layers in Chrome

To view hardware-accelerated layers in Chrome, you can simply type about:flags into the URL bar. This launches the currently available experimental features in Chrome, including composited render layer borders. After you change the setting, you reboot Chrome in order to see the change take effect.

For example, you can apply a green border to any layer that is being composited on the GPU. Figure 1.5 shows the results that Chrome displays when you view a scene from Anthony Calzadilla's impressive CSS3-driven Madmanimation animation (http://animatable.com/demos/madmanimation/).

Figure 1.5   Chrome's composite render layer borders feature in action at http://animatable.com/demos/madmanimation/

Viewing Hardware-Accelerated Layers in Safari

To view hardware-accelerated layers on a Mac, you launch the Terminal application (which can be found at Applications > Utilities > Terminal) and type in the following command:

```
$ CA_COLOR_OPAQUE=1 /Applications/Safari.app/Contents/MacOS/Safari
```

All hardware-accelerated layers are then shaded in red, as shown in Figure 1.6.

Figure 1.6   Safari's hardware-accelerated layer coloring in action at http://animatable.com/demos/madmanimation/

> **Caution**
>
> Use caution when changing these settings in Chrome. It is a good idea to turn these settings on while you are reviewing your pages and then revert to the previous settings when you're done. You would likely do this anyway, as the color scheme makes things a bit difficult to read!

A Final Word on Working with CSS3 Animations

CSS3 animations are, like many other HTML5 features, a standard in flux. Just as one example, the W3C resolved in January 2012 to work on a universal animation spec that would work across CSS, SVG, and HTML (see http://www.w3.org/2012/01/13-svg-minutes.html#action02 and http://www.w3.org/Graphics/SVG/WG/wiki/F2F/Sydney_2012/Agenda/Animations/WebAnimations). But does this mean that we shouldn't move forward with the standards that exist today and enjoy very good support in modern browsers? Of course not. This just means that what we learn today may serve as a building block for future iterations of the specification. And isn't that how technology works, after all? It builds upon itself, and it improves with every change.

This book is all about showing you what's possible now and how to effectively create dynamic, fun effects and animations for your visitors. So let's get started.

Building a Foundation with Transforms

Transforms serve as the foundation for many of the animations described in this book. This chapter introduces the various kinds of two-dimensional transforms that can be accomplished with CSS3. As a sample project, you will create a bicycle using only CSS, and you will use CSS3 transforms to assist in its creation.

Introducing Transforms

With CSS3 transforms, you can manipulate elements by using various transform functions, changing their skew, scale, and rotation, for example. You use the `transform` property together with one or more transform functions that define how to change an element. These are the available transform functions:

rotate: You use this function to rotate an element clockwise or counterclockwise.

scale: You use this function to resize an element by scaling its width up or down, its height up or down, or both.

skew: You use this function to add a slant to an element along a specific axis.

translate: You use this function to move an element along the x- or y-axis.

matrix: You use this function to specify multiple transforms on an element at once.

In this chapter, you will first walk through the basics of each of the available transform properties by manipulating a simple `div` element. Then you will use the concepts reviewed to draw a bicycle using only `div` elements, a handful of CSS, and some transforms.

Browser Support for `transform`

CSS3 transforms enjoy nearly universal support in modern browsers. The main exception is Internet Explorer versions 8 and earlier. (You will hear this many times throughout this book.) The following browsers support `transform` and the transform functions:

Android Browser 2.1+

Chrome 4.0+

Firefox 3.5+

Internet Explorer 9.0+

iOS Safari 3.2+ and Safari 3.1+

Opera 10.5+

The source for this and all other browser support lists throughout this book is the invaluable site http://caniuse.com.

The `transform` Syntax

This is the basic syntax for using transforms:

```
transform: <transform-function>
```

If you would like to apply more than one transform function, you can specify a list of transform functions separated by spaces:

```
transform: <transform-function1> <transform-function2> <transform-function3>
```

As is the case for many of the other CSS3 properties used in this book, you need to use a list of vendor-specific versions of the property before specifying the actual property name. In order to get transforms to work in all supported browsers, you can specify the transform like this:

```
-webkit-transform: <transform-function>;
   -moz-transform: <transform-function>;
    -ms-transform: <transform-function>;
     -o-transform: <transform-function>;
        transform: <transform-function>;
```

At the time of this writing, the standard version (`transform`) is supported by Internet Explorer 10 (Internet Explorer 9 still requires the -ms- prefix, thus we still need to use it to ensure support for that version), Opera 12.5 (Opera 12 and earlier still requires the -o- prefix), and Firefox 16 (earlier versions of Firefox still require the -moz- prefix). Firefox 16 is upcoming at the time of this writing, but new standard syntax support is documented at https://hacks.mozilla.org/2012/07/aurora-16-is-out/.

Fun with Vendor Prefixes

If you are new to CSS3, you may be wondering why the `transform` property is repeated so many times in so many different flavors. As with other new technologies, CSS3 properties are not without their share of challenges. The major one with CSS3 is the use of vendor prefixes. These are the hyphenated abbreviations for a specific browser that you see before a property name. These are the ones you will see most often:

`-webkit-`: This is the prefix for any WebKit-based browser. This is the prefix that both Chrome and Safari use, since both are built with the WebKit open source layout rendering engine.

`-moz-`: This is the prefix for the Firefox browser.

`-ms-`: This is the prefix for the Internet Explorer browser.

`-o-`: This is the prefix for the Opera browser.

Browser vendors introduced their own prefixes to allow developers to use experimental features that are not yet in the specification or that are still in flux in the specification. Implementing their own specific version of a new property allowed browser vendors to implement the new feature *now*, without worrying about the syntax changing later.

One thing that makes this difficult, in addition to the repetition, is that the vendor prefix(es) required varies by property. In some cases, you can use only the actual CSS3 property name, with no vendor prefixes required. In other cases, all vendor prefixes are needed. And in still other cases, some browsers require a prefixed version and other browsers use the standard property name. It's a lot to keep track of.

Luckily, as mentioned in Chapter 1, "Working with CSS3 Animations," there is a website that lets you avoid the need to keep track of any of this: http://css3please.com. Created by Paul Irish and Jonathan Neal, this site allows you to simply edit their prepared samples to match your values and click Copy to Clipboard. You then have the complete list you need for any given property. You could also use the website http://prefixr.com/ by Jeffrey Way. Another option to be aware of is the -prefix-free library by Lea Verou, available at http://leaverou.github.com/pre-fixfree/. -prefix-free is a client-side CSS postprocessor that adds the required vendor prefixes automatically, based on the browser the visitor is using.

Transform Functions

In the following sections, I will walk you through the basics of each of the available transform functions by manipulating a simple `div` element. Then I will have you use the concepts reviewed to build a bicycle with `div` elements, a handful of CSS properties, and some transforms.

The Effect of Transform Functions on Surrounding Elements

Before I get into the specifics of the transform functions, it's important that you know how changes to elements added through transforms differ from changes added through the use of properties such as `margin`, `padding`, `width`, or `height`. Changes to these properties will cause surrounding elements to move as well. Increasing an element's top margin will push an element that precedes it higher up on the page. This is not the case, however, with the transform property.

The W3C spec states that "the transform property does not affect the flow of the content surrounding the transformed element" (http://www.w3.org/TR/css3-transforms/#transform-rendering). This means that the transformed element will not cause other elements around it to move the way margin, padding, and other properties do. In addition, the transformed element will not cause scrollbars to appear if it happens to overflow its parent (even if the parent is set to overflow: auto). If you scale up an element to two times its original height, you may well overlap elements that precede or follow it. This is important to keep in mind, and it comes up again in the sections on the individual transform functions.

rotate

The rotate transform function allows you to rotate an element either clockwise or counter-clockwise. The angle of rotation can be specified in several ways:

Degrees: Likely to be the most familiar way to define an angle. There are 360 degrees in a complete circle. (Example: 90deg)

Gradians: 400 gradians make up a complete circle. (Example: 100grad)

Radians: 2π radians make up a complete circle. (Example: 1.57rad)

Turns: How many turns of the circle. A full circle is one turn. 0.25 turns is equivalent to a 90 degree rotation. (Example: 0.25turn)

Whenever this book uses the rotate transform function, it specifies the angle of the rotation in degrees.

Let's look at an example to demonstrate rotate. Assume that you have a simple HTML file with only a div containing an h1, styled to be a 150-pixel-wide square with a light gray background color and white text. By using padding, you place the h1 element near the center of the div. Listing 2.1 provides the HTML, Listing 2.2 provides the CSS, and Figure 2.1 shows the output.

Listing 2.1   **A Simple div (box.html)**

```
<!DOCTYPE html>
<html lang="en">
  <head>
    <meta charset="utf-8" />
    <title>Examples of CSS3 Transforms</title>
    <link rel="stylesheet" href="css/box.css">
    <script src="js/modernizr.custom.57498.js"></script>
  </head>
  <body>
    <div class="box" id="rotate">
      <h1>hello.</h1>
```

```
      </div>
    </body>
</html>
```

Note

It is important to ensure that you include the HTML5 document type directive, as is done in Listing 2.1. This is especially important for ensuring that Internet Explorer 9 will display the effects of any CSS3 properties. In order for Internet Explorer 9 to properly display a webpage using HTML5 features, the webpage must be displayed in "IE9 Standards mode." Internet Explorer Standards mode is triggered through the use of the HTML5 document type directive `<!DOCTYPE html>`. Make sure you don't forget it! To learn more, see http://msdn.microsoft.com/en-us/library/ie/gg699338(v=vs.85).aspx.

Listing 2.2   **Styling the Simple** `div` **(box.css)**

```
.box {
  width: 150px;
  height: 150px;
  background-color: rgb(211,211,211);
  color: white;
  margin: 100px 0;
}

.box h1 {
  padding: 50px 0 0 30px;
}
```

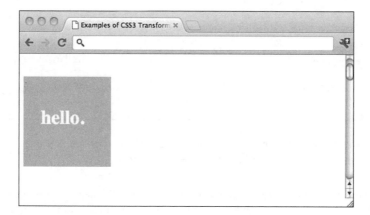

Figure 2.1   The original `div` element

To rotate this element by 15 degrees, and ensure that it works in all modern browsers, you must include all the vendor prefixes for `transform`, as shown in Listing 2.3.

Listing 2.3   **Rotating an Element 15 Degrees (box.css)**

```
/* continued from Listing 2.2 */
#rotate {
  -webkit-transform: rotate(15deg);
    -moz-transform: rotate(15deg);
     -ms-transform: rotate(15deg);
      -o-transform: rotate(15deg);
         transform: rotate(15deg);
}
```

Figure 2.2 shows the results of this rotation. The dashed line in Figure 2.2 represents the original location of the `.box div` element, to make it clear how the element has been transformed. This border is not relevant to the concepts covered in this chapter, but if you'd like to explore the code used to create this dashed border, you can review it at http://alexisgo.github.com/LearningCSSAnimations/ch2code/boxWithBorders.html. This dashed border appears in all subsequent figures of the `.box div` elements, in order to convey the pre-transform location of the `.box div`.

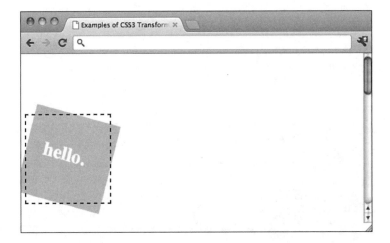

Figure 2.2   The `div` element with `transform:rotate(15deg)` applied. The dashed border represents the original location of the `div`, before the transform.

Notice in Figure 2.2 that the rotation goes off the left edge of the page. This is because the original bounding box for the element hasn't changed. Thus, if you plan on rotating an element, you might want to give it enough of a buffer with `margin` or positioning, or by some other means, so that it does not overlap elements around it.

You may also notice that the rotation has occurred around the center of the element. That is the default anchor point for any rotation. Think of an anchor point as the starting position for the rotation—it is the location on the element that will be anchored down and stay in place as the element rotates. You can manipulate that anchor point to suit your needs by changing the value of the `transform-origin` property.

In Listing 2.4, you add another new `div` element (with the `id` attribute set to `rotateFrom-BottomCorner`) and rotate it by 15 degrees. But this time, you change the anchor point of the `div` element by changing the `transform-origin` property. The default `transform-origin` is in the middle of the element, at 50% of its width and 50% of its height. In Listing 2.4, you change it to the bottom left, or 0% 100%, so that any rotations will happen with the element anchored to the bottom left.

Listing 2.4 **Transforming the Origin of an Element Prior to Rotation (box.css)**

```
#rotateFromBottomCorner {
  -webkit-transform-origin: 0% 100%;
    -moz-transform-origin: 0% 100%;
     -ms-transform-origin: 0% 100%;
      -o-transform-origin: 0% 100%;
         transform-origin: 0% 100%;

  -webkit-transform: rotate(15deg);
    -moz-transform: rotate(15deg);
     -ms-transform: rotate(15deg);
      -o-transform: rotate(15deg);
         transform: rotate(15deg);
}
```

You can see the results of this rotation, after applying the new anchor point, in Figure 2.3.

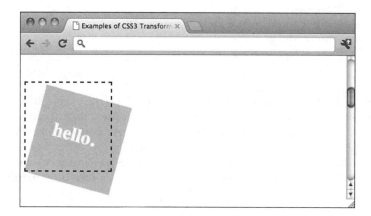

Figure 2.3   The `div` element with `transform:rotate(15deg)` applied after using `transform-origin` to change the anchor point to the bottom-left corner.

scale

The `scale` transform function allows you to increase or decrease the visual size of an element. You can scale evenly across both the width and height of the element, or you can apply different scaling to each dimension. The syntax of `scale` is as follows, where `scale factor` is a number:

```
transform: scale(<scale factor>);
```

To scale an element up to 200% of its original size, you would write this:

```
transform: scale(2);
```

To scale an element down to 50% of its original size, you would write this:

```
transform: scale(0.5);
```

You can also scale horizontally by a different factor than you scale vertically. To scale down to half the size vertically but retain the same width, you specify both values, separated by commas:

```
transform: scale(1, 0.5);
```

Now you can add another `div` element to the page. This `div` will have the `class` attribute `box` and its `id` attribute set to `scale`:

```
<div class="box" id="scale">
```

Next, you should write a new `id` selector, `#scale`, retaining the `div` element's width but making its height 150% of its original size (see Listing 2.5).

Listing 2.5   **Scaling an Element up to 150% of Its Original Height (box.css)**

```
#scale {
  -webkit-transform: scale(1, 1.5);
     -moz-transform: scale(1, 1.5);
      -ms-transform: scale(1, 1.5);
       -o-transform: scale(1, 1.5);
          transform: scale(1, 1.5);
}
```

As with `rotate`, the `scale` transform function does not expand the original bounding box for the element. Thus, as you can see in Figure 2.4, the box after the scale well exceeds the original element's size, represented by the dashed border. To elements before and after the `#scale` div, it's as if the scale didn't take place. Thus, having a healthy amount of `margin` around any element you plan to scale will help you avoid overlapping other elements or running off the edge of the page. The scaling also applies to the `h1` element within the `div`, stretching it out along with the `div` as it scales.

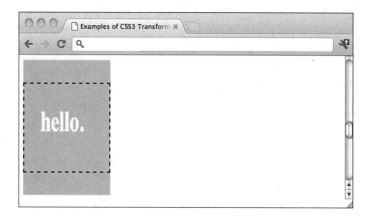

Figure 2.4   The `div` element with `scale(1.0, 1.5)` applied

skew

The `skew` transform function allows you to slant an element along the x- or y-axis. You can specify the skew angle by using the same choices for angles that are available in the `rotate` transform function.

In terms of syntax, you can use several different forms of the `skew` transform function. You can specify a skew only on the x-axis with `skewX`:

```
transform: skewX(15deg);
```

You can specify a skew to the y-axis with `skewY`:

```
transform: skewY(25deg);
```

Or you can specify a skew to both axes simultaneously by using `skew` and specifying the x-axis skew angle first and the y-axis skew angle second, with the two values separated by a comma:

```
transform: skew(15deg, 25deg);
```

You can now add another `div` to the page, with the `class` attribute set to `box` and the `id` attribute set to `skew`:

```
<div class="box" id="skew">
```

Next, as in Listing 2.6, you write a new `id` selector, #skew, and tilt the `div` 50 degrees back from the x-axis.

Listing 2.6   **Manipulating an Element with skew (box.css)**

```
#skew {
  -webkit-transform: skewX(50deg);
    -moz-transform: skewX(50deg);
    -ms-transform: skewX(50deg);
     -o-transform: skewX(50deg);
        transform: skewX(50deg);
}
```

You can see the results of skew in Figure 2.5. As with all the other transform functions, skew does not expand the original bounding box for the element. Thus, the skew transform causes the element to run a bit off the edge of the page.

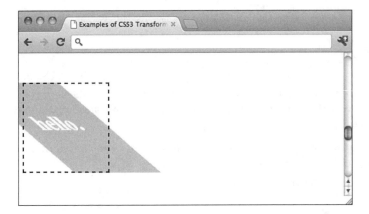

Figure 2.5   The div element with skewX(50deg) applied

To see skew more clearly, and to practice combining two transform functions together into a single transform, you can also scale down the size of the div to 50% of its original size after you apply the skew. In Listing 2.7, you create a new id selector, #skewAndScale, that accomplishes this. The results are displayed in Figure 2.6.

Listing 2.7   **Manipulating an Element with skew (box.css)**

```
#skewAndScale {
  -webkit-transform: skewX(50deg) scale(0.5);
    -moz-transform: skewX(50deg) scale(0.5);
    -ms-transform: skewX(50deg) scale(0.5);
     -o-transform: skewX(50deg) scale(0.5);
        transform: skewX(50deg) scale(0.5);
}
```

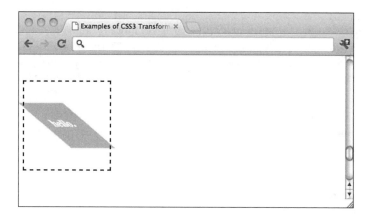

Figure 2.6   The `div` element with `skewX(50deg)` and `scale(2.0)` applied

translate

The `translate` transform function allows you to move an element around the page. There are four different kinds of translates you can use: `translateX`, `translateY`, `translateZ`, and `translate3d`. Chapter 6, "Adding Depth with 3D Transforms," and Chapter 7, "Animating 2D and 3D Transforms," discuss `translateZ` and `translate3d`.

The `translateX` transform function allows you to move elements left and right along the x-axis. `translateY` allows you to move elements up and down along the y-axis. To specify a translation of 100 pixels only on the x-axis, you would write this:

```
transform: translateX(100px);
```

To specify a translation of 250 pixels only on the y-axis, you would write this:

```
transform: translateY(250px);
```

Or you can specify a translation to both axes simultaneously by using `translate` and specifying the x-axis translation first and the y-axis translation second, with the two values separated by a comma:

```
transform: translate(100px, 250px);
```

To demonstrate `translateX`, you can add yet another `div` to the page, with the `class` attribute set to `box` and the `id` attribute set to `translate`:

```
<div class="box" id="translate">
```

In Listing 2.8, you define a new id selector, `#translate`, and define a 400-pixel translation along the x-axis. This will effectively move the element 400 pixels to the right of its original location. You can see the results of this `translate` in Figure 2.7.

As stated previously, transforms do not affect surrounding elements, and the `translate` transform function is no different. Much like with relative positioning, applying a translation via the `transform` property doesn't affect the document's flow. To the surrounding elements, it is as if the translated element is still located at its original bounding box. Thus, you must bear in mind that when you use translation, you may overlap surrounding elements if you don't pay attention.

Listing 2.8   **Moving an Element Across the Screen with `translateX` (box.css)**

```
#translate {
  -webkit-transform: translateX(400px);
    -moz-transform: translateX(400px);
     -ms-transform: translateX(400px);
      -o-transform: translateX(400px);
         transform: translateX(400px);
}
```

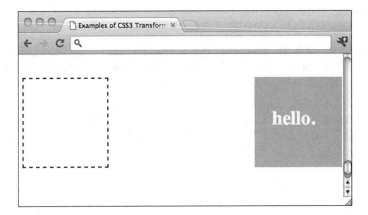

Figure 2.7   The `div` element with `translateX(400px)` applied

Adding a Fallback Message for Older Browsers

In browsers that do not support the new CSS3 transforms, the transforms will be ignored, and all the elements will therefore look identical. In order to warn users that their older browsers (that is, Internet Explorer 8 and earlier) don't support CSS3 transforms, you can add a fallback message.

In Listing 2.9, you add a new `div` element with the `id` attribute set to `unsupported` that holds a message in an `h1` element. The bold lines in Listing 2.9 represent the new code you're adding to the existing code in the file box.html.

Listing 2.9   **Adding a Warning Message for Unsupported Browsers (box.html)**

```
<div id="unsupported">
  <h1>Your Browser does not support
  CSS3 Transforms. You will not be able to see the
  neat transforms applied to the elements below!
  </h1>
</div>

<div class="box">
    <h1>hello.</h1>
  </div>
```

You have now made the #unsupported div element hidden by default, by giving it the style display: none. You can leverage Modernizr (which you'll recall from Listing 2.1 is included in the box.html file) to see whether CSS3 transforms are supported by a visitor's browser.

If CSS3 transforms are supported, the opening html element will have its class attribute set to csstransforms. In Listing 2.10, you will specify that if this class is present, you should set the #unsupported div to display: none.

If CSS3 transforms are not supported, Modernizr will add the class no-csstransforms to the opening html element. In that case, you have another selector defined in Listing 2.10 to specify that #unsupported div should be displayed (display: block). Figure 2.8 shows what this message will look like in a browser that does not support CSS3 transforms.

Listing 2.10   **Displaying an Error Message in Browsers That Do Not Support CSS3 Transforms (box.css)**

```
/* If CSS3 Transforms are supported
 do not display the browser warning*/
.csstransforms #unsupported {
  display: none;
}

/* If CSS3 Transforms are NOT supported
 display the browser warning*/
.no-csstransforms #unsupported {
  display: block;
}
```

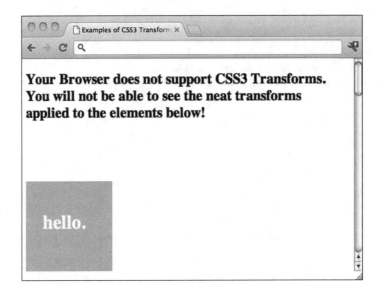

Figure 2.8   The fallback message for browsers that don't support for transforms

matrix

The `matrix` transform function allows the mathematically inclined to specify multiple transforms all at once by using shorter syntax. The `matrix` transform function takes six arguments, which allow you to represent any combinations of a 2D transform with a 3x3 transformation matrix. The syntax looks like this:

```
transform: matrix(a, b, c, d, tx, ty)
```

The values a through d determine the linear transformation, and the values tx and ty describe the x and y translation to apply. Since this book has no math-based prerequisites, I suggest that you go to http://css3please.com and experiment with the visual matrix generator, shown in Figure 2.9.

If you would like to know more about the `matrix` transform function and did not spend your school years taking linear algebra, read the great article by Zoltan Hawryluk called "The CSS3 matrix() Transform for the Mathematically Challenged," which walks slowly through how the `matrix` transform function works: http://www.useragentman.com/blog/2011/01/07/css3-matrix-transform-for-the-mathematically-challenged/.

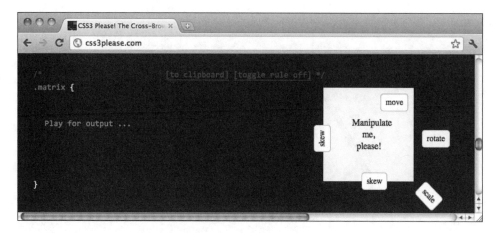

Figure 2.9   css3please's visual matrix generator

Building a Bicycle in CSS3

In this section, you'll apply what you have learned thus far about transforms and the available transform functions to a richer example. You will use a combination of basic HTML, CSS, and some CSS transforms in order to "draw" a bicycle on a webpage, using no images at all. You will tackle this example a few elements at a time, but if you want to get a sense of what you're going to achieve, you can skip ahead to Figure 2.15 to see what the completed bicycle will look like. Or you can take a look at the finished product online, at http://alexisgo.github.com/LearningCSSAnimations/ch2code/bike.html. The source files for this example can be found at this book's GitHub project (https://github.com/alexisgo/LearningCSSAnimations) in the ch2code/ folder.

Laying Out the Basic Skeleton

To create the bicycle, you need a `div` for each of the major components of a bike frame. Figure 2.10 shows the names this chapter uses for the bicycle parts. The parts of the bike you will be building are the forks (which hold the wheels), the top tube, the down tube, the seat stays, and the chain stays.

I will walk you through creating the basic skeleton first, then the wheels, and then each portion of the frame, one at a time. In Listing 2.11, you will start with a basic outline of all the components of the frame.

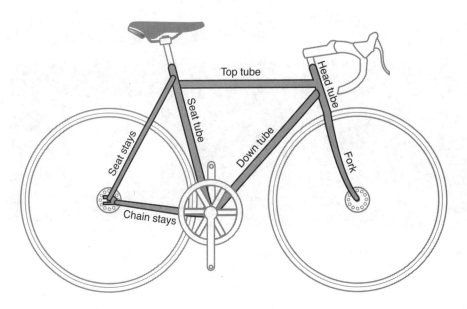

Figure 2.10   The names of bike frame parts

Listing 2.11   **The Basic Bicycle Frame (bike.html)**

```
<!DOCTYPE html>
<html lang="en">
  <head>
    <meta charset="utf-8" />
    <link rel="stylesheet" href="css/bikestyles.css">
  </head>
  <body>
    <div id="bike">
      <div id="frametop"></div>
      <div id="framechainstay"></div>
      <div id="framefork"></div>
      <div id="frameseattube"></div>
      <div id="frameseatstay"></div>
      <div id="framedowntube"></div>
      <div id="seat"></div>
      <div class="handlebars"></div>
      <div id="backwheel"></div>
      <div id="frontwheel"></div>
    </div>
  </body>
</html>
```

In Listing 2.12, you begin to draw the bicycle by styling the elements provided in this basic skeleton, using a combination of basic CSS properties and some of the CSS3 transforms discussed earlier in this chapter.

To begin, you need to give the containing `div id="bike"` element some basic styles. You'll give it a specific size and set the `position` to `relative` so that you can absolutely position the inner `div` elements relative to this outer, containing `div`.

Listing 2.12   **Styling the Containing Bike `div` (bikestyles.css)**

```css
#bike {
  width: 400px;
  height: 250px;
  position: relative;
  margin: 20px 0;
}
```

Creating Bicycle Wheels with `border-radius`

Next, you can style the two `div` elements that will make up the front and back wheels. These styles are laid out in Listing 2.13. First, you'll make both wheels into 125-by-125-pixel squares. You'll give them both black borders to simulate the wheels. You'll absolutely position them, setting the top value of each to be 68 pixels. This will position the wheels 68 pixels from the top of the `div id="bike"` container `div`. You'll set the `left` values for the individual wheels later, in Listing 2.14. Finally, you'll make both the wheels round by setting `border-radius` to be half the width of the wheel. You do so by first using absolute pixel values, and then using the 50% value. You have to do it this way because in some versions of mobile Safari, the 50% value is not recognized.

Listing 2.13   **Styling the Bicycle Wheels (bikestyles.css)**

```css
#backwheel, #frontwheel {
  width: 120px;
  height: 120px;
  border: 8px solid black;
  position: absolute;
  top: 68px;
```

```
/* using border-radius: 50% doesn't work in certain
   versions of mobile Safari, so we're using absolute
   pixel values first, and if 50% isn't understood, these
   absolulte values will be used. */
   -webkit-border-radius: 70px;
      -moz-border-radius: 70px;
           border-radius: 70px;

  -webkit-border-radius: 50%;
     -moz-border-radius: 50%;
          border-radius: 50%;
}
```

To finish up the wheel outlines, you place them each in different locations, by setting the `left` property separately for each wheel, as shown in Listing 2.14.

Listing 2.14   **Placing the Bicycle Wheels (bikestyles.css)**

```
#backwheel {
  left: 35px;
}
#frontwheel {
  left: 278px;
}
```

Drawing the Spokes

Apart from setting `border-radius`, I haven't yet had you do anything interesting in CSS3. But in Listing 2.15, you will add a hub and some spokes for each of the wheels and practice using `transform: rotate` to do so. Each spoke will itself be a very small, thin `div` element. You will use only five spokes per wheel. Once you have applied the changes described, you will have two wheels with hubs in the center and five spokes around each hub, as pictured in Figure 2.11. Note that the lines in Listing 2.15 that are bold are the new lines that you will add inside the HTML elements you've defined previously.

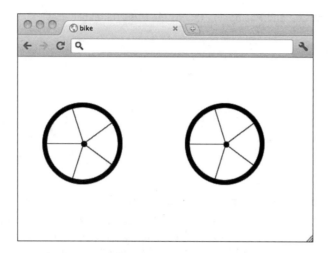

Figure 2.11   Two CSS-created bicycle wheels

Listing 2.15   **The Spokes for the Wheels (bike.html)**

```
/* continued from Listing 2.11 */
<div id="backwheel">
  <div class="center"></div>
  <div class="spoke1"></div>
  <div class="spoke2"></div>
  <div class="spoke3"></div>
  <div class="spoke4"></div>
  <div class="spoke5"></div>
</div>
<div id="frontwheel">
  <div class="center"></div>
  <div class="spoke1"></div>
  <div class="spoke2"></div>
  <div class="spoke3"></div>
  <div class="spoke4"></div>
  <div class="spoke5"></div>
</div>
```

Now you're ready to style the hub of each wheel, using the CSS in Listing 2.16. You should make both of these div elements circular by giving them a 5-pixel border-radius. Next, you position them directly in the middle of the containing div. (Keep in mind that the middle of these div elements is 60 pixels in, but since the center div is 10 pixels wide, you must offset 5 pixels from the center.)

Listing 2.16   **Drawing and Positioning the Wheel Hubs (bikestyles.css)**

```
.center {
  position: absolute;
  top: 56px;
  left: 58px;
  width: 10px;
  height: 10px;
  border-radius: 5px;
  background-color: black;
}
```

Anchoring the Spokes with `transform-origin`

Before you rotate the spoke `div` elements, you need to set up some common styles that they will all share (see Listing 2.17). The spokes will have a common size, color, and position. They will also share a common anchor point that differs from the default anchor point. This will allow you to rotate each spoke around the far right of the `div` instead of the default (at the center of the `div`). Setting `transform-origin` to 100% 50% will make the anchor point be the very right of the `div` horizontally but the middle of the `div` vertically. The transform origin point is visualized by the small square in Figure 2.12. The wheel on the left shows all the spokes before they are individually rotated (which you will do in Listing 2.18), and the wheel on the right shows them after.

Listing 2.17   **Drawing and Positioning the Wheel Hubs (bikestyles.css)**

```
div[class*="spoke"] {
  height: 1px;
  width: 62px;
  background-color: black;
  position: absolute;
  top: 60px;

  -webkit-transform-origin: 100% 50%;
    -moz-transform-origin: 100% 50%;
     -ms-transform-origin: 100% 50%;
      -o-transform-origin: 100% 50%;
         transform-origin: 100% 50%;
}
```

> **Note**
>
> The first selector in Listing 2.17 leverages a new kind of selector that allows you to match on any element whose attribute contains the value specified. `div[class*="spoke"]` will match all `div` elements whose id attribute contains the string `"spoke"`, so it will match `spoke1`, `spoke2`, `spoke3`, `spoke4`, and `spoke5`. Support for this selector is available in all modern browsers and in Internet Explorer versions 7 and later. For more on related selectors and compatibility, see http://www.quirksmode.org/css/contents.html.

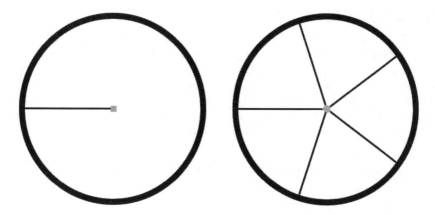

Figure 2.12   Each spoke has its `transform-origin` set to 100% 50%, which is demonstrated by the light square

Rotating the Spokes with `transform: rotate`

Now that you have defined the common styles, the last step is to rotate each spoke in increments of 72 degrees (because you have five spokes, and 360 degrees / 5 = 72). Since the first spoke will have a rotation of 0 degrees, you need not style it. So you begin with `spoke2` and continue to `spoke5`. For the sake of brevity, Listing 2.18 includes all the requisite vendor prefixes in the `.spoke2` style and simply defines the -webkit- vendor prefix in the styles for `.spoke3`, `.spoke4`, and `.spoke5`. You can find the complete styles (with vendor prefixes) in the bikestyles.css file, available in the ch2code/css/ folder at the book's GitHub project (https://github.com/alexisgo/LearningCSSAnimations).

Listing 2.18   **Drawing and Positioning the Wheel Hubs (bikestyles.css)**

```
.spoke2 {
  -webkit-transform: rotate(72deg);
    -moz-transform: rotate(72deg);
     -ms-transform: rotate(72deg);
      -o-transform: rotate(72deg);
         transform: rotate(72deg);
}

.spoke3 { -webkit-transform: rotate(144deg); }
.spoke4 { -webkit-transform: rotate(216deg); }
.spoke5 { -webkit-transform: rotate(288deg); }
```

Drawing the Frame

Now you need to style the bicycle frame and position each part in the right spot. You can begin with what each part of the frame will have in common: its `height`, `background-color`, and `border-radius`. You'll set each portion of the frame to be absolutely positioned, and you'll set the `z-index` to 2 in order to ensure that the frame sits on top of the hub and spokes. As with the spokes, you can target all the frame `div` elements at once by using the substring matching attribute selector, this time looking for any `div` elements whose `id` attribute contains the string `"frame"`. Listing 2.19 outlines all these additions.

Listing 2.19   **Setting the Bike Frame's Default Styles (bikestyles.css)**

```css
#bike div[id*="frame"] {
    height: 10px;
    background-color: red;
    position: absolute;
    z-index: 2;
    -webkit-border-radius: 5px;
      -moz-border-radius: 5px;
          border-radius: 5px;
}

#frametop {
    width: 163px;
    top: 20px;
    left: 158px;
}

#framechainstay {
    top: 131px;
    left: 104px;
    width: 85px;
}
```

Next, in Listing 2.20, you position the two parts of the frame that don't require any rotation at all: the top of the frame and the chain stay.

Listing 2.20   **Styling the Top of the Frame and the Chain Stay (bikestyles.css)**

```css
#frametop {
  width: 163px;
  top: 20px;
  left: 158px;
}

#framechainstay {
  top: 131px;
  left: 104px;
  width: 85px;
}
```

Rotating the Frame Fork and Seat Tube with `transform: rotate`

In Listing 2.21, you create the fork and the seat tube, which are parallel to each other and thus require the same rotation. You can combine most of the styles together into a grouped selector, since they share a common rotation, and then override as needed in the selector for the seat tube.

Listing 2.21   **Styling the Fork and the Seat Tube (bikestyles.css)**

```css
#framefork, #frameseattube {
  top: 75px;
  left: 270px;
  width: 123px;

  -webkit-transform: rotate(75deg);
     -moz-transform: rotate(75deg);
      -ms-transform: rotate(75deg);
       -o-transform: rotate(75deg);
          transform: rotate(75deg);
}

#frameseattube {
  left: 112px;
}
```

As you can see in Figure 2.13, the bicycle is slowly starting to take shape.

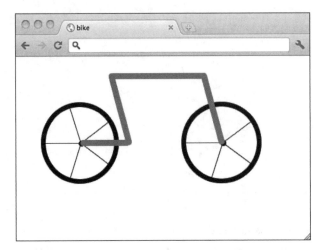

Figure 2.13   The top of the frame, the chain stay, the fork, and the seat tube

Leveraging the Web Developer Toolbar to Determine the Rotation

One tricky part in creating the bike is figuring out the correct degree of rotation for any one part of the bicycle frame. An easy way to determine the proper location of an element and the needed transforms is to use developer tools (for example, Firebug or the Web Developer toolbar in Chrome or Safari). You can utilize the CSS-editing capabilities of such a tool to tweak the values until they are correct. For example, you can determine that 75 degrees is the proper rotation for the fork and the seat tube with trial and error through the Web Developer toolbar, as shown in Figure 2.14.

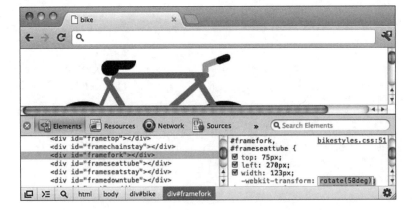

Figure 2.14   Determining the correct rotation through trial and error in the Web Developer toolbar

Completing the Frame

The last parts of the frame are the seat stay (which connects the seat to the rear hub) and the down tube. Each of these will have slightly different rotations and widths, so you need to style them separately, as shown in Listing 2.22.

By default, a rotation occurs clockwise. But for the seat stay and down tube, you need to use negative rotations. To rotate counterclockwise, you can use a negative value. (Or you can use the equivalently large positive value, since circles will eventually come back around to the other side. But I find it easier to determine a small counterclockwise rotation, which is why I chose this approach.)

Listing 2.22   **Styling the Seat Stay and the Down Tube (bikestyles.css)**

```
#frameseatstay {
  top: 78px;
  left: 66px;
  height: 6px !important;
  width: 130px;

  -webkit-transform: rotate(-65deg);
     -moz-transform: rotate(-65deg);
      -ms-transform: rotate(-65deg);
       -o-transform: rotate(-65deg);
          transform: rotate(-65deg);
}

#framedowntube {
  width: 170px;
  top: 78px;
  left: 165px;

  -webkit-transform: rotate(-40deg);
     -moz-transform: rotate(-40deg);
      -ms-transform: rotate(-40deg);
       -o-transform: rotate(-40deg);
          transform: rotate(-40deg);
}
```

Finishing the Bike with a Seat and Handlebars

To put the finishing touches on the bicycle, you should add a seat and handlebars. You'll need to combine two transforms together to achieve the desired effect. For the handlebars, you use three div elements wrapped in a container div. To begin, add a few more div elements to hold both the handlebars and the seat, as shown in Listing 2.23.

Listing 2.23   Adding `div` Elements for the Handlebars and the Seat (bike.html)

```
/* continued from Listing 2.15 */
  <div id="framedowntube"></div>
  <div id="seat">
    <div id="base"></div>
    <div id="nose"></div>
  </div>
  <div class="handlebars">
    <div id="post"></div>
    <div id="bar"></div>
    <div id="handle"></div>
  </div>
```

Styling the Bike Handlebars

To style the handlebars, you will use positioning to determine the correct position of the container `div`. Inside, you'll have a small post, a rotated `div` that will serve as the handlebar, and a final `div` that will represent the black rubber handle.

In Listing 2.24, you first set up the position for the container, `.handlerbars`. Next, you define a position, color, and size to the `#post` div. Then you define styles that the bar and the handle will share, including their basic size, `position`, `border-radius`, and rotation. As in previous examples in this chapter, before you rotate, you change the `transform-origin`. In this case, you change it so you can rotate around the center left edge of this `div`.

Listing 2.24   Styling the Handlebars (bikestyles.css)

```
.handlebars {
  position: relative;
  left: 310px;
}

#post {
  background-color: silver;
  height: 10px;
  width: 10px;
  position: absolute;
  top: 10px;
}

#bar, #handle {
  position: absolute;
  top: 5px;
  width: 50px;
```

```
    height: 10px;
    background-color: silver;

    -webkit-border-radius: 20px;
    -moz-border-radius: 20px;
        border-radius: 20px;

    -webkit-transform-origin: 0% 50%;
    -moz-transform-origin: 0% 50%;
    -ms-transform-origin: 0% 50%;
    -o-transform-origin: 0% 50%;
    transform-origin: 0% 50%;

    -webkit-transform: rotate(-20deg);
    -moz-transform: rotate(-20deg);
    -ms-transform: rotate(-20deg);
    -o-transform: rotate(-20deg);
    transform: rotate(-20deg);
}
```

Finally, you can add a handle to the bar. To do so, you rotate the handle the same amount as you did the bar, but you add a second transform function, translateX, in order to push the handle to the end of the bar. You can combine two transform functions into a single transform by simply separating them with spaces, as in Listing 2.25. Figure 2.15 shows the styles applied with only a rotation on the handle, and Figure 2.16 shows the effect of combining the rotation with translateX.

Listing 2.25 **Styling the Handle (bikestyles.css)**

```
#handle {
  background-color: black;
  width: 25px;
  height: 12px;
  -webkit-transform: rotate(-20deg) translateX(25px);
     -moz-transform: rotate(-20deg) translateX(25px);
      -ms-transform: rotate(-20deg) translateX(25px);
       -o-transform: rotate(-20deg) translateX(25px);
          transform: rotate(-20deg) translateX(25px);
}
```

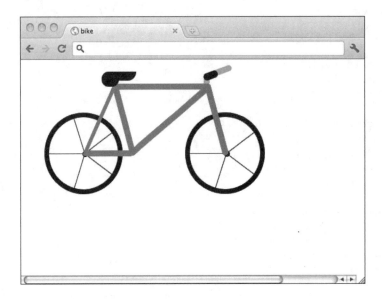

Figure 2.15   The handle, using only the `rotate` transform

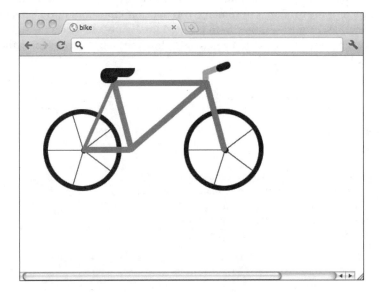

Figure 2.16   The handle correctly positioned by using `rotate` and `translateX` together

Styling the Bike Seat

Finally, you can add a seat to the bike. As with the handlebars, you can style several inner `div` elements in order to achieve the effect you want. The inner `div` `#base` is a relatively large black circle, and the nose is a black rectangle with a single rounded corner, to give the look of the nose of a bike seat. Figure 2.17 shows the finished product. Listing 2.26 presents the code.

Listing 2.26   **Styling the Seat (bikestyles.css)**

```css
#seat {
  background-color: black;
  position: absolute;
  left: 135px;

  z-index: 3;
  -webkit-border-radius: 20px;
  -moz-border-radius: 20px;
      border-radius: 20px;
}

#base {
  width: 30px;
  height: 25px;
}

#nose {
  background-color: black;
  width: 40px;
  height: 15px;
  position: absolute;
  top: 0;
  left: 20px;
  -webkit-border-bottom-right-radius: 15px;
     -moz-border-bottom-right-radius: 15px;
          border-bottom-right-radius: 15px;
}
```

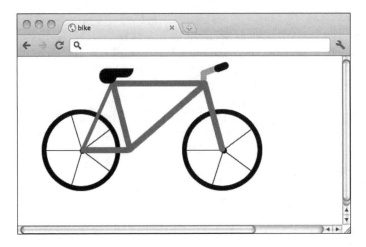

Figure 2.17   The finished CSS-created bicycle

Adding a Fallback Message for Older Browsers

Browsers that do not support CSS3 transforms simply ignore the transforms. Since so much of the bicycle you've just created depends on these transforms, in a browser that doesn't support them, your CSS/HTML-built bicycle will look quite warped. In order to avoid this, you can make some slight modifications to the code in order to hide the bike div in browsers that don't support CSS3 transforms. You can instead show an img element that contains a screenshot of the completed bicycle, along with a message explaining what the user is missing.

Just as you did in Listings 2.9 and 2.10, here you will leverage Modernizr and write some CSS selectors for older browsers. In Listing 2.27 you add the additional HTML necessary to display the error message, and in Listing 2.28 you hide the #bike div element in unsupported browsers and display the screenshot of the bicycle instead.

Listing 2.27   **Adding a Warning Message for Unsupported Browsers (bike.html)**

```
<body>
  <div id="unsupported">
    <h1>Your Browser does not support
    CSS3 Transforms, so we are unable to create
    the HTML/CSS bicycle we planned!
    </h1>
    <p>Here is a screenshot of what you can do with just
      HTML/CSS in a CSS3-ready browser!</p>
    <img src="img/bike.png" alt="screenshot of a bicycle built with HTML and CSS">
  </div>
  <div id="bike">
```

Listing 2.28 **Displaying an Error Message in Browsers That Do Not Support CSS3 Transforms (bikestyles.css)**

```
/* If CSS3 Transforms are supported
 do not display the browser warning*/
.csstransforms #unsupported {
  display: none;
}


/* If CSS3 Transforms are NOT supported
 display the browser warning*/
.no-csstransforms #unsupported {
  display: block;
}


.no-csstransforms #unsupported img {
  border: 2px solid black;
}


/* hide bike if CSS3 transforms are not supported */
.no-csstransforms #bike {
  display: none;
}
```

Additional Resources

To learn more about CSS3 transforms, I recommend the following resources and tutorials:

- CSS Transforms, W3C Working Draft: http://www.w3.org/TR/css3-transforms/
- A Primer on CSS3 Transforms by Louis Lazaris at Sitepoint: http://www.sitepoint.com/a-primer-on-css3-transforms/
- Using CSS Transforms at the Mozilla Developer Network: https://developer.mozilla.org/en-US/docs/CSS/Using_CSS_transforms

Summary

In this chapter you learned the basics of applying CSS3 transforms to elements. You also learned how to change the origin of a transform with `transform-origin` in order to rotate around a desired anchor point. Finally, you learned about the four major transform functions: `rotate`, `skew`, `scale`, and `translate`, and how to use them.

Challenge

Enhance the bicycle by adding two pedals. Adjust the pedals' `transform-origin` and experiment with rotating each pedal to a different angle. Once you have added pedals, use some of the concepts you learned in the bike example to extend the drawing to include front and rear derailleurs, a chain, and a chain ring. Add other parts of a bicycle to the example, using only CSS. You can find a list of all major bike frame parts at Wikipedia: http://en.wikipedia.org/wiki/Bicycle_frame.

Animating Elements with Transitions

CSS transitions allow you to smoothly animate changes to animatable property values. You define which property's value changes should be animated and how long an animation should take, and the browser transitions between the two values. This chapter outlines how you can combine transforms with transitions in order to animate changes made to animatable properties. It also reviews the other CSS properties that can be animated with the use of transitions. In this chapter, you'll enhance the bicycle example from Chapter 2, "Building a Foundation with Transforms," causing the bike to move across the screen and spin its wheels in response to user actions.

Introduction to Transitions

All the transforms you applied in Chapter 2 happened instantly. While that worked for the purposes of drawing a bicycle, often you want transforms—and other changes you make to elements—to happen over a certain amount of time. You can make that happen with transitions. Transitions allow you to define how long any animatable change you make to an element should take.

Transitions make animating easy because they allow you to simply define the property you'd like to animate any changes to, as well as the duration of the animation. The browser manages the rest of the magic. Then, when the value of a property you've set up to transition changes, the browser animates the change from the old property value to the new property value.

Browser Support for `transition`

CSS3 transitions enjoy very good support in modern browsers, with the exception of Internet Explorer 9. Support for CSS3 transitions exists in Internet Explorer starting with version 10. The following browsers currently support transitions:

- Android Browser 2.1+
- Chrome 4.0+

- Firefox 4.0+
- Internet Explorer 10.0+
- iOS Safari 3.2+ and Safari 3.1+
- Opera 10.5+

Creating a Simple Transition

To create a simple transition, you need to define two things: which properties to transition when changes occur to that property's value and how long the transition should take. You define the former via the `transition-property` property. You define the latter via the `transition-duration` property.

For example, say that you want to transition any changes made to the value of the `background-color` property and you want those changes to occur over 1 second. To make all this happen, you write this:

```
transition-property: background-color
transition-duration: 1s;
```

At the time of this writing, Internet Explorer 10, Opera 12.5, and Firefox 16 all support the standard property (`transition-property` or `transition-duration`). All other browsers (and earlier versions of the browsers with standard syntax support) still require the appropriate prefixed value. Thus, to ensure support across all browsers that support transitions, you need to include the -webkit-, -moz-, and -o- vendor prefixes in addition to the standard syntax, as shown in Listing 3.1.

> ### Note
>
> I am not using the -ms- prefix for transitions because Internet Explorer 10 is the first version of Internet Explorer to support them. However, the book will still use the -ms- prefix for transforms. This is because, unlike transitions, support for transforms began in Internet Explorer 9. Thus, in order to ensure support for transforms in both Internet Explorer 9 and 10, we need to use both the prefixed version and the standard version.

Listing 3.1   **Defining a Transition on Changes to the Value of `background-color`**

```
-webkit-transition-property: background-color;
-moz-transition-property: background-color;
-o-transition-property: background-color;
transition-property: background-color;

-webkit-transition-duration: 1s;
-moz-transition-duration: 1s;
-o-transition-duration: 1s;
transition-duration: 1s;
```

The `transition` Shorthand Property

Instead of specifying `transition-property` and `transition-duration` in two separate lines, you can combine them into one line by using the `transition` shorthand property. The shorthand can save you considerable typing, especially when you include all the relevant vendor prefixes. This is the complete shorthand syntax:

```
transition: <transition-property> <transition-duration>
<transition-timing-function> <transition-delay>;
```

I have yet to describe the `transition-timing-function` and `transition-delay` properties (I do so later in the chapter), but both of these properties have default values. Thus, to use the `transition` shorthand with the earlier example of animating background-color changes over 1 second, you can write this:

```
transition: background-color 1s;
```

To use the shorthand with all needed vendor prefixes, you write this:

```
-webkit-transition: background-color 2s;
-moz-transition: background-color 2s;
-o-transition: background-color 2s;
transition: background-color 2s;
```

Triggering a Transition Animation with Hover Events

The `transition-property` and `transition-duration` properties only define *which* property to transition when that property's value changes and how long the transition should take. To actually trigger a transition, you must change the value of the property set as the `transition-property`, which is `background-color` in this example. One way to do this would be to trigger the change when a hover action occurs.

Transitioning Changes to the Background Color

Consider a webpage with only a single `div` element, colored purple, with its `id` attribute set to `animateMe`. Because you will be animating changes to this `div`, this is where you set up the transition, with all appropriate vendor prefixes.

Suppose that you want to change `background-color` from purple to blue when a user hovers over the `div`. Listing 3.2 provides the complete code for doing this, and Figure 3.1 shows the three stages of the transition.

Listing 3.2   **Animating a Background Color on Hover (colorchange.html)**

```
#animateMe {
  width: 100px;
  height: 100px;
```

```
  background-color: rgb(128, 0, 128);

  -webkit-transition: background-color 2s;
  -moz-transition: background-color 2s;
  -o-transition: background-color 2s;
  transition: background-color 2s;
}

#animateMe:hover {
  background-color: rgb(0, 0, 255);
}
```

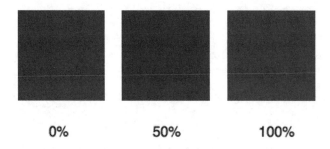

0%   50%   100%

Figure 3.1   The background color at the start of the transition, halfway through, and at the end of the transition

You might wonder why you set up the transition in the #animateMe id selector and not in the #animateMe:hover pseudo-class. If you set up the transition in the :hover pseudo-class, the animation will only occur on hover, *not* when the user moves their cursor away from the element. When you place the transition in the id selector, #animateMe:hover also inherits the transition, so you get the animation effect both on hover and off.

> **Note**
>
> When you transition between two colors, how does the browser determine the intermediate points? In other words, how does the browser know what colors exist between the value purple and the value blue? By interpolating between the two color values.
>
> Interpolation occurs when you provide two points, and a computer program or an algorithm determines all the intermediate points to go from the first point to the next. Interpolation makes computer- or browser-driven animations much easier to achieve than using traditional hand-drawn animation, which requires every frame of the animation to be drawn out in painstaking detail.
>
> The browser interpolates from one rgb value to another. In this example, you go from purple—rgb(128,0,128)—to blue—rgb(0,0,255). To get there, the browser figures out all the intermediate values rgb should go through during the 2-second animation time.

Transitioning Changes to `transform` Values on Hover

In Chapter 2 you learned about the `transform` property. Now you can combine transforms with transitions in order to animate changes to the value of the `transform` property. To demonstrate this, let's revisit the simple blue `div` from Chapter 2.

To begin, you set up the `transition` property to animate any changes to the value of the transform property on the `#box div` (see Listing 3.3). The first property you define in the `transition` shorthand is `transition-property`. Since you want to animate changes to the value of the `transform` property, you set `transition-property` to `transform`. Note that each vendor-prefixed transition is paired with the same vendor-prefixed `transform` property.

Next, you define the pseudo-class `#box:hover`. This sets up the `translateX` that moves the box to the right of the page. When the user hovers over the `#box` element, the box animates 400 pixels to the right. When the users hovers away (from the original bounding box—that is, the location where the element began) the `#box` element moves back to its original position.

Listing 3.3   **Moving the Box to the Right on Hover with `translateX` (box.html)**

```
#box {
  width: 150px;
  height: 150px;
  background-color: blue;
  color:white;
  -webkit-transition: -webkit-transform 2s;
  -moz-transition: -moz-transform 2s;
  -o-transition: -o-transform 2s;
  transition: transform 2s;
}

#box:hover {
  -webkit-transform: translateX(400px);
  -moz-transform: translateX(400px);
  -ms-transform: translateX(400px);
  -o-transform: translateX(400px);
  transform: translateX(400px);
}
```

Triggering a Transition Animation with Click Events

Using hover events is a decent way to trigger transition animations on a desktop computer. The problem with this approach is that the `:hover` pseudo-class isn't supported on mobile devices such as the iPhone or Android.

Earlier in the chapter, in Listing 3.2, you applied a change to the background color of an element when a user hovered over that element; you leveraged transitions to ensure that the color change was animated. A more universal approach that will work on both the desktop and in mobile browsers is to trigger the transitions through events—such as click events—that can be handled through JavaScript.

Triggering the `background-color` Transition in a Mobile Environment

You can revise your earlier code to make it work on mobile devices as well as on desktops. In order to trigger the color change on a mobile device, you need to define two new class selectors, .blue and .purple, and use JavaScript to alternate between these classes when the user clicks the #animateMe element.

To begin, you'll enrich the code from Listing 3.2 that triggers a background color change on hover. In Listing 3.4, you enrich the code to add two new class selectors, .purple and .blue, that also change the background color. You must also update the #animateMe:hover pseudo-class, changing it to #animateMe.purple:hover instead. You do this in order to account for the new #animateMe.purple selector, which will override the #animateMe:hover selector unless we append .purple to it. Listing 3.4 shows the new selectors in bold.

Listing 3.4   **Defining Class Selectors to Change the Background Color (colorchange.html)**

```
#animateMe.purple:hover {
  background-color: rgb(0,0,255);
}

#animateMe.blue {
  background-color: rgb(0,0,255);
}

#animateMe.purple {
  background-color: rgb(128,0,128);
}
```

> **Note**
>
> You might question why you didn't combine the new .blue selector with the #animateMe:hover pseudo-class in Listing 3.4, since they both define the same styles. I did not have you group these selectors together because doing so can cause problems in mobile browsers. As noted by Mozilla in its :hover CSS reference page, "on touch screens :hover is problematic or impossible. The :hover pseudo-class never matches, or matches for a short moment after touching an element" (https://developer.mozilla.org/en-US/docs/CSS/:hover). Grouping the .colorchange selector with the :hover pseudo-class on the iPad results in the first click triggering a transition in color but subsequent clicks being ignored.
>
> Defining these two selectors ensures that the background color changes both when the #animateMe element is hovered over in desktop browsers and when it has the class colorchange applied upon click in mobile browsers.

Now you need a way to alternate between the classes applied to the #animateMe element: blue and purple. You achieve this alternation through JavaScript. In Listing 3.5, you set up an event listener that runs the function transition when the element is clicked. If the class of #animateMe was previously set to blue, you change it to purple. If it was previously set to purple, you change it to blue. You can see this code in action at http://alexisgo.github.com/LearningCSSAnimations/ch3code/colorchange.html.

Listing 3.5   **Adding the Class colorchange When #animateMe Is Clicked (colorchange.js)**

```
var elem = document.getElementById("animateMe");
elem.addEventListener("click", transition, false);

function transition() {
  if (this.className == "purple") {
    this.className = "blue";
  }
  else if (this.className == "blue"){
    this.className = "purple";
  }
}
```

> **Note**
>
> In Listing 3.5, you use the method addEventListener to set up the code you want to run in response to the user clicking the #animateMe element. The method addEventListener is not supported in Internet Explorer versions 6–9. In this case, that's okay because Internet Explorer versions 6–9 don't support the transition property anyway.

Triggering the **translateX** Transition in a Mobile Environment

Instead of using a hover event to make changes to the transform property of the #box div element, you can revise the code sample to trigger the animation via JavaScript. But first, just as you had to do in Listing 3.4, you must first define a new class selector. In Listing 3.6, you define the #box.translate selector, which will transform the #box element 400 pixels to the right once this translate class is applied.

Listing 3.6   **Defining a Class Selector to Apply the Transform (box.html)**

```
#box.translate {
  -webkit-transform: translateX(400px);
  -moz-transform: translateX(400px);
  -ms-transform: translateX(400px);
  -o-transform: translateX(400px);
  transform: translateX(400px);
}
```

In Listing 3.7, you will set up an event listener that watches for the click event. You create a new function called `transition()` that will be called if a user clicks the `#box` element. The `transition()` function adds the class `translate` to the `#box` element if it is missing a class name. If the element already has the class name set, the function removes it. The effect is that the box moves across the screen when you click it, and then it moves back to its original position on the second click. You can see a demo of this code at http://alexisgo.github.com/LearningCSSAnimations/ch3code/box.html.

Listing 3.7   **Triggering the Animation on Click Events (box.js)**

```
var box = document.getElementById("box");
box.addEventListener("click", transition, false);

function transition() {
  if (this.className) {
    this.className = "";
  }
  else {
    this.className = "translate";
  }
}
```

Transition Properties

Now that you've tackled the basics of transitions, you can take a closer look at all the ways you can configure them. There are four properties you can use to customize transitions:

- `transition-property`
- `transition-duration`
- `transition-timing-function`
- `transition-delay`

You have already used `transition-property` and `transition-duration` in examples. You'll now dig deeper into these properties and also learn about the timing and delay properties you haven't yet seen in action.

transition-property

As you learned earlier in the chapter, the `transition-property` property allows you to define which properties to animate. If you would like to transition the opacity for a given element, you would set the following:

```
transition-property: opacity;
```

You can set multiple `transition-property` values by specifying a comma-separated list:

`transition-property: opacity, background-color, transform;`

If you want all changes to occur over the same duration and with the same timing function, you can set the `transition-property` property to the special keyword `all` to ensure that *all* changes to animatable property values animate in the same way:

`transition-property: all;`

`all` is also the default value for `transition-property`, so if you do not specify a `transition-property` value, all your changes will animate according to the values set up in the other transition-related properties.

You can set CSS properties as values to `transition-property` only if they are animatable. The good news is that most of them are. Strictly speaking, the list of animatable properties is in flux and subject to change. However, in practice, almost all of the properties you'd like to animate are currently animatable. If you are curious, and would like to see the current (very long) list of properties that can be animated, take a look at the W3C's Editor's Draft of the CSS Transitions spec: http://dev.w3.org/csswg/css3-transitions/#animatable-properties-. Lea Verou compiled a good visual depiction of 39 of the animatable properties in the very visual, very helpful project "Animatable": http://leaverou.github.com/animatable/.

> **Note**
>
> `transform` is an animatable property—but what about defining a transition only on a `scale` transform? At the time of this writing, there is no way to distinguish one transform type from another in the transition property. You cannot specifically define that on a single element, a `scale` transform takes 2 seconds and a `rotate` transform takes 3 seconds; you can only specify the duration that all transforms on this one element will take.
>
> On the CSS3 W3C mailing list, a question was asked as to whether the transform property could be split into atomic elements in order to support this. In response, Simon Fraser, who is one of the authors of the CSS Transforms draft spec, stated that doing so would be adding too much complexity; see http://lists.w3.org/Archives/Public/www-style/2011Feb/0795.html.

transition-duration

The `transition-duration` property allows you to define how long you want an animation to take, measured in seconds (s) or in milliseconds (ms):

`transition-duration: 2s;`

transition-timing-function

The transition-timing-function property allows you to control the speed at which intermediate points of a transition animation play over its duration. It allows you to specify that certain parts of the transition animation play at different speeds. The timing functions allow you to configure whether you'd like the animation to, for example, run slower at the start, slower at the end, or have a consistent pace throughout. There are several choices of timing functions:

- **linear:** The animation plays at the same rate throughout.
- **ease:** This is the default transition-timing-function function. It is very similar to the ease-in-out timing function but with a sharper acceleration at the start of the animation and with an acceleration slowdown that begins sooner.
- **ease-in:** The animation plays more slowly at its beginning.
- **ease-out:** The animation plays more slowly at its end.
- **ease-in-out:** The animation plays more slowly at the beginning and the end than it does for the middle portion of the animation.
- **cubic-bezier:** This function allows you to specify a custom timing rate for the animation by defining a cubic Bézier curve. It takes four arguments—x1, y1, x2, and y2—which determine the points of the Bézier curve. For an excellent visualization of cubic Bézier curves, see Lea Verou's http://cubic-bezier.com.

If no timing function is explicitly set, the default timing function, ease, is used. To read more about timing functions and how Bézier curves work, see this excellent article on The Art of Web that illustrates the different timing functions: http://www.the-art-of-web.com/css/timing-function/.

transition-delay

When you set a specific change to transition over a given time period, the transition doesn't have to start immediately. You can use the transition-delay property to define how long the browser should wait before the transition begins:

```
transition-delay: 3s;
```

As mentioned previously, you can also specify the transition-delay in milliseconds. If you wanted a half-second delay, you could define it as follows:

```
transition-delay: 500ms;
```

If you use the transition shorthand property and specify only a single timing value, the first supplied value will always be used for the transition-duration property. Thus, in order to add a delay via the transition shorthand property, you must include values for both transition-duration and transition-delay.

Specifying Multiple Transitions in the `transition` Shorthand Property

As discussed earlier, instead of specifying all the separate transition properties, it's best to use the `transition` shorthand. The `transition` shorthand becomes especially helpful when you want to specify multiple transitions.

To specify multiple transitions with the `transition` shorthand, you separate the listings with commas. For example, to change `opacity` over a 2-second duration but `background-color` over a 4-second duration, both utilizing the `ease-in` timing function and a 1-second delay, you would write this:

```
transition: opacity 2s ease-in 1s,
    background-color 4s ease-in 1s;
```

When you use multiple, comma-separated transitions, as you have done here, you can make the code more readable by putting each transition on a new line, as in this example.

Spinning the Bike Wheels

In this section, you'll practice all that you have learned about transitions thus far by taking the code you wrote in Chapter 2 and enhancing it to add animations to your bicycle. You will modify the bike.html file in order to make the bike wheels move when the user hovers over them.

First, you need to define the transition, and you do so in Listing 3.8, adding the transition in the `#frontwheel` and `#backwheel` id selectors. Here you use the `transform` property for the value of the `transition-property`, and you specify that the transition should last 3 seconds. Finally, you set the `transition-timing-function` to `ease-in-out` so the wheels slowly start to spin and slowly stop spinning as the transition animation ends.

Now you need to define the transform you want applied. Say that you want to make the wheel spin two full rotations—720 degrees—when someone hovers over it. Figure 3.2 shows three intermediate points of the spinning wheel—0-degree, 90-degree, and 180-degree rotations applied to the wheels. In order to make the rotation of the wheel more apparent, Figure 3.2 shows the style of one of the spokes changed so that it's larger and has a dashed border.

Listing 3.8   **Defining the Rotation of the Wheels on Hover (bikemotion.css)**

```
#backwheel, #frontwheel {
  -webkit-transition: -webkit-transform 3s ease-in-out;
  -moz-transition: -moz-transform 3s ease-in-out;
  -o-transition: -o-transform 3s ease-in-out;
  transition: transform 3s ease-in-out;
}

#frontwheel:hover, #backwheel:hover {
  -webkit-transform: rotate(720deg);
```

```
 -moz-transform: rotate(720deg);
 -ms-transform: rotate(720deg);
 -o-transform: rotate(720deg);
 transform: rotate(720deg);
}
```

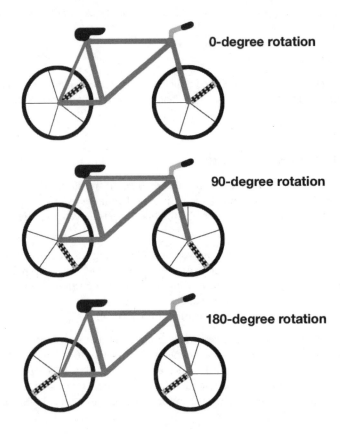

Figure 3.2   Wheels with 0-degree, 90-degree, and 180-degree rotations applied to #frontwheel and #backwheel

Animating the Bike to Move Across the Screen

You've seen how to spin the wheels, and in this chapter's final example, you'll combine spinning wheels with a moving bike, to make the bike appear to move back and forth across the screen. So far, you have been having your bike animation move on hover. Now you'll add a bit of JavaScript so you can listen for a click event and then trigger the bicycle to move across the screen in response.

To begin, you set the up a 3-second transition for any change to a transform that happens to the #bike element, running with the linear timing function (see Listing 3.9).

Listing 3.9   **Setting up a Transition for the Bike (bikemotion.css)**

```
#bike {
  -webkit-transition: -webkit-transform 3s linear;
  -moz-transition: -moz-transform 3s linear;
  -o-transition: -o-transform 3s linear;
  transition: transform 3s linear;
}
```

Next, in Listing 3.10 you define the translation that should occur to the #bike element when it has the class attribute set to move. Initially, the #bike div does not have its class attribute set. You can use JavaScript to programmatically add this new move to the class attribute in response to a user click.

Listing 3.10   **Translating the #bike Element via the move Class Selector (bikemotion.css)**

```
#bike.move {
  -webkit-transform: translateX(500px);
  -moz-transform: translateX(500px);
  -ms-transform: translateX(500px);
  -o-transform: translateX(500px);
  transform: translateX(500px);
}
```

In Listing 3.9 and 3.10, you now have two different selectors (#bike and the #frontwheel, #backwheel grouped selector) that are setting up transitions. You might be tempted to combine this transition setup into a single selector, since they both occur over 3 seconds. However, it is important that they remain apart because each of these transitions uses a different timing function. If you were to define a single transition, you could no longer have the bike's translation occur over a linear timing function. Instead, the wheels would animate with the ease-in-out timing function.

When a given element has more than one selector that matches it, applying a different transition to different matching selectors is also helpful if you want to set up different transition durations for different transform types. As noted earlier, there is currently no way to list a specific `transform` type as a `transition-property`; you are limited to the property `transform`. But with different selectors defining different transitions, as is done in Listing 3.9 and 3.10, you can specify different animation configurations for different `transform` types.

Spinning the Wheels as the Bike Moves

In addition to moving the bike across the screen in response to a user clicking on the bike, you can also spin the wheels. Listing 3.11 defines a class selector, `.spin`, that causes a 1,080-degree rotation when it's applied.

Listing 3.11   **Rotating the Wheels with a `transform` (bikemotion.css)**

```
.spin {
  -webkit-transform: rotate(1080deg);
  -moz-transform: rotate(1080deg);
  -ms-transform: rotate(1080deg);
  -o-transform: rotate(1080deg);
  transform: rotate(1080deg);
}
```

Triggering the Animation

Now you can leverage JavaScript to add the `spin` class to both wheels when the user clicks the bike. In Listing 3.12 you set up an event listener on the click event for the bike `div`. When the bike is clicked, you check whether the bike `div` has a class name present. If it doesn't (which originally it does not), you add the class name `move` to it, and you add the class name `spin` to the front and back wheels. On the subsequent click, because a class name is now present, you remove both class names from the elements, and the bike animates back to the left of the page. You can try this out for yourself by visiting the demo at http://alexisgo.github.com/LearningCSSAnimations/ch3code/bike.html.

Listing 3.12   **Triggering a Class Name Change on Click (bike.js)**

```
var bike = document.getElementById("bike");
bike.addEventListener("click", pedal, false);

function pedal() {
  var frontwheel, backwheel, bike;
  bike = document.getElementById("bike");
  backwheel = document.getElementById("backwheel");
  frontwheel = document.getElementById("frontwheel");

  if (bike.className) {
    bike.className = "";
```

```
    backwheel.className = "";
    frontwheel.className = "";
  }
  else {
    bike.className = "move";
    backwheel.className = "spin";
    frontwheel.className = "spin";
  }
}
```

Additional Resources

To learn more about CSS3 transitions, I recommend the following resources and tutorials:

- CSS Transitions, W3C Working Draft: http://www.w3.org/TR/css3-transitions/
- Transition overview from CSS3 Files: http://www.css3files.com/transition/
- A thorough explanation of timing functions from the Mozilla Developer Network: https://developer.mozilla.org/en-US/docs/CSS/timing-function

Summary

In this chapter you learned how to animate certain CSS properties with transitions. You learned all the configurations available to you: `transition-property`, `transition-duration`, `transition-timing-function`, and `transition-delay`. You also reviewed the particulars of animating transforms with these transitions. You enhanced your bicycle example to add spinning wheels and to move the bike back and forth across the screen in response to clicks.

Challenge

Enhance the bicycle example to include two spinning pedals that rotate at a slightly different pace than the wheels. Once you have added two rotating pedals, try to make the bike do a wheelie as it moves across the screen. To accomplish this, you might want to try changing the `transform-origin` property on the `#bike div` and then rotate the `#bike` element.

4

Keyframe Animations

This chapter outlines the basics of keyframe animations, which give you more fine-grained control over the various stages of an animation than do transitions. You will learn about the many properties you can use with keyframe animations by applying them to a simple animation: an element cycling through various shades of gray. You will also create a bouncing spring and a floating balloon in order to demonstrate the effects that can be achieved through the use of keyframe animations.

Introduction to Keyframe Animations

Keyframe animations enable you to outline multiple key points, or "keyframes," within an animation. You can use them in the same way you used transitions in Chapter 3, "Animating Elements with Transitions," but they also allow you to animate more complex paths and provide more configuration options for tweaking how an animation runs. Like transitions, keyframe animations allow you to take advantage of the browser's ability to interpolate between two points.

Transitions give you the ability to have a starting point and an ending point. In contrast, keyframe animations allow you to define animations with multiple intermediate steps. In these intermediate steps, you can configure an animation in powerful ways, such as using different timing functions throughout the stages of the animation. Keyframe animations also have configuration options that aren't available with transitions: You can specify how many times an animation should play, change the direction of an animation, and apply the styles from an animation to an animated element even after the animation has completed.

Browser Support for Keyframe Animations

The following browsers currently support keyframe animations:

- Android Browser 2.1+
- Chrome 4.0+
- Firefox 5.0+

- Internet Explorer 10.0+
- iOS Safari 3.2+ and Safari 4.0+
- Opera 12.0+

At the time of this writing, there is support for the standard keyframe animation syntax (the non-vendor-prefixed syntax) in Opera 12.5, Firefox 16, and Internet Explorer 10.

Creating a Basic Keyframe

Creating a keyframe animation requires two distinct steps:

1. Set up the keyframes of the animation.

2. Configure the animation by setting properties that control the way the animation plays.

You set up keyframe animations by using the `@keyframes` CSS at-rule. This at-rule allows you to specify, for example, how an animation starts and how it should end. Using a keyframe in this most basic way is not substantially different from using a transition. Indeed, if you simply need to move from one value to another, you are better off using a transition.

To create a new set of keyframes, you begin by adding the `@keyframes` at-rule and giving a name to the keyframe animation you are creating. You need to use the vendor-prefixed version of the keyframe animation syntax to ensure support for WebKit browsers, Firefox version 15 and earlier, and Opera 12. To define a new keyframe animation called `animation-name`, to ensure support in all browsers, you would write this:

```
@-webkit-keyframes animation-name { }
@-moz-keyframes animation-name { }
@-o-keyframes animation-name { }
@keyframes animation-name { }
```

Internet Explorer 10 is the first version of Internet Explorer to support keyframes, so you don't need to worry about the `-ms-` prefix in this case

Next, you define the keyframes that make up your animation. If you are defining only two keyframes, you can use the keywords `from` and `to`, each followed by a block of CSS that contains all the styles you want to apply to that keyframe, as shown in Listing 4.1.

Listing 4.1   **Basic Keyframe Syntax**

```
@-webkit-keyframes animation-name {
  from { /* CSS styles for the first frame */ }
  to { /* CSS styles for the final frame*/ }
}
@-moz-keyframes animation-name {
  from { /* CSS styles for the first frame */ }
  to { /* CSS styles for the final frame*/ }
```

```
}
@-o-keyframes animation-name {
  from { /* CSS styles for the first frame */ }
  to { /* CSS styles for the final frame*/ }
}
@keyframes animation-name {
  from { /* CSS styles for the first frame */ }
  to { /* CSS styles for the final frame*/ }
}
```

The Components of a Keyframe

Per the W3C CSS animations spec (http://www.w3.org/TR/css3-animations/#keyframes), there are three components to a keyframe:

- The @keyframes at-rule
- The keyframe selector
- The keyframe declaration block

The @keyframes at-rule consists of the keyword @keyframes followed by a name for the animation and then a set of CSS style rules, as shown in Listing 4.1.

The keyframe selector is either the keywords from and to (as in Listing 4.1), the percentage value representing where in the animation that frame occurs (as you will see in Listing 4.4), or a comma-separated list of percentage values that define multiple places in the animation where the same frame occurs (as you will see in Listing 4.7).

Finally, the keyframe declaration block is made up of the property/value pairs specified within the keyframe selector.

Here is a summary of how you use @keyframes, the keyframe selector, and the keyframe declarations together to define the keyframes:

```
@keyframes animation-name {
  <keyframe selector>: { <keyframe declaration>; }
}
```

For example, if you wanted to animate a change in the background-color of an element from black to light gray—rgb(211,211,211)—you could set up the keyframes as shown in Listing 4.2.

Listing 4.2   Changing background-color with Keyframes (colorchange.html)

```
@-webkit-keyframes colorchange {
  from { background-color: black; }
  to { background-color: rgb(211,211,211); }
```

```
}

@-moz-keyframes colorchange {
  from { background-color: black; }
  to { background-color: rgb(211,211,211); }
}

@-o-keyframes colorchange {
  from { background-color: black; }
  to { background-color: rgb(211,211,211); }
}

@keyframes colorchange {
  from { background-color: black; }
  to { background-color: rgb(211,211,211); }
}
```

Setting `animation` Properties

Setting up the `@keyframes` at-rule is only the first step in creating a keyframe. Next, you must assign the keyframe you've created to an element and configure how the animation should play. At a minimum, there are two properties you must set in order to play the animation: `animation-name` and `animation-duration`.

For example, assume that you used HTML to define an element with the `id` attribute set to `#animateMe`. You can configure the `colorchange` `@keyframes` defined in Listing 4.2 to act on the `#animateMe` element by setting `animation-name` to `colorchange` (see Listing 4.3).

You must also define how long the animation should last, and you do so with the `animation-duration` property. You can define a value in seconds by following the number with `s`, or you can define the duration in milliseconds by following the number with `ms`. Because no browsers at the time of this writing support the non-prefixed animation property names, you use only the prefixed version of both properties. You can view a demo of this code in action at http://alexisgo.github.com/LearningCSSAnimations/ch3code/colorchange.html.

Listing 4.3   **Configuring a Keyframe Animation with `animation-name` and `animation-duration` (colorchange.html)**

```
<style>
#animateMe {
  width: 100px;
  height: 100px;
  background-color: black;

  -webkit-animation-name: colorchange;
  -moz-animation-name: colorchange;
```

```
  -o-animation-name: colorchange;
  animation-name: colorchange;

  -webkit-animation-duration: 5s;
  -moz-animation-duration: 5s;
  -o-animation-duration: 5s;
  animation-duration: 5s;
  </style>
</head>
<body>
  <div id="animateMe"></div>
</body>
```

`animation-name` and `animation-duration` are only two of the eight animation properties currently defined in the CSS animations specification. You will learn about the rest of the animation properties, all of which are optional, later in this chapter.

Using Percentages in Keyframe Selectors

While you can certainly use keyframe animations in the ways demonstrated so far in this chapter, if you are simply changing between two values, keyframe animations do not provide much benefit over transitions. But one way that keyframes are much more flexible than transitions is that they allow you to animate in only one direction, rather than going full circle, as all transitions do. For example, you can't hover on a transition and have the element preserve the styles applied by the transition; when you hover away, the element's styles return to their original state. With keyframes, as you will see when we discuss the property `animation-fill-mode`, you can specify that the styles added at the end of the keyframe animation persist past the end of the animation.

Another time when keyframe animations come in handy is when you have three or more keyframes you would like to define. In that case, you would not use the `from` and `to` keyframe selectors but rather use percentage values that define at what point in the animation the keyframe should occur. Note that using `from` is the same as using 0% and that using `to` is the same as using 100%. For example, if you want to create an animation with three major frames, each occurring one-third of the way through the animation, you can set up the keyframes as shown in Listing 4.4. Note that the first keyframe, 0%, denotes the starting point of the animation.

Listing 4.4 **Keyframe Animation to Change a Color Multiple Times (bwKeyframes.css)**

```
@-webkit-keyframes rangeOfGrays {
  0% { background-color: black; }
  33% { background-color: rgb(211,211,211); }
  66% { background-color: rgb(105,105,105); /*darkgray*/; }
  100% { background-color: gray; }
}
```

```
@-moz-keyframes rangeOfGrays {
  0% { background-color: black; }
  33% { background-color: rgb(211,211,211); }
  66% { background-color: rgb(105,105,105); /*darkgray*/; }
  100% { background-color: gray; }
}

@-o-keyframes rangeOfGrays {
  0% { background-color: black; }
  33% { background-color: rgb(211,211,211); }
  66% { background-color: rgb(105,105,105); /*darkgray*/; }
  100% { background-color: gray; }
}

@keyframes rangeOfGrays {
  0% { background-color: black; }
  33% { background-color: rgb(211,211,211); }
  66% { background-color: rgb(105,105,105); /*darkgray*/; }
  100% { background-color: gray; }


}
```

It is important to emphasize how the frames in the `@keyframes` at-rule work together. On their own, the frames do not do anything. It is the time *in between* the frames that counts. Two frames always work together in order to define the change that occurs. In Listing 4.4, it is not the 0% styles nor the 33% styles that define the change but the two working in conjunction. The change that will be animated is the difference between the styles in the 0% frame and the styles in the 33% frame. The styles in Listing 4.4 are applied to the element #animation in the HTML, which is a simple `div` element:

```
<div id="animation"></div>
```

Now that you have defined the keyframes, you must also configure the keyframe animation itself. In Listing 4.5, you assign the animation to the `rangeOfGrays` `@keyframes` and set the `animation-duration` to 5 seconds. A demo of this code is available at http://alexisgo.github.com/LearningCSSAnimations/ch4code/bwKeyframes.html.

Listing 4.5   **Configuring the Color Change Animation (bwKeyframes.css)**

```
#animation {
  width: 100px;
  height: 100px;
  background-color: black;

  -webkit-animation-name: rangeOfGrays;
  -moz-animation-name: rangeOfGrays;
  -o-animation-name: rangeOfGrays;
```

```
  animation-name: rangeOfGrays;

  -webkit-animation-duration: 5s;
  -moz-animation-duration: 5s;
  -o-animation-duration: 5s;
  animation-duration: 5s;
}
```

Figure 4.1 shows the resulting animation, as well as the intermediate points between the keyframes.

Figure 4.1   Changing from black to light gray to dark gray to gray, with the intermediate colors shown in the smaller boxes.

> ## Note
>
> The examples so far have always had at least two keyframes specified. However, you are only actually required to specify one keyframe. If a `to` and/or `from` keyframe (or a 0% and/or 100% keyframe) is missing, the browser automatically constructs it. So you could, technically, define only a 50% keyframe, and the browser would construct the 0% and 100% keyframes (based on the original style of the element with the animation applied).
>
> For example, assume that you have a single `div` element with a blue background color, assigned to a keyframe animation called `makeRed`:
>
> ```
>     div {
>       background-color: blue;
>       animation-name: makered;
>       animation-duration: 2s;
>     }
>     @keyframes makeRed {
>       50% {
>         background-color:red;
>       }
>     }
> ```
>
> Because the `makeRed` keyframe animation defines only the 50% keyframe, the browser constructs the 0% and 100% keyframes to both have a background color of blue. Thus, the element will begin blue, change to red, and then halfway through the animation, it will begin to change back to blue again.

Controlling a Keyframe Animation with Properties

You can configure six optional properties in order to more finely control keyframe animations:

- **animation-fill-mode:** This property defines what styles from the animation are applied to the animation's target element before and after the animation executes. The default is none.

- **animation-iteration-count:** This property indicates how many times the animation should be played. The default is one.

- **animation-direction:** This property defines whether the animation should play in reverse (from 100% to 0%) or whether it should play in reverse on certain iterations of the animation. The default is normal, which means the animation will play from start (0%) to finish (100%).

- **animation-timing-function:** This property controls the speed at which intermediate points of the transition animation play over its duration. The default is ease.

- **animation-delay:** This property defines how long the animation should wait before it begins playing once it has been triggered. It is measured in seconds (s) or milliseconds (ms). The default is 0.

- **animation-play-state:** This property defines the current state of an animation—that is, whether it is running or paused. The default is running. Note that this property would be used only in response to an event occurring on the page (such as the user hovering over an element), and it cannot be used as a state within an individual keyframe.

animation-fill-mode

If you review the demo page for Listing 4.4, available at http://alexisgo.github.com/LearningCSSAnimations/ch4code/bwKeyframes.html, you will notice that at the very end of the animation, the element snaps back to its original background-color, black. This is jarring and probably not the effect you want to achieve. In order to prevent this, you can make use of one of the optional animation properties, animation-fill-mode. animation-fill-mode defines what happens to the element being animated either before or after the animation is running. These are the available values for animation-fill-mode:

- none (the default)

- forwards

- backwards

- both

When animation-fill-mode is set to none, whatever style was applied to the animated element before it began animating will be the style applied to it after the animation is complete. In our case, the div element had a black background-color to begin with, so that is what is re-applied once the animation finishes.

Let's suppose that you'd like to make the final value of your animation, the gray background-color, apply to the element even after the animation completes. You can accomplish this by setting animation-fill-mode to forwards. The forwards value applies the styles defined in the final keyframe to the element after the animation is completed. Typically, the final keyframe is either the to keyframe or the 100% keyframe. However, this is not always the case, as you will see later, in Listing 4.7. The final keyframe can also be the from keyframe or the 0% keyframe if the animation is alternating back and forth.

In Listing 4.6, you add the animation-fill-mode property in order to make the final gray background-color apply past the end of the animation. Note that the changes you've specified are in a new file, bwKeyframesStick.html. As with all the other examples in this chapter, the source code for this file is available on the book's GitHub page (https://github.com/alexisgo/LearningCSSAnimations) and a demo of the file can be found at http://alexisgo.github.com/LearningCSSAnimations/ch4code/bwKeyframesStick.html.

Listing 4.6   **Preserving the Style of the Final Keyframe with animation-fill-mode:
forwards (bwKeyframesStick.html)**

```
<head>
  <!-- base css for bw keyframes animations -->
  <link rel="stylesheet" href="css/bwKeyframes.css">

  <!-- custom css for this file -->
  <style>
  #animation {
    -webkit-animation-fill-mode: forwards;
    -moz-animation-fill-mode: forwards;
    -o-animation-fill-mode: forwards;
    animation-fill-mode: forwards;
  }
  </style>
</head>
<body>
  <div id="animation"></div>
</body>
```

Setting animation-fill-mode to backwards causes the styles applied in the first keyframe to apply during the period defined in the animation-delay property. Setting animation-fill-mode to both combines the effects of forwards and backwards. It applies the styles of the first keyframe to the period of delay (if any) before the animation runs, and it also applies the styles of the last keyframe to the element when the animation has finished executing.

Instead of modifying the animation-fill-mode property to make the final keyframe's background-color stick, you could instead simply end the final keyframe with the background-color black. That way, the animation would end on the same color it begins on, and you wouldn't notice the rapid change back to the original color when the animation ends.

If you use this approach, rather than have a separate entry just for 100% to specify black as the `background-color`, you can use the concept of grouping selectors to save some typing. The 0% keyframe already defines black as the `background-color`. So you can apply this style to both the 0% and the 100% keyframes by grouping the selectors together. This is demonstrated in Listing 4.7, with the grouped selectors highlighted in bold for emphasis.

Listing 4.7   **Grouping Keyframe Selectors**

```
@-webkit-keyframes rangeOfGrays{
    0%, 100% { background-color: black; }
    25% { background-color: lightgray; }
    50% { background-color: darkgray; }

@-moz-keyframes rangeOfGrays{
    0%, 100% { background-color: black; }
    25% { background-color: lightgray; }
    50% { background-color: darkgray; }
}
@-o-keyframes rangeOfGrays{
    0%, 100% { background-color: black; }
    25% { background-color: lightgray; }
    50% { background-color: darkgray; }
}

@keyframes rangeOfGrays{
    0%, 100% { background-color: black; }
    25% { background-color: lightgray; }
    50% { background-color: darkgray; }
}
```

animation-iteration-count

With keyframe animations, you are not limited to playing animations a single time. You can configure exactly how many times you would like an animation to play, or you can even make it repeat infinitely.

To specify that an animation should repeat a certain number of times, you can use the `animation-iteration-count` property. If you want the animation to repeat infinitely, you can set `animation-iteration-count` to the keyword `infinite`. If you want the animation to play two full times, you can set `animation-iteration-count` to 2. If you set `animation-iteration-count` to 2, the resulting animation will be a black square that changes to light gray, then dark gray, and then back to black. This color change is then repeated another time. Because you begin and end with black, the two iterations blend together. If the 100% keyframe were gray instead of black, in between the first and second iteration of the animation, the color would jump (without any transition between the colors) from gray back to black. Listing 4.8

demonstrates the use of `animation-iteration-count`. A demo of this code can be found at http://alexisgo.github.com/LearningCSSAnimations/ch4code/bwKeyframesRepeat.html.

Listing 4.8   **Replaying the Color Change Animation with `animation-iteration-count` (bwKeyframesRepeat.html)**

```
<!-- base css for bw keyframes animations -->
<link rel="stylesheet" href="css/bwKeyframes.css">

<!-- custom css for this file -->
<style>
#animation {
  -webkit-animation-iteration-count: 2;
  -moz-animation-iteration-count: 2;
  -o-animation-iteration-count: 2;
}
</style>
```

animation-direction

Setting `animation-direction` to `alternate` causes the animation to play *forward* (from the 0% keyframe to the 100% keyframe) on even-numbered iterations and *backward* (from the 100% keyframe to the 0% keyframe) on odd-numbered iterations. Note that in order to use `animation-direction`, the `animation-iteration-count` property needs to be set to 2 or higher or to `infinite`.

The default value for `animation-direction` is `normal`, which causes the animation to play the way it did in Listing 4.8—that is, from start to finish on each iteration.

To demonstrate this, instead of ending when the section element turns gray, you can make the animation play again in reverse, cycling back through the background colors defined in the keyframes. Listing 4.9 does this by setting `animation-direction` to `alternate`. You can see a demo of the effect this creates at http://alexisgo.github.com/LearningCSSAnimations/ch4code/bwKeyframesReverse.html.

Listing 4.9   **Reversing an Animation with `animation-direction` (bwKeyframesReverse.html)**

```
<!-- base css for bw keyframes animations -->
<link rel="stylesheet" href="css/bwKeyframes.css">

<!-- custom css for this file -->
<style>
#animation {
  -webkit-animation-iteration-count: 2;
  -moz-animation-iteration-count: 2;
  -o-animation-iteration-count: 2;
  animation-iteration-count: 2;
```

```
    -webkit-animation-direction: alternate;
    -moz-animation-direction: alternate;
    -o-animation-direction: alternate;
    animation-direction: alternate;
}
</style>
```

Because you set the `animation-iteration-count` to 2, the `animation-fill-mode: forwards` will set the 0% keyframe as the final keyframe. This is because with two repeats of the animation, the final keyframe before the animation ends is in fact the 0% keyframe.

animation-delay

You can delay the start of an animation by using the property `animation-delay`. `animation-delay` causes the very first run of the animation to wait the specified amount of time before beginning to execute.

Note that the delay will apply *only* to the very first iteration of the animation. The delay will not occur during animation repeats.

If you want to delay the start of the `rangeOfGrays` animation by 2 seconds, you would write this:

```
-webkit-animation-delay: 2s;
-moz-animation-delay: 2s;
-o-animation-delay: 2s;
animation-delay: 2s;
```

animation-play-state

If you would like an animation to pause in response to a user action, you can take advantage of the `animation-play-state` property. `animation-play-state` has two possible values: `paused` and `running`. If you would like to freeze the color-changing element when someone hovers over it, you can accomplish this by setting `animation-play-state` to paused in the `:hover` pseudo-class. Listing 4.10 enhances the bwKeyframesReverse.html file to also include this ability to pause the animation on hover.

Listing 4.10   **Pausing an Animation with `animation-play-state` (bwKeyframesReverse.html)**

```
#animation:hover {
  -webkit-animation-play-state: paused;
    -moz-animation-play-state: paused;
      -o-animation-play-state: paused;
        animation-play-state: paused;
}
```

The `animation` Shorthand Property

Because there are so many properties you can define in order to fine-tune an animation, and because you need to contend with a number of vendor prefixes for any production animation, it makes sense to leverage the `animation` shorthand property. This shorthand allows you to combine nearly all the available animation properties into a single line:

```
animation: <animation-name> <animation-duration> <animation-timing-function>
  <animation-delay> <animation-iteration-count> <animation-direction>
  <animation-fill-mode>
```

If any of the optional properties are absent, they simply revert to their default values.

Note that there is one property the shorthand does not account for: `animation-play-state`. If you want to pause the animation, you cannot do so via the animation shorthand; you must set it via the `animation-play-state` property.

If you'd like to apply more than one keyframe animation to a single element, you can still use the `animation` shorthand property. You must, however, list all the properties you'll apply to the first animation, insert a comma, and then list the next animation name and all the properties associated with it.

Also note that, as with the `transition` shorthand property, if you use the `animation` shorthand and specify only a single timing value, the first supplied value will always be used for the `animation-duration` property. Thus, in order to add a delay via the `animation` shorthand property, you must include values for both `animation-duration` and `animation-delay`.

Listing 4.11 demonstrates an example of how to use the `animation` shorthand property with two different `@keyframes`.

Listing 4.11   **Using the `animation` Shorthand with Multiple `@keyframes`**

```
#animateMe {
  animation: animation1 3s, animation2 4s;
}
```

Listing 4.12 demonstrates again how to use the animation shorthand with two `@keyframes`, but this time specifying all the optional animation properties as well.

Listing 4.12   **Using the `animation` Shorthand with Multiple `@keyframes` and All Properties Defined**

```
#animateMe {
  /* The order of the animation properties is:
    <animation-name> <animation-duration> <animation-timing-function>
    <animation-delay> <animation-iteration-count> <animation-direction>
    <animation-fill-mode>
  */
```

```
animation:
  animation1 3s ease-in 1s 2 alternate,
  animation2 4s ease-in-out 2s normal none;
}
```

As shown in Listing 4.13, you can rewrite the code configuring the `rangeOfGrays` @ `keyframes` to utilize the `animation` shorthand property instead of explicitly listing all the properties used.

Listing 4.13 **Updating the `#animation` Element to Use the `animation` Shorthand (bwKeyframesShorthand.html)**

```
#animation {
  /*animation: name, duration, timing function, delay, iteration count,
            direction, fill mode */
  -webkit-animation: rangeOfGrays 5s linear 0s 2 alternate forwards;
  -moz-animation: rangeOfGrays 5s linear 0s 2 alternate forwards;
  -o-animation: rangeOfGrays 5s linear 0s 2 alternate forwards;
  animation: rangeOfGrays 5s linear 0s 2 alternate forwards;
}
```

Animating a Recoiling Spring

To further practice using keyframe animations, in this section, you'll animate a spring being compressed and then released. When you compress a spring and release it, it bounces back to a length longer than its starting size, due to the force it accumulated—that is, the spring temporarily stretches out (see Figure 4.2). You can view a demo of this at http://alexisgo.github.com/LearningCSSAnimations/ch4code/spring.html.

Figure 4.2   Animating a spring being compressed and then recoiling

You could not easily accomplish this example by using transitions because you need to scale the spring down, up, and then down again. A transition on the `div` element that contains the spring image could only animate between two points. With keyframes, you can modify the spring over and over again, defining all the manipulations you'd like to see in their own keyframe.

To begin, you set up the HTML. The HTML consists of a container `div` and another `div` that uses an image of a spring as its background, as shown in Listing 4.14.

Listing 4.14   **Styling a `div` with a Spring Image (spring.html)**

```
<body>
  <div id="container">
    <div id="spring"></div>
  </div>
</body>
```

Creating the Keyframes for the Spring's Compress and Recoil

To accomplish the compressing and recoil of the spring, you need three keyframes, which are created in Listing 4.15. In Listing 4.15 we also define some basic styles for the `#spring` element.

> **Note**
>
> In this example and all subsequent code listings in this chapter, for the sake of brevity, we use only the `-webkit-` vendor prefix. You can, however, find all the vendor prefixes in the spring.css file inside the ch4code/css/ folder at https://github.com/alexisgo/LearningCSSAnimations.

Listing 4.15   **Compressing and Releasing a Spring (spring.css)**

```
#spring {
  background-image: url('../img/spring.png');
  width: 50px;
  height: 182px;
}

@-webkit-keyframes spring {
  0% { -webkit-transform: scale(1);}
  30% { -webkit-transform: scale(1, 0.5); }
  40% { -webkit-transform: scale(1, 1.5); }
}
```

The first keyframe, 0%, defines the starting point of the spring—the original image with no scaling.

The second keyframe, 30%, defines the end state of the compressed spring—in other words, how far down the spring should be squished before it is released. Here, you scale down the size of the spring image to one-half its original height, leaving the width unchanged. Recall from Chapter 2, "Building a Foundation with Transforms," that if you specify two values in the `scale` transform function, the first value modifies the scaling of width and the second value modifies the scaling of the height. In this and all subsequent keyframes, you will keep the width of the spring the same but scale the height up and down.

In this case, you'll make this (the animation between the 0% and 30% keyframes) the longest point in the animation because compressing a spring down is usually a difficult task that doesn't happen immediately. It is also a task that takes longer than the subsequent recoil of the spring once it's released, which will happen very rapidly.

The browser uses these two keyframes, 0% and 30%, to animate all intermediate points between those two keyframes, thus creating the animation. In terms of duration, the animation will take 30% (from 0% to 30%) of the time of the entire animation to scale down the spring to half of its original size. To be more specific, if the entire animation lasts 3 seconds, the change between the 0% and 30% keyframes will take 0.9 seconds.

In the final keyframe, 40%, you scale up the size of the spring to one-and-a-half times its original height, again leaving the width unchanged. The animation will take 10% (from 30% to 40%) of the time of the entire animation to stretch the scrunched-up spring out to 150% of its original size. Figure 4.3 shows the changes that these first three keyframes trigger.

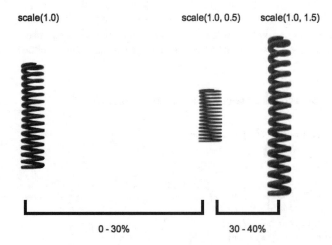

Figure 4.3   The first three keyframes of the spring animation create two actions: a compression and a recoil.

Controlling the Animation's Playback

Now that you have defined the keyframes, you need to set up how the animation will play. You can do so via the `animation` shorthand property (see Listing 4.16). You point the animation to the `spring` `@keyframes` and specify that the `animation-duration` should be 2.8 seconds.

Listing 4.16   **Configuring Animation Properties for the Spring (spring.css)**

```
#spring {
  /* Continued from Listing 4.15  */
  -webkit-animation: spring 2.8s;
  -moz-animation: spring 2.8s;
  -o-animation: spring 2.8s;
  animation: spring 2.8s;
}
```

Adding Additional Compress and Recoil Keyframes

If you were to press a spring down and let go, there would not simply be a single recoil. The spring would recoil, stretching itself out, and then compress down again, then recoil again, compress, and so on, until it finally exerts all of its energy.

In order to create an animation that reflects this, you can add additional keyframes, as shown in Listing 4.17. For the 50% keyframe, you can set the scale transform function to scale the height down to 0.7, or 70% of its original height.

At the 61% keyframe, you can recoil the spring again, this time scaling to 1.4 (140%) of the original height of the spring. Notice that instead of doing the compression over 10% of the animation, you can make this keyframe last a little longer: 11% of the animation (50% to 61%). The idea here is that the very first recoil will be the fastest, and subsequent recoils (and compressions) will last longer.

Listing 4.17   **Adding Another Compression and Recoil to the Spring Animation (spring.css)**

```
@-webkit-keyframes spring {
  0% { -webkit-transform: scale(1);}
  30% { -webkit-transform: scale(1, 0.5); }
  40% { -webkit-transform: scale(1, 1.5); }
  /* compresses in again */
  50% { -webkit-transform: scale(1, 0.7);}
  /* stretches out */
  61% { -webkit-transform: scale(1, 1.4);}
}
```

For each subsequent recoil, you scale the spring by a smaller number (but still scale it above 100% of its original size). In each subsequent compression, you scale up the spring by a slightly larger number (but, again, less than 100% of its original size). Finally, at the final, 100%, keyframe, you return the spring image to its original size by scaling it to 1. Listing 4.18 shows the complete code for this example, and Figure 4.4 shows what the animation looks like.

Listing 4.18   **One Additional Compression/Recoil in the Spring Animation**

```
@-webkit-keyframes spring {
  0% { -webkit-transform: scale(1); }
  30% { -webkit-transform: scale(1, 0.5); }
  40% { -webkit-transform: scale(1, 1.5); }
  /* compresses in again */
  50% { -webkit-transform: scale(1, 0.7); }
  /* stretches out */
  61% { -webkit-transform: scale(1, 1.4); }
  /* compress */
  72% { -webkit-transform: scale(1, 0.8); }
  /*stretch*/
  83% { -webkit-transform: scale(1, 1.2); }
  100% { -webkit-transform: scale(1); }
}
```

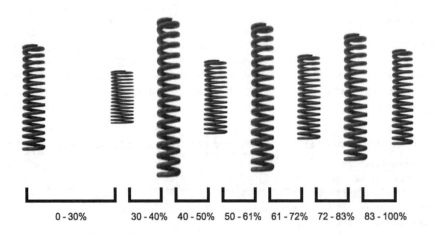

Figure 4.4   The complete set of keyframes that make up the recoiling spring

Animating a Floating Balloon

You don't have to rely on putting all the changes you'd like to apply on one element into a single keyframe. You can take advantage of the fact that the `animation` shorthand property allows a comma-separated list of animations in order to apply multiple keyframe animations to one element. In this example, you will create a floating balloon that applies three different animations on a single element. As with the previous example, you will be using only the -webkit- prefix for brevity, but the sample code on the book's website contains all the prefixes.

First, you set up the base HTML and style for a basic blue balloon. Listings 4.19 and 4.20 provide this code.

Listing 4.19   **Base HTML for the Floating Balloon Animation Page (balloon.html)**

```
<head>
  <link rel="stylesheet" href="css/base.css">
  <script src="js/modernizr.custom.57498.js"></script>
</head>
<body>
  <div id="container">
    <div id="balloon"></div>
    <div id="balloon-tie"></div>
    <div id="string"></div>
  </div>
</body>
```

Listing 4.20   **Styling the Balloon (balloon.html)**

```
#container {
  width: 100px;
  margin: 0 auto;
  position: relative;
}
#balloon
{
  background-color: blue;
  width: 60px;
  height: 70px;
  border-radius: 40px;
}
#balloon-tie {
  border-top: none;
  width: 1px;
  border-left: 10px solid transparent;
  border-right: 10px solid transparent;
  border-bottom: 10px solid blue;
  position: relative;
```

```
    left: 18px;
    top: -1px;
}
#string {
    width: 1px;
    height: 130px;
    background-color:black;
    position: relative;
    top: -1px;
    left: 28px;
}
```

The #container element holds all elements of the balloon: the balloon itself, the small tie at the bottom, and the balloon's string. This #container is also the major element that you will be applying animations to.

Applying Multiple Keyframe Animations to a Single Element

In order to make the balloon float upward in a natural way, you will be applying three different changes to it: a movement straight up, a movement left and right, and a slight rotation back and forth. You could combine all these changes into a single set of keyframes. But it is difficult to combine so many aspects together. To make your life easier, you can define each of these actions as a separate set of keyframes but apply them all to the same #container element. Listing 4.21 shows the keyframes you need to create: float-lr, float-up, and wobble.

Listing 4.21   **Setting up the Keyframes to Float the Balloon (balloon.html)**

```
@-webkit-keyframes float-lr {
    0%, 40%, 80% { left: -100px; }
    20%, 60%, 100% { left: 100px;}
}

@-webkit-keyframes float-up {
    0% { top: 200px; }
    88% { top: 0;}
    92% { top: 10px;}
    96% { top: 0}
    98% { top: 5px;}
    100% { top: 0;}
}

@-webkit-keyframes wobble {
    0%, 40%, 80% { -webkit-transform: rotate(4deg);}
    20%, 60% { -webkit-transform: rotate(-4deg);}
    100% { }
}
```

The `float-lr` keyframe causes the balloon to oscillate back and forth from –100 pixels to 100 pixels. The `float-up` keyframe makes the balloon rise up from 200 pixels from the top up to 0 pixels from the top. And then you have a series of small fluctuations in the distance from the top, to create a bouncing effect. The balloon rises up smoothly until it hits the top of the browser, and then it bounces back down a couple times before settling to a stop. The final keyframe, `wobble`, makes the balloon rotate slightly back and forth, to give a sense of movement.

You might wonder why you would modify the `top` and `left` values instead of using `translateX` or `translate`. You take this approach because of a predicament with the technique of applying multiple animations to a single element: It works only if each `@keyframes` at-rule modifies a different property. For example, if you specified two `@keyframes` at-rules, both of which modify the `transform` property, the second set of keyframes would overwrite the transform of the first set of keyframes. Therefore, you cannot use the `transform` property in both the `float-lr` and `float-up` keyframes, even though they would both use different transform functions. In order to get around this problem, you can simply modify the values of the property `left` in the `float-lr` animation and the values of `top` in the `float-up` animation.

In Listing 4.22, you update the `#container` styles to include the animations you've defined in the keyframes. Note that you set `animation-fill-mode` to `forwards` to ensure that the final state of the balloon persists past the end of the animation.

Listing 4.22   **Assigning the Animation to the Balloon Container**

```
#container {
  -webkit-animation: float-up 10s ease-in-out forwards,
    float-lr 10s ease-in-out forwards,
    wobble 10s ease-in-out forwards;
}
```

You can view a demo of this code at http://alexisgo.github.com/LearningCSSAnimations/ch4code/balloon.html. Figure 4.5 shows the balloon part of the way through the animation.

Figure 4.5   A freeze-frame of the floating balloon animation

Adding a Fallback Message for Older Browsers

Browsers that do not support keyframe animations simply ignore the animations. In order to warn users that their older browsers (that is, Internet Explorer 9 and earlier) don't support CSS animations, you should add a fallback message.

In Listing 4.23, you add a new div element with the id attribute set to unsupported, which holds a message in an h1 element. The bold lines in Listing 4.23 show the new code that you're adding to the existing code in the file balloon.html.

Listing 4.23   **Adding a Warning Message for Unsupported Browsers (balloon.html)**

```
<div id="unsupported">
  <h1>Your Browser does not support
    CSS Animations. You will not be able to see the
    floating balloon animation we've set up here :(
  </h1>

</div>
<div id="container">
  <div id="balloon"></div>
  <div id="balloon-tie"></div>
```

```
    <div id="string"></div>
</div>
```

You hide the #unsupported div element by default by giving it the style display: none. You can use Modernizr (which you linked to in the head section of the balloon.html file in Listing 4.19) to see whether keyframe animations are supported by a visitor's browser.

In browsers that support keyframe animation, Modernizr adds the class csstransforms to the opening html element. If keyframe animations are not supported, Modernizr adds the class no-cssanimations.

In Listing 4.24, you specify that if .csstransforms is present, you should set the #unsupported div to display: none. If .no-csstransforms is present, then the #unsupported div is displayed (display:block). Figure 4.6 shows what this message looks like in Internet Explorer 9.

Listing 4.24   Displaying the Error Message in Browsers That Do Not Support CSS Animations (balloon.html)

```
/* Warning is hidden in browsers with
CSS Animation support */
 .cssanimations #unsupported {
   display: none;
}

/* If CSS Animations are NOT supported
 display the browser warning*/
.no-cssanimations #unsupported {
   display: block;
}
```

Additional Resources

To learn more about CSS keyframe animations, I recommend the following resources and tutorials:

- CSS Animations, W3C Working Draft: http://www.w3.org/TR/css3-animations/
- An Introduction to CSS3 Keyframe Animations by Louis Lazaris: http://coding. smashingmagazine.com/2011/05/17/an-introduction-to-css3-keyframe-animations/
- The Safari Developer Library's animation property reference: http://developer.apple. com/library/safari/#documentation/AppleApplications/Reference/SafariCSSRef/Articles/ StandardCSSProperties.html#//apple_ref/doc/uid/TP30001266-_webkit_animation

Figure 4.6   The fallback message displayed in Internet Explorer 9

Summary

In this chapter you learned the basics of keyframe animations, including how to set up keyframes themselves and how to configure the animation via a series of properties once you've established the keyframes. This chapter explores the many properties that give you more fine-grained control over animations than you have with transitions, and you have practiced combining multiple keyframes in a single element.

Challenge

This spring bounce-and-recoil animation you created in this chapter is a bit simple. In reality, a spring would likely bounce and recoil a few more times than yours does in the example. Start with the spring.html file as a base but modify the keyframes to include at least eight compression-and-recoil combinations, double the example's current four cycles of compression and recoil for the spring.

For another challenge, start with the balloon animation example and make it more realistic by animating the string as well as the balloon. You might want to rotate the string back and forth in a way similar to the rotation of the balloon. If you do this, remember to change the `transform-origin` of the string from its default (50% 50%) to a more realistic anchor point (perhaps 50% 0%).

For one last challenge, try adding a fallback error message for the examples from this chapter for browsers that support CSS animations. Use the fallback you already created for the balloon example as a template and add fallbacks to the `spring.html` example as well as the various color-changing examples early in the chapter.

Creating 3D Effects with Parallax Scrolling

Combining keyframe animations and transforms with parallax scrolling enables you to create rich, engaging content that has a 3D feel without actually doing any 3D manipulation. This chapter walks you through creating an immersive page with a sense of depth in a 2D space.

Introduction to Parallax Scrolling

Parallax scrolling is a technique in which background images move by the camera—or the person viewing the webpage—more slowly than foreground images. By creating a page that has multiple layers and then animating each layer to move across the screen at different speeds, you can create the illusion of depth.

A typical parallax scrolling effect has the background moving at the slowest speed, a midground scene moving faster than the background, and a foreground scene moving at the fastest speed. Because each layer moves at a different speed, the website appears 3D when, in fact, each layer is 2D and lives in a 2D space.

In order to create parallax scrolling in the examples in this chapter, you will combine a few concepts you have previously worked with, including the `transform` property and keyframe animations.

A Three-Layer Parallax Scrolling Animation

In this example, you will create an animation of a robot walking through the desert. It will be a simple, GIF–style animation that scrolls left to right, repeating infinitely. To create the animation, you will leverage keyframe animations and the concept of parallax scrolling. There will be three moving parts to this animation: a background that repeats, a sprite in the foreground, and a sprite in the midground. Each element will move at different speeds, which will create the illusion of depth.

> **Note**
>
> For the sake of brevity in the code samples in this chapter, in this and all subsequent examples, I use only the -webkit- vendor prefixes. As always, you can find all the vendor prefixes in the code available on this book's GitHub page, https://github.com/alexisgo/LearningCSSAnimations. The code relevant to this chapter can be found in the folder ch5code/. You can find demos of the two examples you will be creating at: http://alexisgo.github.com/LearningCSSAnimations/ch3code/.

Listing 5.1 shows the base HTML you use for the desert animation.

Listing 5.1   **The HTML Elements for the Desert Animation (parallaxLoop.html)**

```
<body>
  <div id="desert">
    <div id="tumbleweed"></div>
    <div id="shadow"></div>
    <div id="robot"></div>
  </div>
</body>
```

Creating the Background

The first layer of the animation you need to create is the background. This layer will move the slowest of the three layers. You will make the background repeat by using a keyframe animation that modifies the background-position property of the background image.

The image you use for your background will be repeated over and over. Because of this repetition, the left and right edges of the image need to be identical, so they blend together when the background is repeated. Figure 5.1 shows a photograph of a desert, which you'll use for the background image.

If this image were to repeat horizontally, it would not blend well because the left and right edges are substantially different. To fix this, you first resize the canvas of the image to be twice its original width. Then, you copy and paste the original image and flip it horizontally (see Figure 5.2). You now have a picture of a desert that is created from two mirror images of the same desert picture. Because the two edges of the image are now identical, they will blend together when the image is repeated.

Figure 5.1   The starting background image

In order for any changes you make to the `background-position` property to show up, you need the viewport (in other words, the visible area) of the animation to be smaller than the actual background image. In this case, you are going to make the `#desert` viewport (the size of the area where the animation will live) one-half the size of the background image (see Listing 5.2).

Figure 5.2   The final background desert image, which will blend together when it repeats because the edges are identical

Listing 5.2   **Setting Up the Containing Element (parallaxLoop.html)**

```
#desert {
  background-image: url('img/desert.jpg');
  overflow: hidden;
  width: 400px;
  height: 484px;
  position: relative;
}
```

In Listing 5.3, you set up the keyframes and the background animation. The key to looping the background is a clever use of the `background-position` property.

The vertical position of the background image will not be changing, so this value remains at 0% throughout the animation. You can make the horizontal location of the background image move by setting the final location of the background to the left of the original starting location by 800 pixels (that is, `-800px`). This causes the background image to be pulled to the left until the image is completely offscreen, and then it begins to repeat.

While you are not explicitly setting the `background-repeat` property, since the default is set to `repeat`, this property is the key to making this effect work. At the 100% keyframe, the viewport of the page will be essentially over the repeated image, as the original background image will have been moved entirely offscreen. You make this effect repeat forever by setting `animation-iteration-count` to `infinite` as the last value you provide to the `animation` shorthand. Because you are adding new code to an existing selector, I have highlighted the new code in bold in Listing 5.3.

Listing 5.3 **Making the Desert Background Loop with Keyframes and `background-position`** (parallaxLoop.html)

```
@-webkit-keyframes desertMove {
  0% {  background-position: 0% 0%; }
  100% {  background-position: -800px 0%;}
}

#desert {
  background-image: url('img/desert.jpg');
  overflow: hidden;
  width: 400px;
  height: 484px;
  position: relative;

  -webkit-animation: desertMove 18s linear infinite;
}
```

Animating the Midground Sprite

Now that you have created the background layer, you are going to set up the keyframes for the second layer of this animation: a tumbleweed blowing across the desert. The element itself is the `#tumbleweed` div first used in Listing 5.1. It is absolutely positioned 400 pixels to the left (see Listing 5.4), which is past the bounds of the containing `#desert` element and thus begins offscreen. You can also see from Listing 5.4 that the tumbleweed animation will last for a total of 5 seconds, the initial run of the animation will be delayed by one second, and the animation will repeat infinitely. Recall from Chapter 4 that the animation delay of one second we apply here will apply *only* to the very first iteration of the animation.

Listing 5.4 **Configuring the Tumbleweed's Styles and Animation**

```
#tumbleweed {
  width: 50px;
  height: 56px;
  background-image: url('img/tumbleweed.png');
  position: absolute;
  top: 310px;
  /* begins past the right of the containing element */
```

```
    left: 400px;
    z-index: 2;
    -webkit-animation: tumbleweed 5s ease-in 1s infinite;
}
```

In Listing 5.5 you set up the keyframe animation for the tumbleweed. You have the element starting in its default location and then set the `left` position to –60 pixels. This causes the tumbleweed to move from offscreen on one side (on the right of the container `#desert div`) to offscreen on the other side (at the left edge of the `#desert div`). In other words, it moves the tumbleweed from right to left. In addition to this right-to-left movement, you also set the tumbleweed to rotate three full 360-degree turns, in the counterclockwise direction.

Listing 5.5   **Tumbleweed Keyframes**

```
@-webkit-keyframes tumbleweed {
    0% {  }
    100% {
    /* ends off to the left of the containing element */
    left: -60px;
    -webkit-transform:  rotate(-1080deg);
    }
}
```

You apply a reduced version of the tumbleweed keyframe to add a shadow element that moves along underneath the tumbleweed. Instead of moving the element left and rotating it as you did with the tumbleweed, you simply move the shadow left. Listing 5.6 shows the keyframes, the basic styling (including the use of a radial gradient and a scale transform to create the shadow), and the animation configuration for the shadow.

Listing 5.6   **Styling and Animating the Shadow Under the Tumbleweed**

```
@-webkit-keyframes shadow {
    0% {  }
    100% {  left: -60px;  }
}
#shadow {
    width: 50px;
    height: 50px;
    -webkit-border-radius: 25px;

    position: absolute;
    top: 340px;
    left: 400px;
    z-index: 1;
```

```
/* Color the shadow with black by default,
   a semi-transparent black next, and then with a semi-transparent black
   to transparent radial gradient as the preferred option. */
background: #000000;
background: rgba(0,0,0,0.5);
background: -webkit-radial-gradient(53% 56%,
  circle farthest-side, rgba(0,0,0,0.5),
  transparent 100%);

-webkit-transform: scale(1, 0.2);

-webkit-animation: shadow 5s ease-in 1s infinite;
}
```

Animating a Foreground Sprite

Now you're ready to add a robot who will be wandering through the desert. How did a robot end up in a desert? Who knows? But he is going to keep on moving through it infinitely.

In Listing 5.7, you define the keyframes that make the robot bounce up and down as he walks. You also update the styling of the #robot element to add the configuration of the animation through the animation shorthand property. And with this listing, your Robot in the Desert animation is complete! Figure 5.3 shows a screenshot of the final animation.

Listing 5.7   **Setting Up the Walking Robot Animation**

```
@-webkit-keyframes robotMove {
  0% {  -webkit-transform: translateY(0px);}
  50% { -webkit-transform: translateY(5px);}
  100% { -webkit-transform: translateY(0px);}
}
#robot {
  width: 150px;
  height: 295px;
  background-image: url('img/robotoCropo150.png');

  position: absolute;
  left: 100px;
  top: 230px;
  z-index: 3;
  -webkit-animation: robotMove 1s linear 0 infinite;
}
```

Figure 5.3   A screenshot from the final desert parallax animation

Animating Several Scenes with Parallax Scrolling

Rather than create a single, repeating animation to create a sense of depth, you can apply the techniques of parallax scrolling across several scenes in order to create a more immersive experience.

In order to see how these core concepts can be used together, you will build a sample site with three scenes. In keeping with the robot theme already established for this chapter, you will have three robots making their way down several different city streets, as objects pass by them in the foreground and rooms are revealed through windows in the background. All the robots in this chapter appear courtesy of the artist Tabatha Paterni, whose work can be found at http://tabdesign.etsy.com.

The effect you are aiming to achieve is to move the background, the foreground robot sprites, and the midground sprites all at different speeds, in order to make the animation look 3D even though it is only 2D.

In addition, in the third scene you will have an additional layer, which is a small scene that is inside a window in the background. The background of the third scene is a transparent PNG that includes a window with empty space. This will allow you to peek inside the window and see the chair inside it as you scroll by. Figure 5.4 shows this scene.

You can find the complete code for this example in the ch5code folder on the book's GitHub page (https://github.com/alexisgo/LearningCSSAnimations), and you can find a demo of this example at http://alexisgo.github.com/LearningCSSAnimations/ch5code/robotos.html.

Figure 5.4   The third scene from the parallax scrolling example, with a robot sprite, the primary background, and a secondary background (a chair) inside the window

The Animation's Layout and Basic Styles

The animation you will be building has three scenes in all. The first and the final scene will both have sprites in them, moving across the screen at different speeds. The middle scene (scene two) is a segue scene: it consists of the transition from the background and sprites of the first scene, to the background and sprites of the final, third scene. You'll create links that allow the user to transition between the scenes by clicking.

The Animation's Core HTML

A few major elements make up this page: a containing div (#bgContainer), two background elements (#background1 and #background2), a series of sprites (#skateboard, #robot1, #bikerack, #robot2, #cat, and #inside), and three links. Listing 5.8 shows the complete code.

Listing 5.8   **Base HTML for a Parallax Scene (robotos.html)**

```html
<body>
  <div id="bgContainer">
    <div id="background1" class="bg">
      <div class="robotUnit">
        <div id="skateboard"></div>
        <div id="robot1"></div>
      </div>
      <img id="bikerack" src="img/bikerack.png" width="150">
    </div> <!-- end barground1 -->
    <img src="img/insideApt.png" id="inside">
    <div id="background2" class="bg">
      <div id="robot2"></div>
      <img src="img/cat.png" id="cat">
    </div> <!-- end background2 -->
  </div> <!-- end bgContainer -->
  <nav>
    <a href="#" class="scene one">Move!</a>
    <a href="#" class="scene two">Scene2!</a>
    <a href="#" class="scene three">Scene3!</a>
  </nav>
  <script src="http://ajax.googleapis.com/ajax/libs/jquery/1.7.1/jquery.min.js">
  </script>
  <script src="js/robotos.js"></script>
</body>
```

Base Styles for the Page

Next, you need to apply CSS to some of the major page elements. As shown in Listing 5.9, you will give the page a gray background. You define a containing element, #bgContainer, that will hold all the animations, and give it a white border, a position, and a fixed size. Finally, you define three links with white backgrounds and rounded corners.

Listing 5.9   **Basic Styles for the Page and Its Main Container (robotos.css)**

```css
body {
  background-color: rgb(50,50,50);
}

#bgContainer {
  width: 800px;
  height: 400px;
  overflow: hidden;
  border: 5px solid white;
  margin: 30px auto;
  position: relative;
```

```
}

nav {
  width: 400px;
  height: 40px;
  margin: 0 auto 50px;
  text-align: center;
}

nav a {
  background-color: white;
  padding: 5px;

  -webkit-border-radius: 12px;
          border-radius: 12px;
  -moz-background-clip: padding;
  -webkit-background-clip: padding-box;
  background-clip: padding-box;

  color: gray;
  text-decoration: none;
  font-weight: bold;
  font-size: 1.8em;

}
```

Next, you define the styles for the links that live inside the nav element. These links will appear along the bottom of the #bgContainer element, and they will look and act like buttons that allow you to click and play the next scene.

In Listing 5.10, you set up the basics of the links, all of which share the class .scene. Any changes made to opacity on these links will be transitioned—the change to opacity will occur over the course of one second. And all but the first link (.one) start out with their opacity set to 0. This is because you want to make the link for scene 2 available only after scene 1 has completely finished animating.

You also define how the links that are originally hidden are revealed: You have their opacity change to 1 after the visible class is applied.

Listing 5.10   **Basic Styles for the Scene Links (robotos.css)**

```
.scene {
  -webkit-transition: opacity 1s;
  -moz-transition: opacity 1s;
  -o-transition: opacity 1s;
  transition: opacity 1s;
}
```

```
.one.invisible {
  opacity: 0;
}
/* scene2 and 3 links are initially hidden */
.two, .three {
  opacity: 0;
}

.two.visible, .three.visible {
  opacity: 1;
}
```

For the final bit of styling before you jump into setting up the first scene, you set the two background elements shown in Listing 5.11. Both share a fixed size.

Listing 5.11   **Styling the Two Background Images (robotos.css)**

```
.bg {
  width: 1000px;
  height: 400px;
}
```

Scene 1: Creating a Skateboarding Robot

In the first scene, you have a robot on a skateboard in the foreground that skates past a wall of graffiti. This graffiti wall in the background scrolls a bit more slowly than the skateboarder. There is one more sprite, a bike rack, that moves more slowly than the robot but faster than the background. These varying speeds make the first scene look like it has 3D depth, even though you're working in only two dimensions.

The Background for Scene 1

In Listing 5.12 you will set up the CSS for the first background element, #background1. The image is a bit larger than the containing #bgContrainer element, so you use background-position to adjust which part of the image is shown. You position the element and set up a transition of 2.2 seconds to any changes to background-position and a transition of 1.5 seconds for any changes to the left property.

Listing 5.12   **Styles for Scene 1's Background (robotos.css)**

```
#background1 {
  background-image: url('../img/SFGraffiti.jpg');
  background-position: 0 -200px;
```

```
position: absolute;
left: 0; /* important to set left here or FF, Opera
won't pick up on the change to -1000px later &
won't apply the transition */

-webkit-transition: background-position 2.2s ease-in-out,
    left 1.5s ease-in-out;
-moz-transition: background-position 2.2s ease-in-out,
    left 1.5s ease-in-out;
-o-transition: background-position 2.2s ease-in-out,
    left 1.5s ease-in-out;
transition: background-position 2.2s ease-in-out,
    left 1.5s ease-in-out;
}
```

Styling Scene 1's Sprites

The first scene consists of a couple sprites, one of which is a robot riding a skateboard, as you can see in Figure 5.5. The other sprite is a bike rack, which appears in the midground. The images these sprites use, as well as their sizes, positions, and transitions, are defined in Listing 5.13.

Figure 5.5   Scene 1 from the parallax scrolling example, with two sprites (the robot on a skateboard and the bike rack) and a scrolling background

Listing 5.13   **Styles for the Scene 1 Sprites (robotos.css)**

```
.robotUnit {
  position: absolute;
  left: -300px;
  bottom: 10px;
  -webkit-transition: left 2.7s ease-in-out;
  -moz-transition: left 2.7s ease-in-out;
  -o-transition: left 2.7s ease-in-out;
  transition: left 2.7s ease-in-out;
}
#robot1, #skateboard {
  width: 150px;
  height: 205px;
  z-index: 2;
  bottom: 30px;
  left: 50px;
  position: absolute;
  background-image: url('../img/robot.png');
}

#skateboard {
  background-image: url('../img/skateboard.png');
  width: 250px;
  height: 50px;
  bottom: 0;
  left: 5px;
}

#bikerack {
  left: -300px;
  position: absolute;
  bottom: 10px;
  -webkit-transition: left 2.5s ease-in-out;
  -moz-transition: left 2.5s ease-in-out;
  -o-transition: left 2.5s ease-in-out;
  transition: left 2.5s ease-in-out;
}
```

Moving Scene 1's Elements Across the Screen

Because you have set up the .robotUnit and #bikerack transitions on #background1, the minute you change the left property (or in the case of the background, the left or the background-position property), these elements begin to animate. In Listing 5.14, you change these properties when the move class is applied. Adding the move class is the trigger to begin the transitions defined in Listing 5.13. Moving the background-position property of the

#background1 element as defined in Listing 5.14 makes the background appear to scroll as the sprites start to move.

Listing 5.14   **Moving the First Scene (robotos.css)**

```css
#background1.move {
  background-position: -250px -200px;
}

.robotUnit.move {
  left: 600px;
}
#bikerack.move {
  left: 450px;
}
```

Triggering the Transitions via JavaScript

You have set up the selectors that will change the transition-property properties, but you have yet to apply the class move to the code. You will use jQuery to add the move class, which serves as an animation trigger throughout this example. To see how all of the code listings that you have written thus far work together, scan through Listing 5.15, which is the complete JavaScript code for this example. Don't worry if it seems overwhelming; this is just a preview. We will examine this code one piece at a time.

Listing 5.15   **The Complete JavaScript Code (robotos.js)**

```javascript
$(document).ready(function(){
  $('#background1, #bgContainer, .one').on('click', function() {
    $('.robotUnit, #bikerack, #background1').addClass('move');
});

var transEndEventNames = {
    'WebkitTransition' : 'webkitTransitionEnd',
    'MozTransition'    : 'transitionend',
    // per Ian Lunn at http://www.ianlunn.co.uk/blog/articles/opera-12-
       otransitionend-bugs-and-workarounds/
    // in Opera 12 they changed the case of oTransitionEnd
    // to be otransitionend instead
    'OTransition'      : 'oTransitionEnd otransitionend',
    'msTransition'     : 'MSTransitionEnd',
    'transition'       : 'transitionend'
},
transEndEventName = transEndEventNames[ Modernizr.prefixed('transition') ];

$('.robotUnit').on(transEndEventName, function() {
```

```
  $('.one').addClass("invisible");
  $('.two').addClass("visible");
});

$('.two').on('click', function() {
  console.log('clicked');
  $('#background1').addClass('slideOut');
  $('#background2').addClass('slideIn');
  $('#cat').addClass('visible');
});

$('#background2').on(transEndEventName, function() {
  $('.two').removeClass("visible");
  $('.three').addClass("visible");
});

$('.three').on('click', function() {
  $('#robot2, #cat, #background2, #inside').addClass('move');
});
});
```

Adding the move Class to Scene 1's Elements

In Listing 5.16, you will set up an event listener to watch for the #background1 element, the #bgContainer element, or the very first a element (.one) to be clicked. When any of these elements are clicked, you apply the move class to scene 1's background and sprites, which causes their transitions to begin and starts them moving across the screen to the right.

Listing 5.16   **Triggering Scene 1's Animation on Click (robotos.js)**

```
$(document).ready(function(){
  $('#background1, #bgContainer, .one').on('click', function() {
    $('.robotUnit, #bikerack, #background1').addClass('move');
  });
  // continued in Listing 5.17
});
```

Responding to the End of the Transition

The animation you're creating moves between scenes in response to the user clicking link elements. But you don't want to make all the links available to begin with. You want to reveal the link for scene 2 only after scene 1 has completed. In order to achieve this, you need a way of being notified when the last transition of a scene ends. Luckily, the CSS3 Transitions spec (http://www.w3.org/TR/css3-transitions/#transition-events) provides this event: It's referred to as the transition end event.

There is one issue with the transition end event: Every browser defines its own name for this event. Listing 5.17 shows some helper code that allows you to determine which transition end event name you should be watching for. This code leverages a very helpful method of the Modernizr library, `prefixed()`, in order to look up the appropriate transition end event name in the array defined in the code. This code is taken from code outlined in Modernizr's own documentation, at http://modernizr.com/docs/#prefixed.

Listing 5.17   **Listening for the End of the First Transition (robotos.js)**

```
// continued from Listing 5.16
var transEndEventNames = {
    'WebkitTransition' : 'webkitTransitionEnd',
    'MozTransition'    : 'transitionend',
    'OTransition'      : 'oTransitionEnd otransitionend',
    'msTransition'     : 'MSTransitionEnd',
    'transition'       : 'transitionend'
},
transEndEventName = transEndEventNames[ Modernizr.prefixed('transition') ];
```

Modernizr's `prefixed()` Method

`Modernizr.prefixed()` allows you to pass the CSS property you'd like to use as an argument to the method, and the method will output the appropriate property name. For example, if a user is using Firefox, calling `Modernizr.prefixed('transition')` returns `MozTransition`. If a user is in either Safari or Chrome (both browsers based on the WebKit browser engine), `Modernizr.prefixed('transition')` returns `WebkitTransition`.

Armed with the correct string to represent a transition in the user's current browser, you can look up the name of the transition end event in the `transEndEventNames` dictionary defined in Listing 5.17.

Opera and the Transition End Event

There is one line in Listing 5.17 that is a bit unlike the others—the line for the Opera prefixes:

```
'OTransition'       : 'oTransitionEnd otransitionend',
```

It turns out that while previously Opera's transition end event was `oTransitionEnd`, beginning in Opera version 12, the *case* of this event has changed, and the event is `otransitionend` instead. Thus, you need to look out for both `oTransitionEnd` and `otransitionend` if you want to support older version of Opera as well as versions 12 and beyond. To read more about this issue, see Ian Lunn's article "Opera 12 otransitionend Bugs and Workarounds," at http://www.ianlunn.co.uk/blog/articles/opera-12-otransitionend-bugs-and-workarounds/.

In Listing 5.18, you will use jQuery's on method to listen for the transition end event firing on the robot on the skateboard (.robotUnit). When that robot's transition finishes, you hide the first link and unveil the link to scene 2 (which contains the text Scene2!). Figure 5.6 shows the result of running this code.

Listing 5.18   **Hiding the Scene 1 Link and Revealing the Scene 2 Link (robotos.js)**

```
// continued from Listing 5.17
$('.robotUnit').on(transEndEventName, function() {
    $('.one').addClass("invisible");
    $('.two').addClass("visible");
});
```

Figure 5.6   After scene 1's final transition completes, you hide the first link and reveal the scene 2 link

Scene 2: Moving Between Landscapes

After the first scene finishes, you need to move out the old background and move in the background and sprites present in the next scene. This action starts when the user clicks the Scene2! link, which is labeled in the HTML with the class two (refer to Listing 5.8).

Scene 2's HTML and CSS

In Scene 2's CSS, you will first define how the first background image will be positioned now that it is no longer needed. In the `background1.slideOut` selector, which also triggers a transition, you will set the initial background out to the left, hiding it.

Next, you will focus your attention on the styling of the element `#background2`, shown in Listing 5.19. `#background2` is initially placed offscreen, at `left:1000px`. `#background2` also has a transition defined on both the `left` and `background-position` properties.

You also define `#background1.slideIn`, which changes the `left` value to `0`, thus triggering a transition animation that slides in the second background image.

Listing 5.19   **Scene 2's Styles (robotos.css)**

```
#background1.slideOut {
  left: -1000px;
}
#background2 {
  background-image: url('../img/outsideGatesWindow.png');
  background-position: 0 -200px;
  z-index: 2;
  position: absolute;
  left: 1000px;
  -webkit-transition: background-position 2.2s ease-in-out,
      left 1.5s ease-in-out;
  -moz-transition: background-position 2.2s ease-in-out,
      left 1.5s ease-in-out;
  -o-transition: background-position 2.2s ease-in-out,
      left 1.5s ease-in-out;
  transition: background-position 2.2s ease-in-out,
      left 1.5s ease-in-out;
}

#background2.slideIn {
  left: 0;
}
```

Scene 2's JavaScript

In Listing 5.20, you will add code to ensure that when the Scene2! link is clicked, the class `slideOut` gets added to the first background `div` element (`#background1`), and the class `slideIn` is added to the second background `div` element (`#background2`). Applying the `slideOut` and `slideIn` classes changes the value for the `left` property on both background elements, causing each to animate its changes to left, sliding `background1` out to `left:-1000px` and sliding in `background2` to `left:0`. Figure 5.7 shows this effect.

Listing 5.20   **Running Scene 2 When Link .two Is Clicked (robotos.js)**

```
// continued from Listing 5.18
$('.two').on('click', function() {
  console.log('clicked');
  $('#background1').addClass('slideOut');
  $('#background2').addClass('slideIn');
  $('#cat').addClass('visible');
});
```

Figure 5.7   Moving between backgrounds in scene 2

Scene 3: Making the Robot Walk

The third and final scene consists of three sprites: a black cat in the foreground, a robot in the midground, and an image of a chair in the background. Just as you did in the first scene, you'll have the sprites and the background move at different speeds in order to given a sense of depth.

Scene 3's HTML and CSS

The very last elements that make up this example are shown in Listing 5.21 and 5.22. They include another foreground sprite (#cat), a midground sprite (#robot2), and a background sprite (the element #inside, which is a picture of a chair).

Listing 5.21   **Styles for the Sprites in the Final Scene (robotos.css)**

```
#robot2 {
  position: absolute;
  bottom: 20px;
  left: 0;
  width: 300px;
  height: 277px;
  background-image: url('../img/spriteRobotSpringy.png');
  -webkit-transition: left 2.4s ease-in-out;
  -moz-transition: left 2.4s ease-in-out;
  -o-transition: left 2.4s ease-in-out;
  transition: left 2.4s ease-in-out;
}

#cat, #inside {
  -webkit-transition: left 2s ease-in-out;
  -moz-transition: left 2s ease-in-out;
  -o-transition: left 2s ease-in-out;
  transition: left 2s ease-in-out;
}

#cat {
  opacity: 0;
  left: -400px;
  position: absolute;
  bottom: -70px;
  z-index: 10;
}
```

As previously mentioned, scene 3 has an interior layer that is visible through an open window. The interior layer is an `img` element of a chair, which moves slowly from one end of the open window to another as the scene moves. Listing 5.22 defines the styles for the `#inside` element.

Listing 5.22   **Styles for the Layer Inside the Window (robotos.css)**

```
#inside {
  position: absolute;
  left: 460px;
  bottom: 300px;
  z-index: -1;
}
```

Listing 5.23 shows how you change the `transition-property` properties for `#background2`, `#robot2`, and `#cat` after the move class has been applied. Because they are all properties set to `transition-property` for these elements, these changes cause a transition animation when they are applied.

Listing 5.23   **Triggering Transitions When Class move Is Applied (robotos.css)**

```css
#background2.move {
  background-position: -250px -200px;
}

#robot2.move {
  left: 520px;
}

#cat.move {
  opacity: 1;
  left: 200px;
}

#inside.move {
  left: 300px;
}
```

Scene 3's JavaScript

Just as you did in scene 2, you are going to wait for the previous scene to finish before you display the final link, the Scene3! link. In Listing 5.24, you once again wait for the transition end event to fire, but this time you are listening for it on the #background2 element, which is the last element to finish transitioning in scene 2.

Listing 5.24   **Changing the Link When the Second Transition Ends (robotos.js)**

```javascript
// continued from Listing 5.20
$('#background2').on(transEndEventName, function() {
   $('.two').removeClass("visible");
   $('.three').addClass("visible");
});
```

In the very last lines of the robotos.js file, shown in Listing 5.25, when the Scene3! link (element .three) is clicked, you trigger the third and final scene by adding the move class to scene 3's elements. Figure 5.8 shows an intermediate point of the resulting transition animation.

Listing 5.25   **Triggering Scene 3 upon Clicking the Third Link (robotos.js)**

```javascript
// continued from Listing 5.24
$('.three').on('click', function() {
  $('#robot2, #cat, #background2, #inside').addClass('move');
});
```

Figure 5.8   The Beginning of the Scene 3 Animation

Additional Resources

To learn more about parallax scrolling, I recommend the following resources and tutorials:

- Building a Parallax Scrolling Storytelling Framework, by Stevan Živadinović:
  http://www.netmagazine.com/tutorials/building-parallax-scrolling-storytelling-framework
- For more advanced parallax scrolling techniques, see Richard Shepherd's GitHub project,
  at http://github.com/richardshepherd/Parallax-Scrolling/, and accompanying tutorial, at
  http://coding.smashingmagazine.com/2011/07/12/behind-the-scenes-of-nike-better-
  world/.

A number of sites, including these, have used the parallax scrolling technique to good effect:

- HBO GO: http://www.hbogo.com/product-tour/
- The Hobo Lobo web comic: http://hobolobo.net
- GitHub's 404 page: https://github.com/404

Summary

In this chapter you learned how to combine keyframe animations and parallax scrolling to
make a simple repeating animation. You also used jQuery to build an animation that has
several scenes, each taking advantages of parallax scrolling to convey a sense of depth in the
2D animations.

Challenge

Use the repeating animation of the robot in the desert to practice using keyframe animations in layers with parallax scrolling by adding another repeating background to the animation. Perhaps you could have a series of cacti or other desert flora pass by as the robot walks through the scene.

As another challenge, add to the robotos.html project a fourth button, REPLAY, that appears at the end of the animation. Enhance the robotos.js code to reset all the classes in order to bring the animation back to its original state when the REPLAY button is clicked.

Adding Depth with 3D Transforms

In Chapter 5, "Creating 3D Effects with Parallax Scrolling," you used parallax scrolling—moving different layers at different speeds—to create the illusion of depth. This chapter covers how to change the depth of elements through the use of several 3D transform properties. You will explore an important property called `perspective`, which is crucial to ensuring that the user can properly see the 3D transforms you make. This chapter also covers how to transform in three dimensions by applying rotations to the x-, y-, or z-axis. Finally, you will practice using these properties by creating two examples: a 3D cube and a series of stacked playing cards.

Introduction to 3D Transforms

All the transforms you applied in Chapter 2, "Building a Foundation with Transforms," happened in two dimensions. For example, the `translateX`, `translateY`, and `rotate` (which is a rotation on the z-axis) properties all perform only 2D transforms. However, you can also manipulate elements in three dimensions by using a number of additional properties that explicitly specify the axis on which the transform occurs.

3D Transform Properties

You can use the following properties, which specify the axis on which the transform will occur, to create 3D effects on sites:

- **`rotateX`**: Defines a rotation around the x-axis.
- **`rotateY`**: Defines a rotation around the y-axis.
- **`translateZ`**: Defines a translation around the z-axis. This will bring an element closer to the viewer or push it back farther away.

When working with these properties, it is helpful to visualize how applying the transforms to different axes will look. Imagine holding a piece of paper at the top middle and bottom middle between your thumb and forefinger of each hand. If you were then to rotate the paper left and right, you would achieve rotation around the y-axis. Figure 6.1 illustrates this.

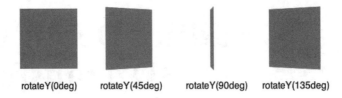

Figure 6.1   Rotation around the y-axis

If, instead, you held the paper in the middle at the right and left edges and then rotated back and forth in a nodding motion, you would achieve rotation around the x-axis. Figure 6.2 illustrates this.

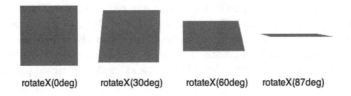

Figure 6.2   Rotation around the x-axis

You use the `translateZ` property to move an element forward or backward along the z-axis. This creates a visual effect of the element moving toward or away from the viewer in space, as illustrated in Figure 6.3. Note that unlike in the previous examples, a large value for `translateZ` can cause the element to move past its containing element (which is represented by the dotted border in Figure 6.3).

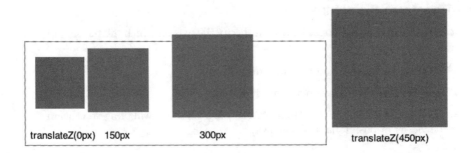

Figure 6.3   Results of several different `translateZ` transforms

In order to be properly applied, these properties must be used in combination with a number of other new properties that will help you configure 3D transforms:

- **perspective:** Sets up a viewing cube that controls how the viewer sees transforms applied to descendent elements. perspective can be thought of as how close or far away the viewer is from the scene, along the z-axis.

- **perspective-origin:** Sets up the starting point for the perspective property.

- **transform-style:** Determines how descendent elements are rendered in space. Are they flattened in the plane of the parent element, or are they positioned in 3D space (preserve-3d)? The default value is flat.

- **backface-visibility:** Determines whether the back of an element is visible when it faces the viewer. Available values are visible and hidden, with visible being the default.

You'll learn more about these properties later in the chapter, as you work through the examples.

Defining Transforms on All Three Axes

Three properties allow you to define transforms on all three axes at once: translate3d, rotate3d, and scale3d.

translate3d(x, y, z)

The translate3d property allows you to simultaneously specify translations on the x-, y-, and z-axes by providing a comma-separated list of translations.

You need not necessarily supply translations to all three axes in order to use translate3d. In fact, you could set two out of the three arguments to 0 and translate only a single axis. For example, translate3d(100px,0,0) is completely valid. The reason you may do this instead of simply using translateX, translateY, or translateZ is because there is an additional benefit to translate3d: It is *hardware accelerated*. You will learn more about this in Chapter 7, "Animating 2D and 3D Transforms," when you begin to animate 3D transforms.

scale3d(scale-x, scale-y, scale-z)

As with translate3d, scale3d allows you to specify scaling on all three axes at once. For example, specifying -webkit-transform: scale3d(0.5, 2, 0); results in an element that is half its original width by twice as tall. The three values you pass to scale3d define a vector whose coordinates define how much scaling is done in each direction (x, y, and z).

rotate3d(x, y, z, angle)

rotate3d works a bit differently than translate3d or scale3d. You specify the angle of rotation as the fourth argument to rotate3d. The first three arguments define the x-, y-, and z-coordinates of a vector, denoting the axis of rotation on each coordinate.

Using this property requires a decent understanding of how matrix multiplication works. This property and its heavy reliance on matrix-related math is beyond the scope of this book, so we don't use `rotate3d` here.

Browser Support for 3D Transforms

CSS3 3D transforms have mixed support in modern browsers. There is good support in the latest versions of Firefox, Safari, and Chrome, but at the time of this writing, Opera does not support them. Support for CSS3 3D transforms is planned in Internet Explorer starting with version 10. The following browsers currently support 3D transforms:

- Android Browser 3.0+

- Chrome 12.0+

- Firefox 10.0+

- Internet Explorer 10, beginning with the Internet Explorer 10 Developer Preview (http://en.wikipedia.org/wiki/Internet_Explorer_10#Release_history)

- iOS Safari 3.2+ and Safari 4.0+

Drawing a 3D Cube

You can practice using the 3D transform properties by drawing a cube. For this example, you are going to orient the cube such that you are looking at it from an aerial view, as if you were peering inside it. In order to be able to actually peer inside the cube, you need to make the topmost face transparent. The HTML for this cube, as you can see in Listing 6.1, consists of a containing element #stage, a second containing element #cube, and then six `div` elements that make up the faces of the cube. For a preview of what the cube will look like when you are finished, either skip ahead to Figure 6.8 or take a look at the completed demo at http://alexisgo.github.com/LearningCSSAnimations/ch6code/cube.html.

Listing 6.1   **Base HTML for the 3D Cube (cube.html)**

```
<div id="stage">
  <div class="cube" >
    <div id="cubetop"></div>
    <div id="cuberight"></div>
    <div id="cubebottom"></div>
    <div id="cubeleft"></div>
    <div id="cubefront"></div>
    <div id="cubeback"></div>
  </div>
</div>
```

Creating a Containing Element for the Scene

After you have your HTML, you define the basic styles of the #stage element, as shown in Listing 6.2. You give the #stage element a margin, position, fixed size, and border. But the most important property you define for #stage is the first one, perspective. The correct use of the perspective property ensures that you can actually see all of the 3D transforms you are going to apply in order to draw a cube.

Listing 6.2   **Applying `perspective` and Other Styles to a Cube's Container (cube.css)**

```
#stage {
  -webkit-perspective: 800px;
  -moz-perspective: 800px;    /* FF10+ */
   -ms-perspective: 800px;    /* IE10+ */
      perspective: 800px;

  -webkit-perspective-origin: 50% 50%;
  -moz-perspective-origin: 50% 50%;
  -ms-perspective-origin: 50% 50%;
  -o-perspective-origin: 50% 50%;
  perspective-origin: 50% 50%;

  margin-top: 100px;
  margin-left: 100px;
  position: relative;
  width: 200px;
  height: 200px;
}
```

In the "CSS Transforms" draft spec (http://www.w3.org/TR/css3-3d-transforms/), the W3C describes the perspective property as a viewing cube that lives inside "a pyramid whose base is infinitely far away from the viewer and whose peak represents the viewer's position. The viewable area is the region bounded by the four edges of the viewport. . . . The *depth*, given as the parameter to the function, represents the distance of the z=0 plane from the viewer."

Just in case this explanation has left you confused, I'll explain it in a different way: Imagine going to a museum and looking at a painting. perspective can be thought of as how close to the painting or how far away from it you are. If you are very close to the painting, you may be able to see the texture of the paint, but you won't be able to see the entire painting. It is only when you take a step back from the painting that you can see the complete composition.

The perspective property allows you to define how close to or far from the painting you are (the viewport of the browser), and this allows you to better see the effects of 3D transforms. To see this, take a look at Figure 6.4, which shows what the final version of your cube (which you are looking into from an aerial view and with a transparent top cube face) would look like with different values for perspective.

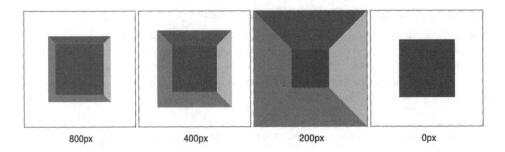

Figure 6.4   The same cube with four different `perspective` values

The spec also states that the use of the `perspective` property establishes a containing block, which is similar to `position: relative`. This is important because it means that if the `perspective` property is applied to a parent element, all descendants of that element will share the same 3D space—the same containing block.

Rendering Nested Elements in 3D Space

Next you will style the `#cube` `div`, which is applied to the `div` that holds all the faces of the cube. The most important style defined in Listing 6.3 is the `transform-style` property. `transform-style` determines how the children of the element this property is applied to are rendered in 3D space. The default is that they will appear `flat`. Setting this property to `preserve-3d` ensures that if you rotate the `#cube` containing `div` along the x- or y-axis, the children of this element will not be flattened into the parent element's plane. It is important to note that this property affects only the children of the element, and not the element itself.

Listing 6.3   **Setting `transform-style` for the Descendants of the Cube Container (cube.css)**

```
.cube {
  position: absolute;
  width: 200px;
  height: 200px;
  -webkit-transform-style: preserve-3d;
  -moz-transform-style: preserve-3d;
  -ms-transform-style: preserve-3d;
  transform-style: preserve-3d;
}
```

The next step is to set up the default styles for the faces of the cube, which you do in Listing 6.4. You position the cube and set the default opacity to 0.7. This will come in handy in Chapter 7, when you add some JavaScript and make this cube movable; the opacity makes the sides semi-transparent, so you can see through them.

You also set the background color of each cube face. You set the front cube face to
transparent so you can see the inside, the cube.

Listing 6.4   **Default Styles for the Cube Faces**

```
.cube div {
  position: absolute;
  top: 0px;
  left: 0px;
  opacity: 0.7;
  width: 100%;
  height: 100%;
  #cubetop {
    background-color: purple;
  }
  #cubebottom {
    background-color: red;
  }
  #cubeleft {
   background-color: green;
  }
  #cuberight {
    background-color: orange;
  }
  #cubefront {
    background-color: transparent;
  }
  #cubeback {
    background-color: blue;
  }
}
```

Rotating the Faces of the Cube

Right now, all the faces of the cube are absolutely positioned in the same spot. You need to
rotate the top, right, bottom, and left faces in order to properly assemble the cube.

You will rotate the top and bottom faces of the cube on the x-axis by 87 degrees. This will
make them nearly perpendicular to the current position of the rest of the cube faces. Figure 6.5
shows the result of this rotation around the x-axis.

Next, you need to rotate the right and left faces of the cube. You will rotate these faces around
the y-axis instead of the x-axis. Figure 6.5 shows the result of these rotations around the x- and
y-axes.

Figure 6.5   The vertical face in the middle has been rotated by 87 degrees on the y-axis, and the horizontal face has been rotated 87 degrees on the x-axis

All faces in this figure share the same size and default position, which is illustrated by the flat, untransformed face in the figure. Listing 6.5 shows the code for these rotations. Because you are adding new content to existing selectors, to distinguish between the existing code and the new code, the new code appears in bold.

> **Note**
>
> These cube faces have no depth; they technically are still 2D elements, even though you are transforming them in a 3D space. Thus, rotating the faces 90 degrees on either the x- or y-axis makes the elements seem to disappear. They don't actually disappear, but if they are lying perpendicular to the flat, visible faces, because they have no depth, you can no longer see them. That is why you are, for the time being, rotating them by only 87 degrees. If you rotated by 90 degrees at this point in the code, the rotated faces would not be visible.

Listing 6.5   **Rotating Cube Faces (cube.css)**

```
/* the left and right faces will rotate around the y-axis */
#cubeleft {
 background-color:green;
  -webkit-transform: rotateY(87deg);
    -moz-transform: rotateY(87deg);
     -ms-transform: rotateY(87deg);
         transform: rotateY(87deg);
}
#cuberight {
  background-color:orange;
  -webkit-transform: rotateY(87deg);
    -moz-transform: rotateY(87deg);
     -ms-transform: rotateY(87deg);
         transform: rotateY(87deg);
```

```
}
/* the top and bottom faces will rotate around the x-axis */
#cubetop {
  background-color: purple;
  -webkit-transform: rotateX(87deg);
     -moz-transform: rotateX(87deg);
      -ms-transform: rotateX(87deg);
          transform: rotateX(87deg);
}
#cubebottom {
  background-color: red;
  -webkit-transform: rotateX(90deg);
     -moz-transform: rotateX(90deg);
      -ms-transform: rotateX(90deg);
          transform: rotateX(90deg);
}
```

Changing Depth with `translateZ`

It is not enough to simply rotate the faces of the cube. You must also reposition these faces in order to properly construct the cube. You can do so via the `translateZ` property. You can begin by applying the `translateZ` property to a face you have already rotated: the cube's left face. But how far should you translate this face of the cube?

Figure 6.5 shows where the `#cubeleft` element is after an 87-degree rotation on the y-axis, as well as where the `#cubetop` element is after an 87-degree rotation on the x-axis. You have accomplished the rotation of these cube faces, but you still need to move them to the proper edge of the cube.

In order to move the `#cubeleft` face to be truly on the left of the cube, you also need to translate it along the z-axis by 100 pixels—one-half the width of the face itself, as shown in Listing 6.6. To move the `#cubetop` face to be truly on top of the cube, you must also translate it by 100 pixels along the z-axis. This is because the `transform-origin` properties of the faces of the cube are all using the default value: `50% 50%` (because they are using the default, we didn't need to specify them in code, and thus you don't see them in the code Listings). Any rotations happen from the center of the face. This results in transformed elements that still sit in the middle of the container. In order to move them out to the edges, you must translate them, along the z-axis, by one-half of the cube face's width. Figure 6.6 shows the result of adding `translateZ(-100px)` to the `#cubeleft`'s transform property and `translateZ(100px)` to `#cubetop`. Note that you are again updating the styles inside existing selectors, so the new or modified code is shown in bold to distinguish it from preexisting code.

While you are revising the code, you can also change the 87-degree rotation to a pure 90-degree rotation. The combination of the translation and the rotation will ensure that you can see the cube face, even with a 90-degree rotation applied. This wasn't previously true; remember that applying a 90-degree rotation without an additional translate (or other) transform would have made the faces invisible.

Listing 6.6   **Adding Translates to the Left Face and Top Face**

```
#cubeleft {
 background-color: green;
  -webkit-transform: rotateY(90deg) translateZ(-100px);
    -moz-transform: rotateY(90deg) translateZ(-100px);
     -ms-transform: rotateY(90deg) translateZ(-100px);
         transform: rotateY(90deg) translateZ(-100px);
}
#cubetop {
  background-color: purple;
  -webkit-transform: rotateX(90deg) translateZ(100px);
    -moz-transform: rotateX(90deg) translateZ(100px);
     -ms-transform: rotateX(90deg) translateZ(100px);
         transform: rotateX(90deg) translateZ(100px);
}
```

Figure 6.6   Setting the #cubeleft face to translateZ(-100px) and the #topcube face to translate(100px) makes them align with the edges of the flat cube face

But why are you translating along the z-axis for this left cube face? When you move things left and right, you tend to translate along the x-axis. But remember, you have already applied a transform: You have rotated the #cubeleft element along the y-axis. The transform means that the axes are no longer where you might expect them to be. Figure 6.7 illustrates the #cubeleft face with its axes both before and after the y-axis rotation.

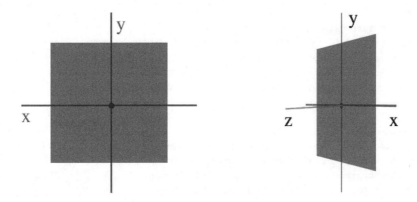

Figure 6.7   Location of x- and y-axes before and after a 90-degree rotation on the y-axis

Next, you can tackle moving the rest of the faces of the cube into place, as shown in Figure 6.8, by enriching the existing transforms with the appropriate values for `translate`. (Note that you need to apply the code in Listing 6.7 before you can see the results shown in Figure 6.8.)

Figure 6.8   All faces of the cube in place

Note that neither the back face nor the front face of the cube (whose background color you have left transparent in order to be able to see into the cube) requires any rotations. They only need a `translateZ` to push the face backward or forward. Also note that you have set the background color of the `#cubefront` face to `transparent`, so you will not actually see the front face of the cube. Listing 6.7 shows the complete transforms needed to assemble the cube. As before, you are updating existing selectors, so to distinguish the modified or added code from the old code, new or modified code appears in bold.

Listing 6.7   **Finalized Transforms on All Six Cube Faces (cube.css)**

```
#cubeleft {
 background-color: green;
  -webkit-transform: rotateY(90deg) translateZ(-100px);
     -moz-transform: rotateY(90deg) translateZ(-100px);
      -ms-transform: rotateY(90deg) translateZ(-100px);
          transform: rotateY(90deg) translateZ(-100px);
}
#cubetop {
  background-color: purple;
  -webkit-transform: rotateX(90deg) translateZ(100px);
     -moz-transform: rotateX(90deg) translateZ(100px);
      -ms-transform: rotateX(90deg) translateZ(100px);
          transform: rotateX(90deg) translateZ(100px);
}
#cubebottom {
  background-color: red;
  -webkit-transform: rotateX(90deg) translateZ(-100px);
     -moz-transform: rotateX(90deg) translateZ(-100px);
      -ms-transform: rotateX(90deg) translateZ(-100px);
          transform: rotateX(90deg) translateZ(-100px);
}
#cuberight {
  background-color: orange;
  -webkit-transform: rotateY(90deg) translateZ(100px);
     -moz-transform: rotateY(90deg) translateZ(100px);
      -ms-transform: rotateY(90deg) translateZ(100px);
          transform: rotateY(90deg) translateZ(100px);
}
#cubefront {
  background-color: transparent;
  -webkit-transform: translateZ(100px);
     -moz-transform: translateZ(100px);
      -ms-transform: translateZ(100px);
          transform: translateZ(100px);
}
#cubeback {
  background-color: blue;
  -webkit-transform: translateZ(-100px);
     -moz-transform: translateZ(-100px);
      -ms-transform: translateZ(-100px);
          transform: translateZ(-100px);
}
```

Changing the Camera Angle with `perspective-origin`

The property that controls how you view the scene is `perspective-origin`. The default value for `perspective-origin` (`50% 50%`) leaves the viewer looking at the scene straight on. But if you adjust this value, you can alter the "camera angle" and change how you view the page. `perspective-origin` can take both absolute values and percent values. Figure 6.9 illustrates the results of applying various `perspective-origin` values to the cube.

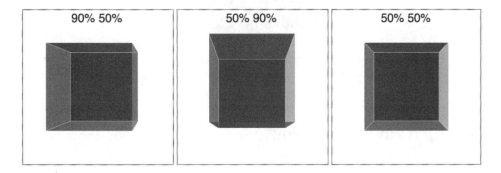

Figure 6.9   Varying the `perspective-origin` property

> **Note**
>
> You may not have noticed this when you first set up the `#stage` containing element, but you gave the parent element a fixed size (refer to Listing 6.2). This is typical, but it is worth emphasizing how important this step is when you apply 3D transforms to its children.
>
> Giving the containing element a size is key to keeping the descendent elements from moving around as the window size changes. If no width or height is specified on the containing element, as the window size grows or shrinks, the descendent cube will move around as if its perspective is changing.

It is important to give the containing element, `#stage`, a fixed size because this element determines both the `perspective` and the `perspective-origin` properties of the descendent elements that make up the cube. If the containing element doesn't have a fixed size, and `perspective-origin` is set to the center of the element (as it is by default), as the window grows or shrinks, the center of the element and `perspective-origin` both change.

This causes the angle at which you view the 3D elements to move around and the window to grow and shrink. You can see this by growing or shrinking the window on the demo page cubeMovesWithWindow.html, which is available at http://alexisgo.github.com/LearningCSSAnimations/ch6code/diagrams/cubeMovesWithWindow.html. Figure 6.10 shows this, as well as the result of widening the browser window on a cube whose containing element does not have a fixed size.

Figure 6.10 Without a fixed size for the containing element, the same cube will look very different in a wider window, due to the changing `perspective-origin` property

Creating a House of Cards

In this section, you'll apply what you've learned so far to a whimsical example. Here you'll create a house of cards by leveraging some 3D transform properties and combining them with some CSS3 styling to draw the cards themselves.

You begin with the HTML in Listing 6.8. You start with a containing element, again called #stage. Next, you have two containing divs, #toprow and #bottomrow. #toprow will hold three cards, and #bottomrow will hold six. A common class called card will be used to provide some base styling, and a series of custom classes—left, right, flat, and secondcol—will distinguish the cards from one another.

Listing 6.8 **Base HTML for the House of Cards (houseOfCards.html)**

```
<div id="stage">
  <div id="toprow">
    <div class="card left"></div>
    <div class="card right"></div>
    <div class="card flat"></div>
  </div>
  <div id="bottomrow">
    <div class="card left"></div>
    <div class="card right"></div>
    <div class="card flat"></div>
    <div class="card left secondcol"></div>
    <div class="card right secondcol"></div>
    <div class="card flat secondcol"></div>
  </div>
</div>
```

Styling the Containing Element for the House of Cards

To style the containing element, `#stage`, as shown in Listing 6.9, you set the perspective to 900 pixels, so you can see the 3D transforms you'll be performing. You also set `perspective-origin` to be angled at 100% horizontally (the leftmost edge) and 0% vertically. This makes it seem as though you are looking at the scene from the rightmost and topmost edge of the page.

Note that this example includes only the `-webkit-` vendor prefix for the sake of brevity. The complete code, with all vendor prefixes, can be found at the book's GitHub page, https://github.com/alexisgo/LearningCSSAnimations/ in the ch6code/ folder. You can find a completed demo of what you are going to build here at http://alexisgo.github.com/LearningCSSAnimations/ch6code/houseOfCards.html.

Listing 6.9   **Setting Up the Default Styles for the Containing Element (houseOfCards.css)**

```
#stage {
  -webkit-perspective: 900px;
  -webkit-perspective-origin: 100% 0%;
  width: 500px;
  height: 300px;
  margin: 10%;
}
```

Positioning and Styling the Cards

Listing 6.10 sets the position of the cards within the two containing elements `#toprow` and `#bottomrow`. You position both rows of the house of cards to be 100 pixels from the left, in order to push them away from their default position at the left edge of the browser. You position the `.right` cards 40 pixels from the left of the parent, `#toprow`. You position the `.flat` cards 20 pixels from the left and 50 pixels from the top of the parent `#toprow`. You also apply positioning to the `#bottomrow` and its descendent elements (which aren't detailed in this chapter but are shown in Listing 6.10).

Finally, you set the positions for the second set of stacked cards (`.secondcol`) in `#bottomrow`, moving them all slightly to the left of the first set of cards in `#bottomrow`.

Listing 6.10   **Positioning the Cards According to Their Row or Type (houseOfCards.css)**

```
#toprow, #bottomrow {
  position: relative;
  left: 100px;
}

#toprow .right {  left: 40px;  }
#toprow .flat {
  top: 50px;
  left: 20px;
```

```
}
#bottomrow {
  top: 100px;
  left: 60px;
}
#bottomrow .right { left: 40px; }
#bottomrow .flat {
  top: 50px;
  left: 15px;
}
#bottomrow .secondcol {  left: 100px; }
#bottomrow .left.secondcol { left: 80px; }
#bottomrow .right.secondcol { left: 120px; }
```

Listing 6.11 defines the default styles for all cards. You give each one an absolute position and fixed size, as well as a border-radius of 10 pixels to make the edges of the cards rounded. You give them a silver border and a default background color of light blue. For cards on the left (with the class left), you set the background color to white, to represent the face of the card (where the numbers or drawings for the face cards would normally be). At this point, since you have yet to transform any of the cards, they all appear to lay flat, as illustrated in Figure 6.11.

Listing 6.11 **Basic Styles for the Playing Cards (houseOfCards.css)**

```
.card {
  position:absolute;
  width: 70px;
  height: 100px;
  -webkit-border-radius: 10px;
  -moz-border-radius: 10px;
  border-radius: 10px;
  border: 5px solid rgb(179,179,179);
  background-color: rgb(102,102,255);
}
.left {
  background-color: white;
}
```

Figure 6.11   The cards before any transforms are applied

Transforming the Cards

Now you need to set up the transforms you want to apply to your cards (see Listing 6.12). You will rotate all the cards 90 degrees on the y-axis. Next, for the cards that will lean together to form a peak, you rotate one by 22 degrees and the other by –22 degrees. The two cards meet at their peaks (see Figure 6.12). You also set the background color of the left cards—which will have their front faces visible to the user—as white.

The flat cards also have an additional transform applied. You rotate the flat cards along the z-axis by 90 degrees. You can think of this as making them appear in landscape rather than portrait view.

Listing 6.12   **Setting Up the Default Transforms for Each Card Type (houseOfCards.css)**

```
.left {
  background-color: white;
  -webkit-transform: rotateY(90deg) rotateX(-22deg);
}
.right {
  -webkit-transform: rotateY(90deg) rotateX(22deg);
}
.flat {
  -webkit-transform: rotateZ(90deg) rotateY(90deg);
}
```

Figure 6.12   The house of cards after you transform the cards

Adjusting the Ordering of the Stacked Cards

There is an issue with the way the house of cards looks at the moment. The bottom parts of the stacked cards appear *behind* the cards that lay flat, that they are supposed to be stacked on top of. You may have noticed this effect in Figure 6.12, but in case you did not, I have highlighted the issue in Figure 6.13.

Figure 6.13   Stacked cards appear behind flat cards

The effect you see in Figure 6.13 is due to transform-style. The default transform-style is flat, and so that is what #toprow and #bottomrow are currently set to. This means the descendants of the #toprow and the #bottomrow elements are all flattened into the plane of #toprow and #bottomrow, leading to the effect you see in Figure 6.13. They are flattened in the order in which the elements appear, which is why the #bottomrow's stacked cards appear behind the #bottomrow's flat cards.

In Listing 6.13, you fix this by setting transform-style to preserve-3d. Changing transform-style to preserve-3d ensures that the cards that are inside #toprow and #bottomrow are positioned in 3D space rather than flattened.

Since you are updating a selector that you previously defined in Listing 6.10, the new code that you add here is highlighted in bold, to make it clear which new line you need to add to the code. Figure 6.14 shows two images: On the left, you see the way the cards looked before this change, and on the right, you see the result of adding `transform-style: preserve-3d` to the cards.

Listing 6.13   **Fixing Incorrect Element Overlapping with `preserve-3d` (houseOfCards.css)**

```
#toprow, #bottomrow {
  position: relative;
  left: 100px;

  -webkit-transform-style: preserve-3d;
}
```

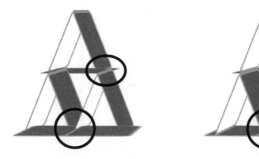

Figure 6.14   The left image shows the cards *before* `transform-style: preserve-3d` is applied, and the right image show them *after* it is applied

As you can see in Figure 6.14, the cards are still not quite right: The very peak of the cards on the left of the second row are standing in front of the flat card that's supposed to be sitting on top of it. The problem is highlighted explicitly in Figure 6.15.

Figure 6.15   The left cards in the bottom row appear in front of the flat card they're supposed to be stacked under.

You can fix the issue shown in Figure 6.15 with one last tweak to the code. In Listing 6.14, you set `z-index` of the #toprow to 2 in order to ensure that it is displayed in front of the second row, which it is stacked on top of.

Listing 6.14   **Moving `#toprow` in front of `#bottomrow` with `z-index` (houseOfCards.css)**

```
#toprow {
  z-index: 2;
}
```

Figure 6.16 shows the result of Listings 6.13 and 6.14 combined (adding *both* `preserve-3d` and the `z-index:2`).

Figure 6.16   The house of cards after the fixes to `z-index` and `transform-style`

Adding a Pattern to the Card Backs

As a final step, you can add a custom double-striped gradient to the backs of the cards in order to give them a more realistic diamond pattern. The base code for this double-striped gradient (Listing 6.15) comes from a series of excellent examples of gradients by Estelle Weyl, on her CSS gradients example page, which is available at http://standardista.com/cssgradients.

Listing 6.15, like all the other code listings in this chapter, provides only the `-webkit-` vendor prefix, but you can find the complete code with all the prefixes at the book's GitHub page. Figure 6.17 shows the final house of cards.

Listing 6.15   **Adding a Double-Striped Gradient to the Cards (houseOfCards.css)**

```
.card {
/* double striped gradients example from Estelle Weyl:
  http://standardista.com/cssgradients/ */
background-image:
  -webkit-linear-gradient(135deg,
    rgba(255, 255, 255, 0.2) 25%,
    rgba(255, 255, 255, 0) 25%,
```

```
      rgba(255, 255, 255, 0) 50%,
      rgba(255, 255, 255, 0.2) 50%,
      rgba(255, 255, 255, 0.2) 75%,
      rgba(255, 255, 255, 0) 75%,
      rgba(255, 255, 255, 0) 100%
      ),
    -webkit-linear-gradient(45deg,
      rgba(255, 255, 255, 0.2) 25%,
      rgba(255, 255, 255, 0) 25%,
      rgba(255, 255, 255, 0) 50%,
      rgba(255, 255, 255, 0.2) 50%,
      rgba(255, 255, 255, 0.2) 75%,
      rgba(255, 255, 255, 0) 75%,
      rgba(255, 255, 255, 0) 100%
    );
}
```

Figure 6.17   The completed house of cards

Additional Resources

To learn more about 3D transforms, I recommend the following resources and tutorials:

- CSS 3D Transforms Module Level 3, W3C Working Draft: http://www.w3.org/TR/css3-3d-transforms/

- 3D transforms article in the Internet Explorer 10 Guide for Developers: http://msdn.microsoft.com/library/ie/hh673529.aspx

- Intro to CSS3 3D Transforms, by David DeSandro: http://desandro.github.com/3dtransforms/docs/card-flip.html

- 3D transforms article from the WebKit blog, by Simon Fraser: http://www.webkit.org/blog/386/3d-transforms/

Summary

In this chapter, you learned how to manipulate elements in 3D space by using the `translateZ`, `rotateX`, and `rotateY` properties. You saw the importance of having a containing element with a fixed size and setting `perspective`. You also looked at how to get the right "camera angle" with the `perspective-origin` property.

Challenge

Enhance the house of cards example so that you have a messy pile of scattered cards next to the house. The cards toward the bottom of the pile should have various `rotateZ` angles set. The cards toward the top should be leaning on top of the lower level of the pile and should utilize rotations on the x-axis, y-axis, or both.

Animating 2D and 3D Transforms

In this chapter, you will work through two examples that demonstrate how you can combine 2D and 3D transforms with CSS3 transitions and keyframe animations to create interesting effects. To begin animating 3D transforms, you'll start in familiar territory, taking the 3D cube that you built in Chapter 6, "Adding Depth with 3D Transforms," and applying transitions, a few HTML5 `range` input type elements, and a bit of JavaScript to rotate the cube about each of the three axes.

Basic 3D Transform Animations with Transitions

In Chapter 6, you built a 3D cube using CSS3 transforms. You can enrich that example to allow the user to change the rotation of the cube, animating any changes made.

In order to do this, you can create a slider for each axis to allow the user to rotate the cube around the x-, y-, or z-axis. You will add some JavaScript to listen to a change event on the sliders. When a change occurs, you will update the rotation on the appropriate axis. In order to animate these changes to the degree of rotation, you'll leverage CSS3 transitions. Figure 7.1 shows the end result of this example.

As with previous chapters, for brevity the listings in this chapter include only the `-webkit-` vendor prefix. However, you can find the code samples, complete with all vendor prefixes, at this book's GitHub page, https://github.com/alexisgo/LearningCSSAnimations, in the ch7code folder.

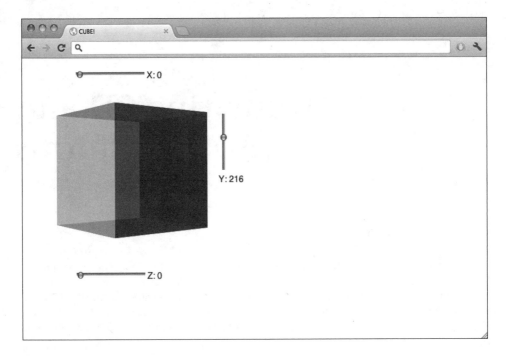

Figure 7.1   The finished cube rotator

Adding HTML5 Sliders to Control Rotation

HTML5 includes many new input types, one of which is the `range` input type. The `range` input type creates a slider in supported browsers. In unsupported browsers, a slider created in this manner simply appears as a text field (`input type=text`).

With the `range` input type, you can define the minimum and maximum input values. In this case, because you want to rotate fully around each axis, the minimum value will be 0 and the maximum value will be 360.

You can also define the attribute `step` for the slider's increment. The increment defines how much the input's value is incremented for each tick of the slider. Listing 7.1 shows the setup for the x-axis slider. It includes only the setup of the x-axis for brevity, as the HTML of the y- and z-axes mimics that of the x-axis.

> **Note**
>
> At the time of this writing, the `range` input type and the `step` attribute are not supported by Firefox, Mobile Safari, or the Android browser. They are supported by Internet Explorer 10 but no previous versions. The good news, however, is that in browsers that don't support the `range` input type, the input type is treated as a text field, and you can simply enter your desired rotation into the text field and press Enter to rotate the cube.

Listing 7.1 **Setting Up the Slider for the x-axis (cube.html)**

```
<div id="xslider">
  <input  name="range" id="slider" type="range" min="0" max="360" step="36" value="0"/>
  <label for="slider">X: </label>
  <span id="xdegrees">0</span>
</div>
```

Rotating a 3D Object as the Slider Changes

You can use JavaScript to set up the appropriate event handlers to listen for changes to each slider. You can do so in an `init` function that runs when the window finishes loading. In Listing 7.2, you create an event handler for the `onchange` event on each of the three sliders. When any of the sliders is changed, the `rotate` function is called.

Listing 7.2 **Setting Up Event Handlers for Changes to the Sliders (cube.js)**

```
window.onload = init;

function init() {
  document.getElementById("slider").onchange = rotate;
  document.getElementById("verticalslider").onchange = rotate;
  document.getElementById("nearnessslider").onchange = rotate;
}
```

Next, you will define the `rotate` function, which has three main parts that the next few sections examine.

Updating the Axis Labels with the Rotations Specified in the Sliders

The first part of the `rotate` function, shown in Listing 7.3, takes the value of each slider and stores those values in the variables `xRotation`, `yRotation`, and `zRotation`. You then update the text beside each slider to indicate how much the cube has been rotated around that axis.

Listing 7.3 **Updating the Labels to the Current Value of the Sliders (cube.js)**

```
function rotate(e) {
  var xRotation = document.getElementById("slider").value;
  var yRotation = document.getElementById("verticalslider").value;
  var zRotation = document.getElementById("nearnessslider").value;

  //update labels
  document.getElementById("xdegrees").textContent = xRotation;
  document.getElementById("ydegrees").textContent = yRotation;
  document.getElementById("zdegrees").textContent = zRotation;

  // code continues in Listing 7.4
}
```

Storing the Values of Previous Rotations

In the second part of the rotate function, shown in Listing 7.4, you construct strings to store the values of the 3D transforms you will be applying to the cube. You will use the variables xRotation, yRotation, and zRotation (defined in Listing 7.3) to store these values, and surround each of these values with the appropriate string in order to define the rotation. For example, you insert the xRotation variable, which holds the current rotation on the x-axis, inside the string rotateX(). You do this for each of the axes, storing each complete string in the variables rx, ry, and rz. See Listing 7.4.

Listing 7.4   **Creating Strings of the Rotation Values for the Transform (cube.js)**

```
function rotate(e) {
  // continued from Listing 7.3

  var rx = "rotateX(" + xRotation + "deg) ";
  var ry = "rotateY(" + yRotation + "deg) ";
  var rz = "rotateZ(" + zRotation + "deg)";
}
```

Transforming the Cube in All Browsers with Modernizr's `prefixed()`

In the final part of the rotate function (see Listing 7.5), you apply to the cube the 3D transforms you've stored in the rx, ry, and rz variables. In order to apply these transforms appropriately in all browsers that support them, you can leverage Modernizr's prefixed() method, introduced in Chapter 5, "Creating 3D Effects with Parallax Scrolling," in order to generate the appropriate vendor prefix to the CSS you'll be adding to the cube element.

In the final part of the rotate function, you apply a new style to the cube element by populating the style attribute. You can do this via JavaScript by assigning a value to cube.style. Which vendor prefix you use in the style attribute depends on the result of Modernizr. prefixed('transform'). In order to look up the appropriate vendor-prefixed property name, you pass the result of Modernizr.prefixed('transform') to cube.style. The bracket notation allows cube.style to select the CSS vendor-prefixed property needed from the result of Modernizr.prefixed('transform'). Finally, the concatenation of the rx, ry, and rz variables is assigned as the value of the prefixed transform property.

Listing 7.5   **Applying Transforms to the Cube with the Correct Vendor Prefix (cube.js)**

```
function rotate(e) {
  // continued from Listing 7.4

  var cube = document.getElementById("cube");
  cube.style[Modernizr.prefixed('transform')] = rx + ry + rz;
}
```

Note

Throughout this book, we have been using a custom build of Modernizr that includes `prefixed()` method. When you download your own custom builds of Modernizr, should you wish to use the `prefixed()` method, you should know that it's not included by default, but that you can specify its inclusion. The method is available under the Extensibility section of the Modernizr build customization site—it's the choice called `Modernizr.prefixed()`—as shown in Figure 7.2.

To learn more about the `Modernizr.prefixed()` method, you can reference the Modernizr documentation at http://modernizr.com/docs/#prefixed or review the excellent tutorial for using the method by Andi Smith, available at http://www.andismith.com/blog/2012/02/modernizr-prefixed/.

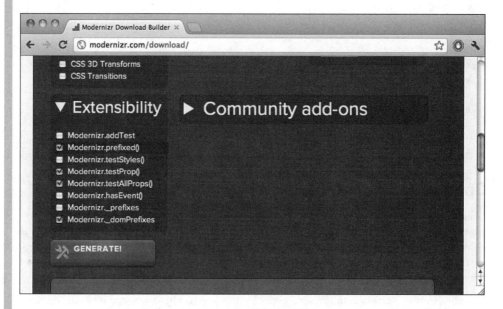

Figure 7.2   Updating the Modernizr build to include `prefixed()`

Adding Basic Styles

Now you need to create some basic styles for the sliders and place the cube appropriately. Since the cube will be rotated around one or more axes as the user moves the sliders, you need to provide ample space around the cube. You accomplish this by absolutely positioning the sliders to leave enough space for all the various combinations of 3D rotations that the cube can take (see Listing 7.6).

You also need to style the sliders themselves, as well as the labels that are associated with each. The trickiest slider to style is for the y-axis, which you want to make a vertical slider. In order to accomplish this, you can use the -webkit-appearance property. Setting -webkit-appearance to slider-vertical makes the slider appear vertical rather than horizontal in supported browsers. In unsupported browsers, the slider simply appears as a regular horizontal slider.

Listing 7.6   **Styling the Sliders (cube.css)**

```css
#slider {
  left: 30px;
}

#yslider {
  position: absolute;
  right: -110px;
}

#verticalslider {
  -webkit-appearance: slider-vertical;
  width: 20px;
  height: 100px;
  top: 40px;
}
```

Optimizing Performance

Combining 3D transforms with CSS animations can make for some very powerful effects on pages. In the next section, we outline how to combine 3D transforms with CSS animations in order to make complex animations. But as the examples get more complex, you need to begin to think about performance. The more animations on a page, and the more complex they are, the more you need to pay attention to page performance and see what can be optimized.

One approach you can take to improve performance is to use hardware acceleration. Hardware acceleration involves moving work normally done by software into the hardware (the CPU or GPU), where it can be done faster. In the realm of web development, when we talk about hardware acceleration, we are often specifically talking about the ability of certain devices to offload work from the CPU to the GPU (the graphics processing unit, more commonly referred to as simply the *graphics card*).

Using Transitions Instead of Keyframe Animations to Improve Performance

An important performance optimization trick to make your animations play as smoothly as possible is using CSS3 properties that can take advantage of hardware acceleration. In CSS3 there are several properties that take advantage of hardware acceleration: CSS3 transitions and `translate3d` and `translateZ`.

Because the browser interpolates (that is, finds the intermediate point) between the start and end of every transition, a transition is faster than an equivalent keyframe animation (with only a 0% and 100% keyframe) and may offload some of the work required to the GPU, which is optimized to do this sort of graphics work. Thus, whenever possible, you should use transitions instead of keyframe animations in order to maximize performance.

There are many cases, though, in which you cannot avoid using keyframe animations. If you want an animation to repeat, for example, you must use a keyframe animation. And if you want to define multiple points in the animation, as discussed in Chapter 4, "Keyframe Animations," you want to use keyframe animations because they allow you to define animations that transitions simply cannot achieve.

Leveraging Hardware Acceleration with `translate3d` and `translateZ`

When you need to use keyframe animations, what can you do to improve the performance of your animations? You can make use of the `translate3d`, `scale3d`, `rotate3d`, and `translate` properties. Also, you can use these properties even if you don't have reason to. For example, you can simply add `translate3d(0,0,0)` to any keyframe animation to implement hardware acceleration.

This method is rather hacky, but Thomas Fuchs, creator of script.aculo.us, and Paul Irish, of Google's Chrome Developer Relations team, have both discussed it. Remy Sharp also has a stunning video of a before and after, showing a dramatically smoother transition in the zoom-in after adding `translate3d(0,0,0)`; see http://www.youtube.com/watch?v=IKl78ZgJzm4. You will be utilizing this method of using `translate3d` to improve performance in the next example (see, for example, Listing 7.12).

As discussed in Chapter 1, "Working with CSS3 Animations," the best way to see if using these properties is having an effect is to color any hardware-accelerated layers in a distinctive way so you can easily see them. Chapter 1 provides directions for how to enable the viewing of hardware-accelerated layers in Chrome and Safari.

For further discussion of performance techniques in HTML5 and CSS3, see the excellent article "Improving the Performance of Your HTML5 App" by Malte Ubl, at http://www.html5rocks.com/en/tutorials/speed/html5/, as well as the video "HTML5, CSS3, and DOM Performance" by Paul Irish, at http://www.youtube.com/watch?v=q_O9_C2ZjoA.

Blowing in the Wind: Animating Dandelion Seeds

In this section, you will build a graphic of a dandelion, using some basic HTML, CSS, and one small PNG image of a dandelion seed that you will duplicate and transform many times to form a dandelion bloom out of many seeds. Once this is constructed, you will apply a set of animations to the dandelion to make it look like the seeds are being blown off and away by the wind. Figure 7.3 shows what the dandelion looks like before any of the animations are applied.

For this example, the CSS file with all the prefixed code is available as a separate file, dandelion_prefixed.css, on the book's GitHub page: https://github.com/alexisgo/ LearningCSSAnimations. To view a condensed version of the CSS that matches the listings in this chapter, review dandelion.css. Note also that all files relevant to this example are found in the ch7code/ folder, under a folder called dandelion/.

Figure 7.3   The completed dandelion, before animation is applied

The Base HTML

You'll initially construct the dandelion from seven elements: the containing element #dande-lion; an element representing the stem; an element for the seed head, where all the seeds sit until they are blown away; a containing div element called #looseSeeds; and three individual seeds with id attributes (see Listing 7.7).

Listing 7.7   **The Base HTML for the Dandelion (dandelion.html)**

```html
<div id="dandelion">
  <div id="stem">
    <div id="seedhead"></div>
  </div>
  <div id="looseSeeds">
    <div class="seed" id="zoomseed"></div>
    <div class="seed" id="floatupseed"></div>
    <div class="seed" id="flipseed"></div>
  </div>
</div>
```

To begin styling, you can give the dandelion, the stem, and the seed head a fixed size, absolute position, and background color (see Listing 7.8). The stem will have a white background color by default, with a semi-transparent white applied via the rgba property for the browsers that support it. (Note that this example defines only the -webkit- vendor prefixes. All vendor prefixes are available in the dandelion_prefixed.css file mentioned above.)

Listing 7.8   **Styling the Dandelion's Stem and Seed Head (dandelion.css)**

```css
body {
  background-color: rgb(44, 44, 44);
}

#dandelion {
  position: absolute;
  width: 100%;
  height: 600px;
  overflow: hidden;
  border-bottom: 5px solid white;
  border-bottom: 5px solid rgba(255,255,255,0.3);
}

#stem {
  width: 10px;
  height: 352px;
  background-color: rgb(255,255,255);
  background-color: rgba(255,255,255,0.7);
  position: absolute;
  bottom: 0;
  left: 205px;
}

#seedhead {
  width: 20px;
  position: absolute;
```

```
    left: -5px;
    bottom: 350px;
    height: 20px;
    border-radius: 10px;
    background-color: white;
}
```

Animating the Stem Blowing in a Gust of Wind

To give the impression that a gust of wind has just blow from the left of the screen, you are going to bend the dandelion stem toward the right by applying an animation that rotates the element on the z-axis.

In Listing 7.9 you first set the `transform-origin` of the `#stem` element to be halfway across and all the way at the bottom of the element (`50% 100%`). This ensures that the stem rotates from the bottom when you begin to animate it. You also assign `#stem` to the animation `stemBlow`, which is also defined in Listing 7.9.

The `stemBlow` keyframe animation first rotates the stem 18 degrees in the clockwise direction. Then, beginning at 7% into the animation, the stem swings back to the left, rotating all the way to 3 degrees past its original location. Finally, it swings back to the right, to 3 degrees in the clockwise direction. These small rotations are meant to simulate a small wobble before the stem completes its movements and goes back to its original position.

> **Note**
>
> One thing to note about Listing 7.9 and subsequent listings in this dandelion example is that when you are rotating elements on the z-axis, you'll be using the transform function `rotate` rather than `rotateZ`. The reason for this is that `rotate` is a 3D transform, and some browsers (namely Opera 12 and Internet Explorer 9 and earlier) do not support these 3D transforms. To make this example have slightly closer to its intended effect in those browsers, you use `rotate` so that Internet Explorer 9 and Opera 12 can at least see a subset of all the many transforms you will be applying to the dandelion seeds.

From 45% to 100%, there is no change. The reason for this prolonged period of no change is that you want the stem-blowing animation to take less time than subsequent animations that will involve blowing the seeds. But to make coordination of these animations easier, you'll be using the same duration (6 seconds) for all animations. Thus, in order to make the `stemBlow` animation more brief than subsequent ones, it needs to spend part of its time not performing any changes.

Listing 7.9   **Bending the Stem (dandelion.css)**

```
#stem {
    /* continued from Listing 7.8 */
    -webkit-transform-origin: 50% 100%;
```

```
  -webkit-animation: stemBlow 6s forwards ease-in;
}

@-webkit-keyframes stemBlow {
  0%{}
  7% {
    -webkit-transform: rotate(18deg);
  }
  25% {
    -webkit-transform: rotate(-3deg);
  }
  35% {
    -webkit-transform: rotate(2deg);
  }
  45% {
    -webkit-transform: rotate(0deg);
  }
  100% {
    -webkit-transform: rotate(0deg);
  }
}
```

Placing and Animating the Seeds

Next, you'll add some base styles to the three seed elements defined in Listing 7.7. All seeds will share the class seed, which sets their background-image and gives them a specific transform-origin that sits at the bottom middle of the seed image. You also define a selector that absolutely positions the containing #looseSeeds element. And the animation blowRight is assigned to this containing element.

The animation blowRight, the last item defined in Listing 7.10, creates an animation that moves the #looseSeeds element (and all its children) across the screen by increasing the value of the left property. There is an intermediate keyframe at 7% so that you can ensure that when the stem blows to the right, the seeds move to the right as well, at a similar pace. Note that Listing 7.10 uses the animation shorthand and sets animation-fill-mode to forwards in that shorthand. This ensures that the seeds stay off the screen even after the animation completes.

Listing 7.10   **Styling the Seeds (dandelion.css)**

```
.seed {
  -webkit-transform-origin: 35px 98px;
  background-image: url('../img/DandelionSeed.png');
  width: 100px;
  height: 100px;
  position: absolute;
```

```
}
#looseSeeds {
  position: absolute;
  bottom: 442px;
  left: 171px;
  -webkit-animation: blowRight 6s forwards ease-in-out;
}

@-webkit-keyframes blowRight {
  0% {  }
  7% {  left: 290px; }
  100% { left: 1600px; }
}
```

Placing the Loose Seeds and Assigning Custom Animations

In order to position each seed contained in the #looseSeeds containing div in a different location, you give two of them (#zoomseed and #flipseed) a custom rotate value, placing them at different angles along the #seedhead element (see Listing 7.11). #floatupseed does not have a rotate value defined and will remain unrotated. (It may appear slightly rotated, but that is because the seed in the background-image itself is slightly rotated.) Figure 7.4 shows the results of the collective seed placement.

In addition, each seed uses its own unique animation: zoomSeed, flip, and float. (These animations will be defined in Listings 7.12, 7.13 and 7.14, respectively.) You give each of these loose seeds its own animation, each lasting 6 seconds, to customize their movement in the burst of wind. Bear in mind that each unique-to-the-seed animation will be combined with the blowRight animation applied to the seeds' shared parent element, #looseSeeds.

Listing 7.11 **Styling Animations for the Initial Seeds (dandelion.css)**

```
#zoomseed {
  -webkit-transform: rotate(-80deg);
  -webkit-animation: zoomSeed 6s forwards;
}

#floatupseed {
  -webkit-animation:  float 6s forwards ease-in-out;
}
#flipseed {
  -webkit-transform: rotate(-190deg);
  -webkit-animation:  flip 6s forwards ease-in-out;
}
```

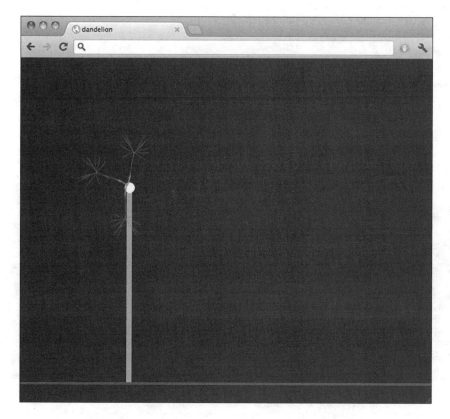

Figure 7.4   Three seeds placed via transforms

Animating a Seed to Move Toward the Viewer with `scale`

The three custom animations are assigned to the seeds in Listing 7.11. Here we examine the `zoomSeed` animation, outlined in Listing 7.12. Three changes happen in this animation, all of which take the full 6 seconds to complete. First, you scale up the seed to three times its original size. Next, you push the seed upward by subtracting 105 pixels from its y-position. You do this via `translate3d` instead of `translate` in order to take advantage of hardware acceleration. Finally, you rotate the seed 120 degrees in the counterclockwise direction.

Figure 7.5 shows the animation at 7% and 30%, respectively. Note that this figure displays both the result of the `zoomseed` animation and the `blowRight` animation on the `#zoomseed` element and its parent, as well as the effect of the `stemBlow` animation on the `#stem` element.

Listing 7.12   **Scaling a Seed Up (dandelion.css)**

```
@-webkit-keyframes zoomSeed {
  0% { }
  100% {
    -webkit-transform:
      scale3d(3,3,3) translate3d(0,-105px,0) rotate(-120deg);
  }
}
```

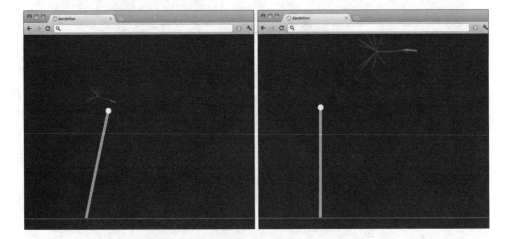

Figure 7.5   Two stages of the `zoomSeed` and `stemBlow` animations

Floating a Seed Upward

In the custom animation `float`, which is assigned to the `#floatupseed` element, the main change is from no translation on the y-axis to a negative 330–pixel translation on the y-axis. (This animation is defined in Listing 7.13.) This has the ultimate effect of moving the seed upward. You leverage the `translate3d` transform function rather than `translateY` in order to glean the benefits of hardware acceleration. You also scale up the element and rotate it along the z-axis before the end of the animation.

Listing 7.13   **Floating a Seed Up and Off Screen (dandelion.css)**

```
@-webkit-keyframes float {
  0% {
    -webkit-transform-origin: 50% 100%;
    -webkit-animation-timing-function: ease-in;}
  7% { -webkit-transform: translate3d(0, 15px, 0) rotate(15deg);}
  100% {
    -webkit-transform:
```

```
      scale3d(4,4,4) rotate(120deg) translate3d(-330px, 10px, 0);
  }
}
```

Rotating a Seed

The last custom seed animation is `flip`, which is assigned to the `#flipSeed` element. In this animation, defined in Listing 7.14, you rotate the element about the x-axis. You also bump this seed up slightly during the 7% keyframe by increasing the y-value through the change to `translate3d`. You also rotate the element 190 degrees counterclockwise at the 7% keyframe, but you don't persist that change to the 100% keyframe. This results in the seed rotating back to its original z-axis position, making for a nice sway movement. Figure 7.6 shows two frames of this animation.

Listing 7.14   **Flipping a Seed About the x-axis (dandelion.css)**

```
@-webkit-keyframes flip {
  0% { -webkit-transform-origin: 50% 50%; }
  7% { -webkit-transform: translate3d(0, 25px, 0) rotateX(5deg) rotate(-190deg); }
  100% { -webkit-transform: rotateX(160deg); }
}
```

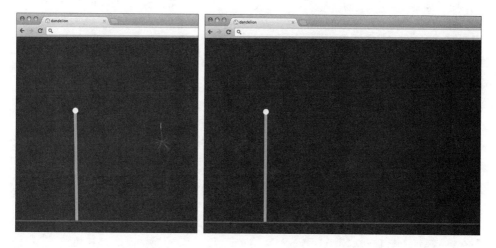

Figure 7.6   The `flip` animation in action, rotating the seed around the x-axis

Adding More Seeds

In this section, you'll enhance your HTML to add additional seeds and make your dandelion look more complete. Listing 7.15 adds five *quadrant* elements. Within each quadrant are have four seeds.

The idea of the quadrants is to reuse the placement of seeds by simply rotating a containing quadrant element around to save some time and avoid the need to position each seed individually.

Listing 7.15   Enriched HTML with Additional Dandelion Seeds (dandelion.html)

```html
<div id="dandelion">
  <div id="stem">
    <div id="seedhead"></div>
  </div>
  <div id="looseSeeds">
    <div class="seed" id="zoomseed"></div>
    <div class="seed" id="floatupseed"></div>
    <div class="seed" id="flipseed"></div>
  </div>
  <div id="quadrant1" class="quad">
    <div class="seed"></div>
    <div class="seed"></div>
    <div class="seed"></div>
    <div class="seed"></div>
    <div class="seed"></div>
  </div>
  <div id="quadrant2" class="quad">
    <div class="seed"></div>
    <div class="seed"></div>
    <div class="seed"></div>
    <div class="seed"></div>
    <div class="seed"></div>
  </div>
  <div id="quadrant3" class="quad">
    <div class="seed"></div>
    <div class="seed"></div>
    <div class="seed"></div>
    <div class="seed"></div>
    <div class="seed"></div>
  </div>
  <div id="quadrant4" class="quad">
    <div class="seed"></div>
    <div class="seed"></div>
    <div class="seed"></div>
    <div class="seed"></div>
    <div class="seed"></div>
  </div>
  <div id="quadrant5" class="quad">
    <div class="seed"></div>
    <div class="seed"></div>
    <div class="seed"></div>
```

```
    <div class="seed"></div>
    <div class="seed"></div>
  </div>
</div>
```

Placing Additional Seeds by Transforming Their Quadrants

Now you will set up one quadrant with four seeds placed, and then you will add additional quadrants and rotate and position the quadrants and all the seeds they contain. This will save you the trouble of placing each seed individually.

In Listing 7.16, the quadrants are, by default, all be set to run the same blowRight animation that was defined and used on the individual seeds earlier (in Listing 7.10). This causes each quadrant to move steadily to the right until it is entirely offscreen, making it look like all the seeds are blowing in the wind.

In Listing 7.16, you will also give a custom rotation and position to the seeds in #quadrant3 and #quadrant5.

Listing 7.16   **Animating Each Quadrant (dandelion.css)**

```
div[id^="quadrant"] {
  position:absolute;
  bottom: 339px;
  left: 171px;
  -webkit-transform-origin: 100% 100%;
  width: 120px;
  height: 120px;
  -webkit-animation: blowRight 6s forwards ease-in;
}
#quadrant3 {
  -webkit-transform: rotateX(180deg);
  bottom: 378px;
  left: 171px;
}
#quadrant5 {
  -webkit-transform-origin: 100% 50%;
  -webkit-transform: rotateY(40deg) scale3d(.8,.8,.8);
  bottom: 32;
  left: 137px;
}
```

Customizing the Animation for Quadrants with Transforms

One of the challenges of working with and animating transforms is that once you've transformed an element about the z-axis—as you will in quadrants 2 and 4 in Listing 7.17—setting them to a given `left` position (left: 290 pixels in this case) will not result in the same positioning as it will on an element whose z-axis rotation has not been transformed.

To be more explicit, consider that using the `blowRight` animation for quadrants 2 and 4 does not work very well at present. They jump ahead too far at the 7% keyframe, resulting in the result shown in Figure 7.7.

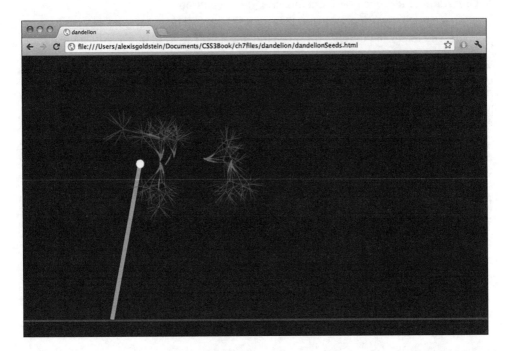

Figure 7.7   Quadrants 2 and 4 not aligned with the others when the animation begins

In order to ensure that all quadrants move together in sync, at the same pace as the stem blows, you can define custom quadrant animations for both quadrant 2 and quadrant 4 (see Listing 7.17). These custom animations will provide the appropriate value at the 7% keyframe to keep both `#quadrant2` and `#quadrant4` aligned with the others.

Listing 7.17   **Animating Quadrants 2 and 4 (dandelion.css)**

```
@-webkit-keyframes blowRightQuad2 {
  0% {  }
  7% {  left: 190px; }
  100% { left: 1600px; }
}

#quadrant2 {
  -webkit-transform: rotate(89deg);
```

```
   left: 78px;
   bottom: 280px;
   -webkit-animation: blowRightQuad2 6s forwards ease-in;
}

@-webkit-keyframes blowRightQuad4 {
   0% {  }
   7% {  left:140px; }
   100% { left:1600px; }
}

#quadrant4 {
   -webkit-transform: rotate(180deg);
   bottom: 382px;
   left: 10px;
   -webkit-animation: blowRightQuad4 6s forwards ease-in;
}
```

Animating Groups of Seeds

Even though you are now moving all the quadrants across the screen and off to the right, you can still make this animation better. It is not very interesting to keep all the new seeds in their original position, apart from moving them to the right en masse. When a gust of wind blows on a dandelion, the seeds tend to move in many different directions, not just in the direction of the wind.

You could take the approach you took previously, giving each seed its own custom animation. But this is cumbersome and not necessary in order to get the overall effect of the seeds being blown about. Rather than animate all the new seed elements individually, you can leverage the nth-of-type pseudo-class to make all first, second, third, and so on seeds in a given quadrant animate in the same way.

Customizing the First Seed in Each `.quad` Element

In Listing 7.18, you rotate the first seed in each element with the class of quad by 20 degrees in the counterclockwise direction. You also push it 5 pixels along the x-axis in the positive direction and 5 pixels up the y-axis in the negative direction (pushing the seed up and out).

You also assign the first seed in each `.quad` element to run the animation seedChange1. This animation rotates the seed from its starting position (–20 degrees on the z-axis) to a 60-degree rotation by the end of the animation. It also pushes the seed up farther than it began, up to 50 pixels above its original position.

Listing 7.18 Configuring the First Seed for Each `.quad` Element (dandelion.css)

```
.quad div:nth-of-type(1) {
   -webkit-transform:rotate(-20deg) translate3d(5px,-5px,0);
   -webkit-animation: seedChange1 6s;
```

```
}
@-webkit-keyframes seedChange1 {
  0% {}
  100% { -webkit-transform: rotate(60deg) translate3d(5px,-15px,0);}
}
```

You'll apply the same concept to all subsequent seeds—from the second in each `div class="quad"` to the fifth seed in each `div class="quad"`. Rather than go through each one individually, the following sections look at the remaining definitions together.

Giving the *n*th Seed in Each Quadrant Its Own Animation

In Listing 7.19, you define the initial degree of rotation for the second, third, fourth, and fifth seed in each `.quad` element, and then you assign a different keyframe animation to each. For the third and fifth seeds, you also add translations to the seeds. The idea here is to vary the path the seeds take in order to make their dispersion look semi-random.

Listing 7.19   **Setting the Animation per Seed (dandelion.css)**

```
.quad div:nth-of-type(2) {
  -webkit-transform: rotate(-30deg);
  -webkit-animation: seedChange2 6s;
}
.quad div:nth-of-type(3) {
  -webkit-transform: rotate(-76deg) translate3d(-5px,0,0);
  -webkit-animation: seedChange3 6s;
}
.quad div:nth-of-type(4) {
  -webkit-transform: rotate(-50deg);
  -webkit-animation: seedChange4 6s;
}
.quad div:nth-of-type(5) {
  -webkit-animation: seedChange5 6s;
  -webkit-transform: rotate(-100deg) translate3d(-5px,-5px,0);
}
```

In Listing 7.20, you define all the remaining keyframe animations for how the second through fifth seed in each `.quad div` element should behave.

The way these animations work is that the second, third, fourth, and fifth seed in each `.quad div` element will all run their respective animation. For example, the fourth seed in every quadrant (which is five seeds total, since there are five quadrants) will all run the animation seedChange4. However, since each seed is in a different quadrant, and they all have different absolute positions, `translate3d` applies to wherever the seed happens to begin. So while seed 2 in quadrant 3 will to some extent appear like a mirror image of seed 2 in quadrant 1, the combination of these animations with the earlier variations in the animations to move the seeds right across the screen will provide enough diversity to keep these animations interesting. Figure 7.8 shows the completed animation at the 50% keyframe.

Listing 7.20   **Individual Seed Animations (dandelion.css)**

```
@-webkit-keyframes seedChange2 {
  0% {}
  100% { -webkit-transform: rotate(40deg) translate3d(5px,5px,0);}
}
@-webkit-keyframes seedChange3 {
  0% {}
  100% { -webkit-transform: rotate(20deg) translate3d(50px,-5px,0);}
}
@-webkit-keyframes seedChange4 {
  0% {}
  100% { -webkit-transform: rotate(10deg) translate3d(5px,-5px,0);}
}

@-webkit-keyframes seedChange5 {
  0% { -webkit-transform-origin: 100% 50%; }
  30% { -webkit-transform: rotateX(60deg) scale3d(2,1.2,2);}
  100% { -webkit-transform:
    rotate(-10deg) rotateX(85deg) translate3d(5px,-5px,0);}
}
```

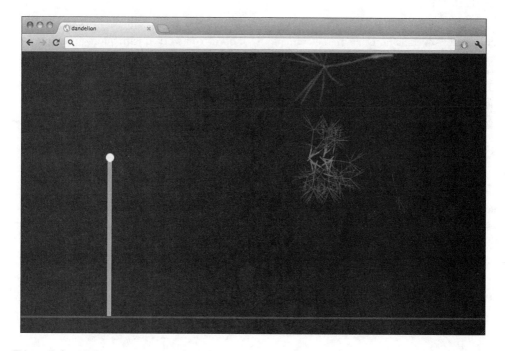

Figure 7.8   Halfway through the animation

Additional Resources

For more information on hardware acceleration, I recommend the following resource:

- Let's Play with Hardware-Accelerated CSS by Martin Kool: http://mobile.smashingmagazine. com/2012/06/21/play-with-hardware-accelerated-css/

For more projects that demonstrate the animation of 3D transforms, see the following demos and examples:

- idzr.org's 404 page, which leverages 3D transforms and CSS animations to create a cloud of spinning letters: http://idzr.org/404

- Surfin' Safari's blog entry Morphing Power Cubes: http://www.webkit.org/blog-files/3d-transforms/morphing-cubes.html

- Surfin' Safari's blog entry 3D Transforms: http://www.webkit.org/blog/386/3d-transforms/

- The Art of the Web's CSS: 3D Transforms and Animations: http://www.the-art-of-web.com/css/3d-transforms/

- Wheel of Kittens demo: http://www.cancelbubble.com/github/wheel_of_kittens/ (source: https://github.com/cancelbubble/Absolutely-Astounding-Wheel-of-Kittens–Safari-)

Summary

In this chapter, you combined 2D and 3D transforms together into examples that you then animated with transitions, keyframe animations, or both. You worked with adding multiple animations to elements to make them move in complex ways. And you explored the difficultly of applying the same animation to elements that have undergone transforms. You saw that in some cases, if you want elements to move in sequence, you must set up multiple animations to account for any transforms.

Challenge

Modify one of the seedChange animations to make some of the seeds float up more than the others. Try adjusting the transformation along the y-axis for one or two seed positions (the second seed in each section, for example) in order to add more diversity of movement to the seed-blowing animation.

Using Transitions and Transforms to Animate Text

In this chapter you will combine keyframes, transitions, transforms, and a bit of jQuery to create a text-driven animation. You will use CSS3 to do some basic styling on elements to make them look like part of a typewriter, and then you'll animate the text and the typewriter's roller to give life to a much-loved quote by Virginia Woolf.

Introduction to the Typewriter Example

In this example, you will take a quote by Virginia Woolf, from her famous essay "A Room of One's Own" (the full text of which can be found at http://ebooks.adelaide.edu.au/w/woolf/virginia/w91r/), and give life to it by animating the words as if they were being typed out on a typewriter. You'll also leverage some CSS3 styles to make your elements look like the roller of a typewriter and a paper wrapped around it. Figure 8.1 shows a freeze-frame from the final animated page. You can see the complete demo at http://alexisgo.github.com/LearningCSSAnimations/ch8code/woolf.html. The source code is in the ch8code folder on this book's GitHub site: https://github.com/alexisgo/LearningCSSAnimations.

"A Room of One's Own"

The quote you will animate in this chapter is from Virginia Woolf's essay "A Room of One's Own." The essay is most well known for Woolf's insistence that, to write, a woman (or any other writer) must have some semblance of financial stability (for Woolf, it was £500 a year) and a room of one's own.

The quote you will animate also speaks to a need of writing—namely, that writing, as well as many other things, requires a decent meal. The quote is "A good dinner is of great importance to good talk. One cannot think well, love well, sleep well, if one has not dined well."

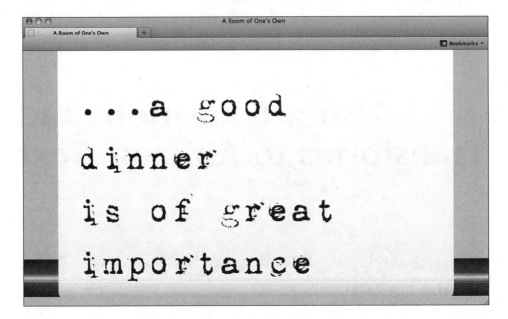

Figure 8.1   A scene from the final typewriter animation

You will use jQuery in this chapter for convenience. You will use a number of jQuery methods in this chapter, including `each()`, `removeClass()`, and `addClass()`, but mostly, you'll be leveraging the power and flexibility of jQuery's selectors.

The Animation's Layout and Basic Styles

Before you begin to animate any piece of this chapter's example, let's review the HTML and the basic CSS styles that make it up. You'll be giving the elements descriptive IDs such as `#paper` and `#roller` for the paper in the typewriter and the roller moving the paper, respectively. And you'll also leverage classes that will serve as triggers, moving the animation from scene to scene. There will be five scenes total in this animation, and thus you will make use of five scene-related classes: `scene1` through `scene5`.

Note that this chapter, for the sake of brevity, uses only the `-moz-` vendor prefix for any CSS3 properties. You can find the code with all the appropriate vendor prefixes in the folder ch8code at the book's GitHub site: http://alexisgo.github.com/LearningCSSAnimations.

The Animation's Core HTML

The example's HTML is split into two main section elements: #quote and #subscenes.
#quote holds two paragraphs, each of which stores one portion of the quote. The first para-
graph inside #quote serves as the basis for scene 1. The elements inside #subscenes form
scenes 2 through 4, and then the second (and final) paragraph inside #quote makes up scene 5.
Listing 8.1 shows the relevant HTML elements.

Listing 8.1   **The Base HTML for the Quote Animation (woolf.html)**

```html
<div id="container">
  <div id="roller"></div>
  <div id="paper">
    <div id="quote">
      <!-- first part of quote will be populated via JavaScript -->
      <p id="one"></p>
      <p id="two">
        One cannot<br class="skip">
        think well,<br class="skip">
        love well,<br class="skip">
        sleep well<br class="skip">
        <!-- remaining portion of quote will be populated via JavaScript -->
      </p>
    </div> <!-- end quote -->
    <div id="subscenes">
      <div id="think">
      THINK
      </div>
      <div id="well">
        WELL
      </div>
      <div id="love">
        <p>LOVE WELL</p>
      </div>
      <div id="sleep">
        <span>SLEEP</span>
        <span>WELL</span>
      </div>
    </div>
  </div>  <!-- end paper -->
</div> <!-- end container -->
```

Using a Custom Font with `@font-face`

To make the letters in the animated quote look like they were produced by a typewriter, you can use the font 1942Report, by Johan Holmdahl, which can be found at http://www.fontsquirrel.com/fonts/1942-report. From that link, you can download the `@font-face` kit to save time.

The way the `@font-face` at-rule works is that you define the font family you want to use, and then in the `src` property, you define the URL where that font lives. If your user doesn't have the font on his or her computer, the browser will visit the URL provided and download the font for use in the browser (and *only* for use in the browser—it will not be available for use in other applications, such as Microsoft Word).

Not all browsers support the same font file type. For example, EOT is the only file type that works in Internet Explorer version 8 and earlier. In order to account for all browsers, you must provide all relevant file types for the chosen font. This is where a tool like Font Squirrel comes in handy. Rather than having to generate all the code from scratch, you can simply choose the font you like and download a `@font-face` kit from http://www.fontsquirrel.com. When you download the `@font-face` kit, not only will you have all the needed font file types (which come in the `@font-face` zip file), but the required CSS will also be provided in a file called stylesheet.css.

For this example, you can move all the font files into a dedicated folder called fonts, rename the stylesheet.css file to font.css, and update the path to the fonts to reflect their new location. Listing 8.2 shows the final `@font-face` rule.

Listing 8.2   Defining the `@font-face` At-Rule for the Custom Font (font.css)

```
@font-face {
    font-family: '1942report1942report';
    src: url('../fonts/1942-webfont.eot');
    src: url('../fonts/1942-webfont.eot?#iefix') format('embedded-opentype'),
         url('../fonts/1942-webfont.woff') format('woff'),
         url('../fonts/1942-webfont.ttf') format('truetype'),
         url('../fonts/1942-webfont.svg#1942report1942report') format('svg');
    font-weight: normal;
    font-style: normal;
}
```

Because this is the only font you'll be using for the page, you assign it to the font family in the body selector, as shown in Listing 8.3. In this listing, note that you also add a basic light gray background color to the body element.

Listing 8.3   Styling the Body's Font and Background Color (woolf.css)

```
body {
  background-color: #D3D3D3;
  font-family: '1942report1942report', sans-serif;
}
```

Styling the Typewriter Roller and Paper Elements

To make it appear as if a typewriter roller is moving, you're going to later use a keyframe animation that moves the `background-position`. Thus, in the base styling, it is important that the `#roller` element have an uneven pattern that can be moved around to simulate turning. You accomplish this with a gradient that gives you a streak of light in the middle and fades to black on the top and bottom (see Listing 8.4). (For the sake of brevity, only the `-moz-` vendor prefix is included in the code listing.)

Listing 8.4   **Styling the `#roller` Element (woolf.css)**

```
#roller {
  width: 100%;
  height: 80px;
  position: absolute;
  bottom: 0px;

  background: rgb(66,65,65); /* Old browsers */
  background: -moz-linear-gradient(top,
    rgba(66,65,65,1) 0%, rgba(66,65,65,1) 6%,
    rgba(109,108,108,1) 38%, rgba(234,232,232,1) 50%,
    rgba(109,108,108,1) 64%, rgba(66,65,65,1) 94%,
    rgba(66,65,65,1) 100%); /* FF3.6+ */
}
```

Next, you can style the `#paper` element on which the quote will be typed. To make it appear as if the paper is wrapped around the typewriter's roller, you'll use a CSS3 gradient that goes from white to light beige, with most of the darker color appearing toward the bottom of the element. This will gives the illusion of a curling paper, wrapped around the roller. In addition, you'll set `border-radius` on the bottom-left and bottom-right corners, making the paper appear to curl ever-so-slightly inward, which provides a sense of perspective. Listing 8.5 presents this code, and Figure 8.2 shows a close-up of the bottom of the paper.

Listing 8.5   **Styling the `#paper` Element (woolf.css)**

```
#paper {
  width: 85%;
  margin: 0 auto;
  height: 500px;
  padding-bottom: 25px;
  overflow: hidden;
  position: relative;

  background: rgb(255,255,255); /* Old browsers */
  background: -moz-linear-gradient(top,
    rgba(255,255,255,1) 0%,
    rgba(249,247,247,1) 88%, rgba(249,248,247,1) 92%,
```

```
    rgba(239,233,222,1) 97%, rgba(219,215,210,1) 99%,
    rgba(211,207,201,1) 100%); /* FF3.6+ */

  border-bottom-right-radius: 5px 20px;
  border-bottom-left-radius: 5px 12px;
}
```

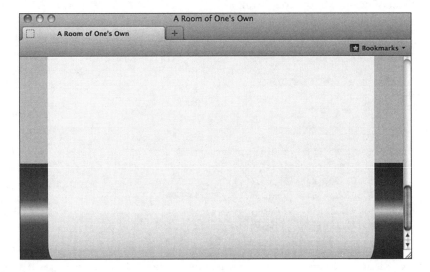

Figure 8.2   Close-up of the bottom of the `#paper` element

Scene 1: Making the Quote Rise Up the Screen

As stated earlier in this chapter, the animation you'll be building is divided into five main scenes. The first scene displays the first five lines of the quote, pushing the paper up one line at a time to reveal each new portion of the quote. At the same time, you will animate changes to the `background-position` of the typewriter's roller. This will give the illusion that the typewriter roller is turning and pushing the paper up as it does so.

In order to achieve the desired effect, you will need several animations. Each transition from one line to the next will require a separate animation. In order to make them play one right after another, you need to ensure that there is an appropriate delay between earlier animations and later ones.

All the lines of the quote that will be displayed live inside the `div` called `#quote`. This `div`'s `top` property will be modified for each line, gradually pulling the `div` up higher and higher to reveal more text.

Using Keyframe Animations to Move the Quote Upward

At this point, you must determine how far up to move the paper in order to give the impression of a typewriter typing. The hardest part about this is determining the correct value for top. The easiest way to determine this is to use a tool such as Firefox's Firebug (http://getfirebug. com) or the built-in Web Developer Toolbar in Chrome or Safari. If you are unfamiliar with these tools, a good tutorial of Chrome's Developer tools is available at https://developers. google.com/chrome-developer-tools/docs/overview#window.

In Firebug, you can experiment with different starting values for top until you find the appropriate location for the div in order to show each line. You need to find the right value in order to display the large font that you will use for the quote you're going to display. For example, in Figure 8.3, you can see that the appropriate location to display the third line of the quote is top: 100px.

Figure 8.3   Using Firebug to determine the appropriate top value for each sentence

Once you have determined the correct placement of the #quote div for each line (and, for the font type and size chosen, those values are 300, 200, 90, –20, and -140 pixels for the first five lines), you can set up the appropriate keyframes.

You don't need to set up an animation for the first line, as the first sentence will already be in view when the page loads. The second line needs to move the #quote div from the top:300px position, which shows only the first line ("a good dinner") to the top:200px position, which reveals the next line ("is of great"). Listing 8.6 shows the code.

Listing 8.6   **Moving the #paper Element Up to Reveal the Second Line (woolf.css)**

```
@-moz-keyframes line2 {
  0% {top: 300px;}
  100% { top: 200px;}
}
```

Next, you use the basic pattern established with the line2 keyframe and define how to continue moving the paper up to reveal one line at a time (see Listing 8.7).

Listing 8.7   **Setting Up the Keyframes for Subsequent Lines (woolf.css)**

```
@-moz-keyframes line3 {
  0% {top: 200px;}
  100% { top: 90px;}
}
@-moz-keyframes line4 {
  0% {top: 90px;}
  100% { top: -20px;}
}
@-moz-keyframes line5 {
  0% {top: -20px;}
  100% { top: -140px;}
}
```

Chaining Together Multiple Keyframe Animations

The key to playing each animation in sequence is to appropriately manage the delay between them. The delay between the first line and the second line needs to be only enough time to read the first line since there is no animation played on the first line. But to approximate the time it takes to move from the second line to the third line, you must take into account two things: the delay that was applied before the line2 animation played and the duration of the line2 animation itself.

What makes this tricky is that, as you'll see later, you are going to eventually animate the appearance of each letter, as if you were actually typing. Listing 8.8 shows the delays applied to each line, along with comments. This code's use of the delays will become clearer after the next section, when you use the letters() function to add in the typing effect. The chained animations, with appropriate delays, are detailed in Listing 8.8.

Listing 8.8   **Chaining Together the Line Feed Animations (woolf.css)**

```
#quote #one.scene1 {
   position: absolute;
  top: 300px;
  -moz-transition: opacity 0.8s;

  -moz-animation:
  /* '...a good dinner:'
  takes 3.6 seconds for all letters to appear */

  /* 'is of great' letters start typing at: 5250*/
  line2 1s 3.6s forwards ease-in-out,

  /* 'importance' starts at: 9000 */
  line3 1s 8000ms forwards ease-in-out,
```

```
/* 'to good talk' letters start at 13000 */
line4 1s 12000ms forwards ease-in-out,

/* 'one cannot' letters start at: 17250 */
line5 1s 16250ms forwards ease-in-out;
}
```

Using JavaScript to Trigger the Animation

You've now set up all the animations for the first scene, but you haven't yet triggered any of them. Neither the #one element nor the #roller element currently contains the class scene1. To amend that, you will define a JavaScript function called setup to configure the time at which each class should be applied to these elements, as well as elements in later scenes. This function is called as soon as the page finishes loading. Listing 8.9 shows the beginning of the function setup. The text and text2 variables contain the first and second parts of the quote you are animating and will be used later in the function. The final line in Listing 8.9 calls the letters function, which you define next.

Listing 8.9   **Triggering Animations with JavaScript's setTimeoutFunction (woolf.js)**

```
$(document).ready(setup);

function setup() {
  var text = "...a good dinner/is of great/importance/to good talk./One cannot/";
  var text2 = "if one has not/dined well./-Virginia Woolf";

  $('#roller, #one').addClass('scene1');
  letters(250, "#one span, #one br", "#one", text);
}
```

Revealing the Letters One at a Time with JavaScript and Keyframe Animations

Next, you will set up the code you need in order to make your animation look like someone is actually typing the quote, with each letter appearing on the paper element one at a time. You will do this through a function called letters. Note that at this point—before you add the letters function—the code will not work properly. You will use a slightly modified version of the approach you took to move the paper: You will use keyframe animations with the appropriate animation-delay in place to ensure that each animation plays at the appropriate time. However, unlike with the previous approach, where you set up the delays in the CSS, you will leverage JavaScript and jQuery to dynamically add the animation property, including its delay value. You will do this in a loop so you can easily add the proper delay for each and every letter.

The `letters` Function

The `letters` function will do the heavy lifting for you by revealing the letters one at a time. To give you a sneak peek of what you'll be building, Listing 8.10 shows a complete version of the function `letters()`. This is a long function, and we will review it one piece at a time.

Listing 8.10   **The Complete `letters()` Function (woolf.css)**

```
function letters(initialDelay, selector, element, text) {
 var re = /[-.\w]/;
 for (var i in text) {
   if (text[i].match(re)) {
     var el = document.createElement("span");
     var letter = document.createTextNode(text[i]);
     el.appendChild(letter);
     $(element).append(el);
   }
   else if (text[i] === "/") {
     $(element).append(document.createElement("br"));
   }
   else {
      $(element).append(document.createTextNode(text[i]));
   }
 }
 var delay = initialDelay;
 $(selector).each(function() {
   if ($(this).is('span')) {
     this.style[Modernizr.prefixed('animation')] = "letterAppear 100ms " + delay +
     ➥"ms forwards";
     delay += 250;
   }
   // If this is a br element, but NOT a br element with the class "skip"
   else if ($(this).is('br') && ( ! $(this).is('.skip'))) {
     delay += 1500;
   }
 });
}
```

You will begin to define the `letters` function in Listing 8.11. `letters` is first called right after the `#roller` and `#one` elements have had their first scene triggered, when the class `scene1` is added (see Listing 8.9). The `letters` function is called so that you can take each and every letter in the quote and wrap it in a `span` element so that you can apply an animation with a different start time to each letter. As you will see in Listing 8.11, `letters` takes four arguments.

Leveraging Regular Expressions

In order to wrap each letter, hyphen, and period in a `span` element, you must be able to parse them out of the `text` and `text2` variables. You also want to replace any forward slashes (/) with a `br` element. To do this, you can leverage JavaScript's support for regular expressions.

Regular expressions allow you to set up a pattern, and then the result includes only the characters that match the pattern. The regular expression that corresponds to the pattern you describe is stored in the re variable (see Listing 8.11). To get a sense of what the regular expression defined in Listing 8.11 matches, try adding the regular expression /[-.\w]/ to the tool reg, explained by Lea Verou at http://leaverou.github.com/regexplained/, and see what it matches.

Listing 8.11 **Setting Up the Quotes and the Regular Expression (woolf.js)**

```
function letters(initialDelay, selector, element, text) {
  var re = /[-.\w]/;
  // continued in Listing 8.12
}
```

Wrapping Each Letter in a span Element

Next, you will use a for loop to wrap each letter from the quote in a span element and every forward slash character inside the quote in a br. This is detailed in Listing 8.12.

First, you loop through each letter in the results of the regular expression. For each letter, you create a new span element and then insert that letter inside the span. Then you append the span to the element specified in the element parameter.

Next, you check for the presence of a forward slash. Any forward slashes in the results get turned into br elements.

Listing 8.12 **Appending the HTML-Enriched Quotation (woolf.js)**

```
function letters(initialDelay, selector, element, text) {
  // continued from Listing 8.11

    for (var i in text) {
      if (text[i].match(re)) {
        var el = document.createElement("span");
        var letter = document.createTextNode(text[i]);
        el.appendChild(letter);
        $(element).append(el);
      }
      else if (text[i] === "/") {
        $(element).append(document.createElement("br"));
      }
      else {
        $(element).append(document.createTextNode(text[i]));
      }
    } // end for
  // continued in Listing 8.14
}
```

Applying the Correct `animation-delay` for Each Letter

Now that you have your `span` elements for each letter, you're going to apply the same animation to each, with a different `animation-delay` for each letter. This will stagger the appearance of each letter so that the effect looks like typing. Every `span` element will use the animation `letterAppear`. Listing 8.13 shows this keyframe animation's code. The animation fades in each letter quickly and then leaves it opaque for the rest of the animation.

Listing 8.13   **The Typing Keyframe Animation (woolf.css)**

```
@-moz-keyframes letterAppear {
  0% { opacity: 0;}
  10% { opacity: 1;}
  100% {opacity: 1;}
}
```

Listing 8.14 includes the last pieces to the `letters()` function. To keep track of the delay each element should have, you create the variable `delay`. You set the value of `delay` to be equal to the `initialDelay` variable that was passed as a parameter to the `letters` function. Next, you need to iterate through all the elements that are matched by the selector you passed in. You achieve this with the jQuery function `each()`.

In the first `if` statement, you check whether the current element is a `span`. If it is, in the first line of the `if` statement, you add the keyframe animation `letterAppear` as an inline style to that `span`. You choose the proper prefix for the animation shorthand property by using the Modernizr method `prefixed`. For a discussion of this method and how it works, see Chapter 7, "Animating 2D and 3D Transforms."

Listing 8.14   **Adding Animation to Each Letter (woolf.css)**

```
function letters(initialDelay, selector, element, text) {
  // continued from Listing 8.12
  var delay = initialDelay;
  $(selector).each(function() {
    if ($(this).is('span')) {
      this.style[Modernizr.prefixed('animation')] =
        "letterAppear 100ms " + delay + "ms forwards";
      delay += 250;
    }
    // If this is a br element, but NOT a br element with the class "skip"
    else if ($(this).is('br') && ( ! $(this).is('.skip'))) {
      delay += 1500;
    }
  });
} // end letters()
```

animation-delay (which appears midway through this line because you're using the animation shorthand property) is set to the current value of the variable delay. In the second and final line of the if statement, you increment the delay variable by 250 so that the next element's letter will animate 250 milliseconds after the current letter.

In the else if statement, you check for the presence of a br element that does *not* have the class skip. This is because later on, in scene 5, there are preexisting portions of the quote that you do not want to be animated. These br elements thus should not add any delays to the typing of the letters. So these br elements are labeled with the class skip. The delay in the case of a br element is 1500 milliseconds. This allows time for the simultaneous animation, which moves the #paper element line by line, to finish before the next set of letters begins animating and appearing (refer to Listing 8.14).

Determining the Post-Typing Timing

The trickiest part of the animation in this chapter is getting the timing correct. Since each scene after the first one needs to ensure that the previous scene has finished, you'll be using the JavaScript function setTimeout to specify a delay before the next scene is applied. Determining the proper delay requires keeping track of how long the prior animation lasts and adding a bit of a buffer where desirable.

The first delay you need to determine is how long to wait before applying the class hide to the #one quote element, which sets the opacity to 0, as follows:

```
#quote #one.hide { opacity: 0; }
```

In this case, the delay is fairly simple to discover. Since you've added a series of span elements (one for each letter), each with its own animation-delay, you simply look at what the delay is in the very last span element inside the #one element—which happens to be 19,250 milliseconds. So you can give a 300-millisecond buffer and hide the first part of the quote after 19,550 milliseconds (see Listing 8.15).

Listing 8.15 **Triggering Animations with JavaScript's setTimeout Function (woolf.js)**

```
function setup() {
  // continued from Listing 8.9

  // last letter appears at 19250, so give it a few
  // more milliseconds before hiding
  setTimeout(function () { $('#one').addClass('hide'); }, 19550);
}
```

You can see an approximation of the typing animation in Figures 8.4 and 8.5, which show what the scene looks like halfway through the first line being typed and what it looks like when the first line is complete.

Figure 8.4   Halfway through the first line's chaining of `letterAppear` across multiple `span` elements

Figure 8.5   The first line of typing completed

In the next three scenes, you will have a bit of fun with each line from the quote and animate them in a more dramatic fashion than simply mimicking the behavior of a typewriter. You will leverage 3D transforms as well as keyframe animations and transitions to bring the text to life.

Scene 2: Making Text Fall

Rather than continue with the typewriter-driven animation, at this point you can change things up a bit by doing something a bit more dramatic with the next few lines of the quote. You can start with the words "THINK WELL," which is the next line, and give it a bit of life and playfulness by having "THINK" fall forward, down, and around, as if the bottom of the words are on a hinge. In order to achieve this, you need to use 3D transforms.

Listing 8.16 outlines the initial styles of the "THINK WELL" quote.

Listing 8.16   **Initial Styles of "THINK" and "WELL"**

```
#think, #well {
  font-size: 8em;
  width: 100%;
  margin-top: 0;
  opacity: 0;
  -moz-transform-origin: 0% 100%;
}

#think { margin-left: 10%;}
#well {
  position: absolute;
  top: 0;
  left: 520px;
}
```

Animating Falling Words

As described earlier, now you will fade in a larger version of the words "THINK WELL" and then cause the word "THINK" to fall downward and then swing back and forth, as if on a hinge. You will do this by using rotateX and a keyframe animation.

You need to bring the elements #think and #well, which hold the next part of the quote, into view. In both cases, you bring them into view by changing the opacity to 1 from 0 over time in a keyframe animation.

Start with the #think element. Once the JavaScript has added the class scene2 to the #think element, the think keyframe animation is triggered. The animation's first step is to fall from its original position to a position –200 degrees away on the x-axis. The result of this transform is that the word "THINK" falls toward the user and then swings away from the user as it passes –180 degrees on its way to –200 degrees.

Next, the #think element swings back toward the user, to –160 degrees. Finally, the #think element settles exactly opposite its original position, or –180 degrees from where it started. Listing 8.17 outlines the entire animation, and Figure 8.6 shows the 50% keyframe.

Listing 8.17   **Animating "THINK" to Fall (woolf.css)**

```
@-moz-keyframes think{
  0% { }
  35% { -moz-transform: rotateX(-200deg); }
  50% { -moz-transform: rotateX(-160deg); }
  80% { -moz-transform: rotateX(-180deg); }
  100% { -moz-transform: rotateX(-180deg); }
}

#think.scene2 {
  /* delay slightly to allow main text to fade out*/
  -moz-animation:
    fadeIn 0.6s 0.5s forwards,
    think 1.8s 1s forwards;
}
```

Figure 8.6   The #think element halfway through the think keyframe animation

The #well element's animation is more straightforward: You simply need to fade it in slightly behind the fade of the #think element. You accomplish this by calling the fadeIn keyframe animation, as detailed in Listing 8.18.

Listing 8.18   **Fading in "WELL" (woolf.css)**

```
@-moz-keyframes fadeIn { 0% {opacity:0;} 100% { opacity:1;}}

#well.scene2 {
  -moz-animation:
    fadeIn 0.5s 1s forwards;
}
```

Triggering Scene 2's Animation

As you did earlier, here you will rely on JavaScript's setTimeout function to apply the classes that serve as triggers to each scene. You trigger this animation by adding the class scene2 to both #think and #well. The delay in this case is the same as was used in Listing 8.15 previously—19,550 milliseconds—which determines when to fade out the text from the previous scene.

Scene 2's animation (defined in Listing 8.17) takes 2.8 seconds total, so you should wait an extra 150 milliseconds before triggering the hide class, which will hide the #think and #well elements (see Listing 8.19).

Listing 8.19   **Triggering the Animation with JavaScript's setTimeout Function (woolf.js)**

```
function setup() {
  // continued from Listing 8.15
  setTimeout(function () { $('#think, #well').addClass('scene2'); }, 19550);
  // THINK animation takes 2800ms--we'll give a 150ms buffer before hiding
  setTimeout(function () { $('#think, #well').addClass('hide'); }, 22500);
}
```

The JavaScript trigger used here works to hide the two elements because in woolf.css, the class hide has been defined to change the display of both elements to none:

```
#think.hide, #well.hide { display: none; }
```

Scene 3: Scrolling Text

In scene 3, you will run the words LOVE WELL quickly across the screen from right to left. You begin, as shown in Listing 8.20, by increasing the size of the font substantially, to 3400% of its original size.

Listing 8.20   **Adjusting the Font for LOVE WELL (woolf.css)**

```css
#love {
  -moz-transform-origin: 50% 40%;
  font-size: 3400%;
}
```

Next, when the `setup` JavaScript function triggers `scene3`, you apply the `loveWell` keyframe animation to the paragraph inside the `#love` element. You force the (very large) words to be all on one line by changing the width of the paragraph to 1000%. You also position the text offscreen initially. The `loveWell` keyframe moves the words from being hidden past the right edge of the browser to being placed on the left off the left edge of the browser. The entire animation takes just 2 seconds. When the animation is complete, adding the class `hide` to the `#love` element will have the style `display:none` applied, hiding it. Listing 8.21 outlines the CSS, and Listing 8.22 shows the JavaScript that controls the timing of the triggers. Figure 8.7 shows the animation toward its beginning, to give you a sense of the scale of the letters.

Listing 8.21   **Scrolling LOVE WELL from Right to Left (woolf.css)**

```css
@-moz-keyframes loveWell{
  0% { left: 951px;}
  100% { left: -3500px;}
}

#love.scene3 p {
  width: 1000%;
  position: absolute;
  top: -200px;
  left: -1251px;
  margin-top: 0;
  -moz-animation: loveWell 2s forwards linear;
}

#love.hide { display: none; }
```

Figure 8.7   The #love element toward the beginning of the loveWell animation

Listing 8.22   **Defining the Timing Triggers for Scene 3 (woolf.js)**

```
function setup() {
  // continued from Listing 8.19

  setTimeout(function () { $('#love').addClass('scene3'); }, 23000);
  setTimeout(function () {$('#love').addClass('hide');}, 25800);
}
```

Scene 4: Growing Text

Scene 4 consists of two words, SLEEP and WELL, that each grow in size, one at a time. Initially, the scene fades in when scene4 is triggered, due to the combination of the transition set for opacity in the #sleep selector and the change to opacity:1 in the #sleep.scene4 selector (see Listing 8.23).

Listing 8.23   **Base Styles for the SLEEP WELL Scene (woolf.css)**

```
#sleep {
  opacity: 0;
  font-size: 6em;
  margin-left: 5%;
  -moz-transition: opacity 1s;
}
```

```
#sleep.scene4 { opacity: 1; }
```

Next, Listing 8.24 defines a keyframe animation called `growWords` that enlarges the font size by 1.4 ems over 0.5 second. Both of the `span` elements that are nested inside the `#sleep` element have this animation applied.

Finally, you use the `:nth-of-type` pseudo-class to stagger the animations. The first word, SLEEP, will grow first. Figure 8.8 shows the result of growing just the SLEEP text.

The second word, WELL, which is the second `span` element inside `#sleep`, will have a longer `animation-delay` applied, as defined in the selector `#sleep.scene4 span:nth-of-type(2)`. This selector will select the second `span` element inside the `#sleep` element.

Listing 8.24   **Leveraging the `nth-of-type` to Stagger Animations (woolf.css)**

```
@-moz-keyframes growWords { 0% {} 100% { font-size:1.4em;} }
```

```
#sleep.scene4 span {
  /* delay by 1s to allow fade in */
  -moz-animation: growWords 0.5s 1s forwards;
}
```

```
/* the second span (which holds the word "well") is delayed
by 0.7 seconds so that it runs a little after the first word animates */
#sleep.scene4 span:nth-of-type(2) { -moz-animation-delay:1.7s;}
}
```

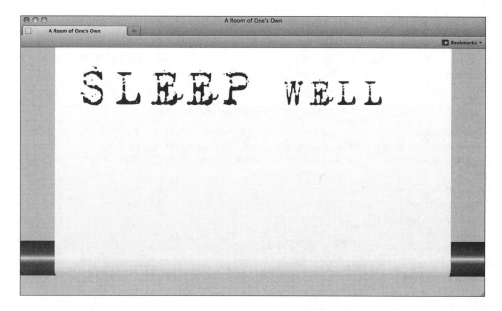

Figure 8.8   The #sleep element after the animation growWords has been applied to the first span element

As with all the earlier scenes, the code in the setup function defines when scene4 begins and ends, according to the delay set in the appropriate setTimeout function (see Listing 8.25).

Listing 8.25   **Defining the Timing Triggers for Scene 4 (woolf.js)**

```
function setup() {
  // continued from Listing 8.22

  setTimeout(function () { $('#sleep').addClass('scene4'); }, 26500);
  // animation lasts 2.7 secs , 300ms buffer
  setTimeout(function () { $('#sleep').addClass('hide'); }, 29500);
}
```

Scene 5: Continuing the Animation

In the final scene of the animation, you repeat the same concepts used in scene 1 to once again turn the typewriter roller, move the paper, and continue typing the letters, one at a time.

Moving the Second Part of the Quote Upward

Because you now need to move the #paper element even farther up, you define a few new keyframe animations with specific top positions, ensuring that each new line is made visible as the #paper element moves further and further upward (see Listing 8.26).

Listing 8.26   **Moving the Final Part of the Quote Upward (woolf.css)**

```
@-moz-keyframes line6 { 0% {top: -25px; } 100% { top: -130px;} }
@-moz-keyframes line7 { 0% {top: -130px;} 100% { top: -240px;} }
@-moz-keyframes line8 { 0% {top: -240px;} 100% { top: -450px;} }

#quote #two.scene5 {
  display: block;
  position: absolute;
  top: -25px;
  opacity: 0;

  -moz-animation:
  fadeIn 1s forwards linear,
  /* 'if one has not' letters start at 1500 */
  line6 1s 0.5s forwards ease-in-out,
  /* 'dined well' letters start at 5750 */
  line7 1s 4.75s forwards ease-in-out,
  /* V woolf starts at 9750 */
  line8 1s 8.75s forwards ease-in-out;

  -moz-transition: opacity 1s;
}
```

Repeating the Turn of the Roller

Just as with the animations on the #quote element inside the #paper element, you can reuse the same keyframe animations you defined in scene 1 for the #roller. The only difference will be the delays that you use. Listing 8.27 matches the delays for the #roller animation to exactly those defined in the movement of the quote so that the two sets of animations play in sync.

Listing 8.27   **Turning the Typewriter Roller in Scene 5 (woolf.css)**

```
#roller.scene5 {
  -moz-animation:
    turn1 1s 0.5s forwards ease-in-out,
    turn2 1s 4.75s forwards ease-in-out,
    turn3 1s 8.75s forwards ease-in-out;
}
```

Setting Up the Timing for the Rest of the Animation

In this last scene, you must, as before, set up the appropriate delays on the triggers to the scene (see Listing 8.28). And because you are going to have this final scene repeat the typewriter animation, you must call the `letters` function one last time, varying the selector you pass to it, the element you should append new HTML to (#two), and the text you want to display (the second half of the quote). Listing 8.29 shows the complete `setup()` function that you have built piece-by-piece in this chapter.

Listing 8.28 **Triggering the Final Scene (woolf.js)**

```
function setup() {
  // continued from Listing 8.25

  setTimeout(function () { $('#two').addClass('scene5'); }, 30500);
  setTimeout(function () { $('#roller').addClass('scene5'); }, 30500);
  letters(1500, "#two span, #two br", "#two", text2)
}
```

Listing 8.29 **The Complete `setup()` Function (woolf.js)**

```
function setup() {
  var text = "...a good dinner/is of great/importance/to good talk./One cannot/";
  var text2 = "if one has not/dined well./-Virginia Woolf";

  $('#roller, #one').addClass('scene1');
  letters(250, "#one span, #one br", "#one", text);
  // last letter appears at 19250, so give it a few more milliseconds before hiding
   setTimeout(function () { $('#one').addClass('hide'); }, 19550);
  setTimeout(function () { $('#think, #well').addClass('scene2'); }, 19550);
  // THINK animation takes 2800ms--we'll give a 150ms buffer before hiding
  setTimeout(function () { $('#think, #well').addClass('hide'); }, 22500);

  setTimeout(function () { $('#love').addClass('scene3'); }, 23000);
  setTimeout(function () { $('#love').addClass('hide'); }, 25800);

  setTimeout(function () { $('#sleep').addClass('scene4'); }, 26500);
  // animation lasts 2.7 secs , 300ms buffer
  setTimeout(function () { $('#sleep').addClass('hide'); }, 29500);

  setTimeout(function () { $('#two').addClass('scene5'); }, 30500);
  setTimeout(function () { $('#roller').addClass('scene5'); }, 30500);
  letters(1500, "#two span, #two br", "#two", text2)
}
```

Summary

This chapter combined many techniques and properties used in previous chapters to create one continuous, text-driven animation. You leveraged CSS3 effects to make your animation look more realistic (with rounded corners and gradients). And you used JavaScript's regular expressions and jQuery's selectors to add a dynamic effect of letters being typed on a typewriter.

Challenge

Add a sixth scene to the typewriter animation that picks up where the quote left off. The next line of the quote is "The lamp in the spine does not light on beef and prunes." See if you can make the paper raise up by adding a new keyframe animation and also extend the typing animation added in the `letters` function.

Building Flash-Style Animations with Keyframe Animations

This chapter presents a cartoon-style animation of a cat that combines the approaches discussed in previous chapters. You will learn how to build a character piece by piece, ensure that its movements across the screen are smooth by aligning the "joints" via `transform-origin`, and trigger a series of animations by using JavaScript timers.

Introduction to the Meow Street Fat Cat Animation

The star of the brief animation you will create in this chapter is a feline named Morgan Diamond. He is a resident of Meow Street, the financial center of downtown Catsville. He's a fat cat with a bit of a reputation for being ruthless, even criminal. Today, while doing his typical speedy reading of the morning paper, he sees that long-awaited justice may be coming his way.

Like Chapter 8, "Using Transitions and Transforms to Animate Text," this chapter splits an animation up into scenes. You will style the scenes on one or more elements by using class selectors that match the name of each scene. As you did in Chapter 8, you will trigger the changes to the class names via JavaScript.

Your animation will have seven scenes. The animation will start zoomed in on Morgan reading the newspaper. It will then move outside, using animated transforms to achieve a zooming-out look. This will reveal Morgan's mansion, as he sits inside with the window open. Next, a police cat appears on the scene, knocking several times on Morgan's door. Morgan's gaze moves down toward the police cat outside. In the final scene, a spinning newspaper zooms in and finally stops, revealing Morgan's fate. Figure 9.1 shows one of the scenes to give you an idea of what you will be building. You can also view a demo of the completed project at http://alexisgo. github.com/LearningCSSAnimations/ch9code/cat.html.

Figure 9.1   Scene 1 from the animation you'll build

I am most indebted to Herbert Hoover, a brilliant artist and designer, who created the original image of Morgan the cat. You can learn more about Herb's work by visiting his site, http://www.potus31.com/.

The Animation's Layout and Basic Styles

Before you begin to animate any piece of this animation, let's review the HTML and the basic CSS styles that make it up. You'll be defining major elements with ids, for the containing #stage element that will hold the entire animation, as well as main characters in the animation such as the #cat element that will hold Morgan Diamond and the #murphy element that will make up Murphy, Meow Street's toughest cop on the beat. You'll also use classes that will serve as triggers, moving the animation from scene to scene, just as you did in Chapter 8. There will be seven scenes in this animation, and thus you will use seven scene-related classes: scene1 through scene7.

Note that this chapter, for the sake of brevity, uses only the -webkit- vendor prefix for any CSS3 properties. The complete code, with all the appropriate vendor prefixes, can be found in the ch9code folder at the book's GitHub page: https://github.com/alexisgo/LearningCSSAnimations/.

The Basic HTML Elements for the Animation

This animation is composed of several different actors and objects. Rather than review all the elements at once, this chapter reviews the relevant HTML on a scene-by-scene basis. Listing 9.1 lists the first few major elements for this animation: the #stage containing element, the #house, and the #window element through which you can see Morgan the cat.

Listing 9.1   **HTML Elements for Morgan the Cat (cat.html)**

```
<div id="stage">
  <div id="house"></div>
  <div id="window">
    <div id="cat">
      <div id="eyes">
        <div id="lefteye"></div>
        <div id="righteye"></div>
      </div>
      <div id="head"></div>
      <div id="neck"></div>
      <div id="newspaper">
            <!-- continued in Listing 9.6 -->
      </div> <!-- end newspaper -->
    </div> <!-- end cat -->
  </div> <!-- end window -->
</div> <!-- end stage -->
```

I want to explain a few unintuitive element placements. The #window element is not nested inside the #house element because you will want to apply different transforms to them, and transforms applied on a parent are inherited by its descendants. Therefore, you keep the #window element as a sibling to house since the #cat element, which holds Morgan, will need to be transformed differently. To make this more clear, take a look first at the styles for the element #house in Listing 9.2. Morgan's house has a fixed height, is positioned a bit to the left, and has a background image of Morgan's Meow Street townhouse—a mansion relative to other residences in the neighborhood.

What's unusual about this CSS, is the transform that's applied. This is the starting CSS for the #house element, so you may question why you scale the house up to three times its regular size (-webkit-transform: scale3d(3,3,3);) before any animation has even begun. The reason you do this is so that later, in scene 4, when you zoom out to reveal the entire mansion, you can shrink the house down at the same time that you shrink Morgan the cat.

> **Note**
>
> Because you will be using 3D transforms in this code, it makes sense to leverage Modernizr and apply the styles defined in Listing 9.2 only if Modernizr has indicated that 3D transforms are supported (which it does by adding the class csstransforms3d to the opening html tag). Toward the end of this chapter, I'll discuss strategies for browsers without 3D transform support.

Listing 9.2   **Styles for Morgan's House (cat.css)**

```
.csstransforms3d #house {
  width: 100%;
  height: 700px;
  position: absolute;
  left: 315px;

  background-image: url('../img/house.png');
  background-repeat: no-repeat;

  -webkit-transition: 2s;
  -webkit-transform: scale3d(3,3,3);
  -webkit-transform-origin: 50% 0%;

  z-index: -3;
}
```

The Basic Elements and Styling for Morgan the Cat

The next relevant set of elements is #window—through which you can see Morgan the cat—and all the other elements that make up Morgan. Listing 9.3 defines styles for the outermost element, #cat, and its first two nested elements, #head and #neck. The #cat element has its perspective property set so that the 3D transforms you will apply shortly can be viewed properly (as discussed in Chapter 6, "Adding Depth with 3D Transforms"). The #head element has its background-image set to an image of just Morgan's face—and this image is transparent in the section for Morgan's eyes. This way, you can construct Morgan's eyes out of elements and then easily animate them. The #neck element also utilizes a background-image of another section of Morgan—his neck, which is wrapped up in a collared shirt and bowtie. You set z-index of the head to 2 so that the head sits on top of the neck in the event of any overlaps.

Listing 9.3   **Styles for Morgan the Cat (cat.css)**

```
#cat {
  -webkit-perspective: 600px;
  position: absolute;
  left: 100px;
}

#head {
  background-image: url('../img/AristocatHead2.png');
  width: 350px;
  height: 400px;
  background-repeat: no-repeat;
  z-index: 2;
}
```

```
#neck {
  background-image: url('../img/AristocatNeck2.png');
  width: 350px;
  height: 400px;
  background-repeat: no-repeat;
  position: absolute;
  top: 0;
  z-index: 2;
}
```

Next, in Listing 9.4, you draw Morgan's eyes and paws. You use the properties `top` and `left` to set initial positions for Morgan's pupils (which are defined in the combined styles for the two elements). The most crucial line in Listing 9.4 is the one that sets the `z-index` to `-2`. Without this line, you would get an effect like that shown later, in Figure 9.2, when you begin to animate Morgan's pupils. (We revisit this in Listing 9.10.)

Listing 9.4   **Drawing and Placing Morgan's Pupils (cat.css)**

```
#lefteye { top: 144px; left: 98px; }
#righteye { top: 140px; left: 178px; }

/* the z-index here is crucial; without it, the pupils appear above */
#lefteye, #righteye {
  width: 4px;
  height: 40px;
  background-color: black;
  border: 4px solid black;
  border-bottom-left-radius: 10px 15px;
  border-bottom-right-radius: 10px 15px;
  position: absolute;
  z-index: -1;
}
```

One thing that's important to note about the way that Morgan is constructed is that his head consists of a PNG image with a transparent space where his eyes will go. This allows you to draw his pupils from HTML elements, as shown in Listing 9.4. But this becomes problematic if you lack a background behind Morgan, as any colors will bleed through his eyes.

In order to avoid this, you can make use of the fact that Morgan's elements are positioned inside a parent element (called #window) and style that window to have a background (see Listing 9.5). Specifically, you can use a radial gradient that goes from white to gray. That way, the transparent part of Morgan's head image will overlap the white portion of the window's background. As with almost all the other gradients in this chapter, you can use the free online tool by Colorzilla to generate this gradient: http://www.colorzilla.com/gradient-editor/.

In Listing 9.5, we include only the `-webkit-` vendor prefixes for brevity, but you can, as mentioned previously, find the complete code in the ch9code folder at the book's GitHub page: https://github.com/alexisgo/LearningCSSAnimations/.

Listing 9.5   **Styling Morgan's Window (cat.html)**

```
#window {
  width: 550px;
  height: 564px;
  position: absolute;
  top: 30px;
  left: 220px;
  overflow: hidden;
  z-index: -1;
  -webkit-transition: all 1.5s;
  border: 2px solid black;
  border-radius: 15px;

  background: rgb(253,255,255);
  background:
    -webkit-radial-gradient(center, ellipse cover,
      rgba(253,255,255,1) 0%,
      rgba(247,247,247,1) 47%,
      rgba(211,211,211,1) 86%,
      rgba(196,197,198,1) 100%); /* Chrome10+,Safari5.1+ */
}
```

Setting Up Morgan's Newspaper

Listing 9.6 shows the major elements that make up Morgan's newspaper—but without the text elements, such as p, h1, and h2, for the sake of brevity. The newspaper is made up of two main elements, #page1 and #page2. An important point to note here is that the elements for Morgan's paws are inside the newspaper. Listing 9.6 does do this to make the transformations on the newspaper itself easier and to require less coordination with Morgan's paws.

Listing 9.6   **The HTML for Morgan's Newspaper (cat.html)**

```
<div id="newspaper">
  <div id="page1">
    <!-- newspaper text -->
    <img id="rightpaw" src="img/pawRight.png" width="100">
  </div>
  <div id="page2">
    <!-- more newspaper text -->
    <img id="leftpaw" src="img/pawLeft.png" width="100">
  </div>
</div>
```

The styling for Morgan's newspaper is lengthy, due in part to the use of gradients in both #page1 and #page2. Listing 9.7 excerpts only the styles for #page1 and #page2 because the #newspaper and related selectors primarily define visual styles such as gradients or border radii.

While the properties defined in the individual #page1 and #page2 selectors are the same, you'll notice that the values are often the opposite between #page1 and #page2. This is because these two pages are meant to be mirror images of each other. For example, #page1 (which happens to be the paper on the right, not the left) is rotated 10 degrees by default, with transform-origin set to the middle of the leftmost edge of the element. #page2 is rotated by –10 degrees and has its transform-origin set to the opposite edge: the middle of the right edge of the element.

Listing 9.7   **Styling for Morgan's Newspaper (cat.css)**

```
#page1, #page2 {
  -webkit-transition: all 2s;
  background-image:
    -webkit-radial-gradient(center top, circle cover,
        rgba(255, 255, 255, 0) 70%,
        rgba(255, 255, 255, 0.9)),
      -webkit-linear-gradient(150px 0px, rgba(0, 0, 0, 0.15),
      transparent);
}

#page1 {
  left:208px;
  -webkit-transform-origin: 0% 50%;
  -webkit-transform: rotateY(10deg);
  -webkit-box-shadow: -2px 1px 4px rgba(0, 0, 0, 0.27);
}

#page2 {
  left:-33px;
  top:0px;
  -webkit-transform-origin: 100% 50%;
  -webkit-transform: rotateY(-10deg);
  -webkit-box-shadow: 2px 1px 4px rgba(0, 0, 0, 0.27);
}
```

Staggering the Scenes of the Animation with JavaScript

There are many different scenes within this animation, and you need to appropriately time the start and end of each scene in order for them to flow well together. To set up this timing, you have a choice. You could utilize the animation-delay property—as you did in many places in Chapter 8—and trigger all the animations at once but delay each one by the appropriate time. Or you could combine your CSS3 animations and transitions with a bit of JavaScript, using a combination of JavaScript and CSS classes to trigger the animation's start time. The latter is the approach you'll be utilizing for the remaining scenes and acts.

The approach you're taking here requires two parts: First, you to create a CSS class selector that holds the animation's definition on the element to be animated. Second, you use JavaScript's `setTimeout` function to define when that class is added to the element to be animated, effectively determining when the animation starts to play.

Listing 9.8 shows the JavaScript that kicks off the first animations. First, you leverage a bit of jQuery to wait for the DOM to be ready before firing any of the code. When the page finishes loading, you call the `setup` method. You then assign the class `scene1` to the containing element `#stage`, the newspaper and its first page, as well as both of Morgan's pupils.

Because these triggers are all occurring in the very first scene of the animation, the delay you need to apply is very minimal. You can wait only one-tenth of a second (100 milliseconds) before displaying the stage element. And you can wait just one-half second before triggering the first animation on the newspaper and on Morgan's eyes.

Listing 9.8   Triggering the Newspaper Movements with JavaScript (cat.js)

```
$(document).ready(setup);

function setup(){
  setTimeout(function () { $('#stage').addClass('scene1'); }, 100);
  setTimeout(function () { $('#newspaper').addClass('scene1'); }, 500);
  setTimeout(function () { $('#page1').addClass('scene1'); }, 500);
  setTimeout(function () { $('#lefteye, #righteye').addClass('scene1');}, 500);
}
```

Scene 1: Moving the Newspaper

To begin the animation, you use the approach described earlier to animate Morgan moving his newspaper so he can see and read the first page. Morgan will first move the paper closer and then lower the first page slightly. You animate Morgan moving the paper closer by rotating it on the y-axis. You animate the lowering of the paper by applying a `rotateZ` to the bottom-left corner of the paper. The key to this animation is determining the proper `transform-origin` location.

To trigger these two motions, you add the class `scene1` to several different elements, as outlined in Listing 9.9.

Listing 9.9   Animations to Move the Newspaper (cat.css)

```
#newspaper.scene1 { -webkit-transform: rotateZ(-2deg); }

#page1.scene1 { -webkit-transform: rotateY(40deg); }
```

```
#lefteye.scene1, #righteye.scene1 { -webkit-transition: all 1s; }

#lefteye.scene1 { left: 102px;}
#righteye.scene1 { left: 182px; }
```

Scene 2: Reading the Newspaper

Now that Morgan has the paper in view, you can move the elements that make up his pupils—moving them back and forth to simulate reading. In Listing 9.10, you set up the actual animation, which you define in a keyframe animation named `reading`.

Listing 9.10   **Keyframe Animation to Move Morgan's Eyes (cat.css)**

```
@-webkit-keyframes reading {
  0% {  }
  30% { -webkit-transform: translate3d(-3px,2px,0);}
  50% { -webkit-transform: translate3d(3px,2px,0);}
  80% { -webkit-transform: translate3d(-3px,2px,0);}
  100% { -webkit-transform: translate3d(3px,2px,0);}
}

#lefteye.scene2,
#righteye.scene2 {
  -webkit-animation: reading 1s both 3 linear; }
}
```

Combining Animations on Two Separate Elements

You use `translate3d` in Listing 9.10 instead of positioning with the `left` property because this allows you to apply the same keyframe animation to both the left eye and the right eye. If you were to use `left`, it would move both pupils to the same horizontal spot—moving one pupil out of one eye and into another! You could define a selector for each, but using `translate3d` gives you an easier way. If you specify to look just at keyframe 30%, no matter where the left or right pupil is, this animation moves it –3 pixels.

As before, you need to trigger these new class changes via JavaScript. From here on out, you'll need to keep track of the length of the previous animation in order to properly time subsequent animations. Scene 1 triggers a change to the `#newspaper` element, whose transitions are set to 2 seconds for any changes. Thus, you should wait at least 2 seconds plus the initial delay (500 milliseconds) before moving on to the next scene. You can see in Listing 9.11 that you give yourself an additional 300-millisecond buffer, waiting a total of 2,800 milliseconds before proceeding to scene 2. Before you do anything else, though, you first remove the class `scene1` from Morgan's left and right eyes.

Listing 9.11   **Triggering the Reading Animation (cat.js)**

```
function setup(){
  // setup() code continued from Listing 9.8
  setTimeout(function () { $('#lefteye, #righteye').removeClass('scene1'); }, 2700);
  setTimeout(function () { $('#lefteye, #righteye').addClass('scene2'); }, 2800);
}
```

The Effect of Transforms on the Stacking Context and Containing Block

Now that you have applied to the pupils an animation with a transform on it, let's go back to something mentioned with Listing 9.4: The z-index value is very important. The reason it's important is that if you do *not* set a low z-index value in Listing 9.4, upon animating, you see the pupils move forward, in front of all the other elements when the reading animation is applied (see Figure 9.2). This happens *only* if you try to use -webkit-transform and apply a transform function. If you don't use any transforms in the keyframe animation, you don't have this problem. Why is this?

Figure 9.2   The effect of transforms on the stacking context

The W3C's spec on transforms tells us, "Any value other than 'none' for the transform results in the creation of both a stacking context and a containing block." Before, the #lefteye and #righteye elements were stacked according to their order. Since they came before the

#head element (with the transparent eyes), their implicit z-index would be lower, and thus they should appear behind the #head element. But once a transform has been applied via the animation, a new stacking context is created, and the eyes are at the top of that new context. It's essentially taken them out of their normal flow. Thus, to compensate, you need the z-index : -1 that is defined in Listing 9.4. It is also important that the other elements (such as the house) are stacked appropriately. So because you set z-index : -1 on the eyes, you will set z-index: -3 on the house (refer to Listing 9.2) to ensure that the eyes are not behind the house.

To read more about the stacking context, see https://developer.mozilla.org/en/CSS/ Understanding_z-index/The_stacking_context.

Scene 3: Moving to and Reading Page 2

In scene 3, you take the same approach you took in scene 1 to have Morgan read the second page of the paper, and you simply apply different transforms to move the second page of the paper toward Morgan. In Listing 9.12, you rotate the second page of the paper along the y-axis by –30 degrees to move it toward Morgan. You also move the paper a bit to the left and turn it slightly counterclockwise to approximate the tilting up of a newspaper that happens when you switch to the opposite page.

The reading2 keyframe animation is quite similar to the earlier reading animation, with different numeric tweaks to the translate3d you're applying. Both the left eye and the right eye have the reading animation applied, making the pupils race back and forth to read this second newspaper page. Figure 9.3 shows the results of the rotated newspaper and Morgan's eyes moving to take in the new page.

Listing 9.12   **Animating Page 2 (cat.css)**

```
#newspaper.scene3 {
  -webkit-transform-origin: 0% 0%;
  -webkit-transform: rotateZ(-2deg) translate3d(-50px,0,0);
}

#page2.scene3 {
  -webkit-transform: rotateY(-30deg);
}

@-webkit-keyframes readingPage2 {
  0% { -webkit-transform: translate3d(-5px,3px,0);}
  30% { -webkit-transform: translate3d(-8px,3px,0);}
  50% { -webkit-transform: translate3d(-5px,3px,0);}
  80% { -webkit-transform: translate3d(-8px,3px,0);}
  100% { -webkit-transform: translate3d(-5px,3px,0);}
}
```

```
#lefteye.scene3,
#righteye.scene3 {
  -webkit-animation: readingPage2 1s both 3 linear;
}
```

Figure 9.3   The newspaper rotated to page 2

As before, the animation is triggered by the addition of a class name—scene3 in this case (see Listing 9.13). The delay on scene 3 is a little over 6 seconds. That is because the reading animation that just played (and was defined in Listing 9.10) ran three times, for 1 second each time. That's 3 seconds, plus the delay to scene 2, which was applied via the setTimeoutFunction to be 2.8 seconds. Thus, you add a 1-second buffer between the end of the reading animation and the start of scene 3 by delaying it by 6,800 milliseconds. Listing 9.13 contains this code. The new code you need to add to the setup() function is displayed in bold, the existing code is formatted normally.

Listing 9.13   **Triggering Scene 3 via JavaScript (cat.js)**

```
function setup(){
  setTimeout(function () { $('#stage').addClass('scene1'); }, 100);

  setTimeout(function () { $('#newspaper').addClass('scene1'); }, 500);
  setTimeout(function () { $('#page1').addClass('scene1'); }, 500);
```

```
setTimeout(function () { $('#lefteye, #righteye').addClass('scene1'); }, 500);

setTimeout(function () { $('#lefteye, #righteye').removeClass('scene1'); }, 2700);
setTimeout(function () { $('#lefteye, #righteye').addClass('scene2'); }, 2800);

// After reading is done
setTimeout(function () { $('#newspaper').removeClass('scene1'); }, 5800);
setTimeout(function () { $('#page1').removeClass('scene1'); }, 5800);

setTimeout(function () { $('#newspaper').addClass('scene3'); }, 6800);
setTimeout(function () { $('#page2').addClass('scene3'); }, 6800);
setTimeout(function () { $('#lefteye, #righteye').addClass('scene3'); }, 8100);
}
```

Scene 4: Moving the Animation Outside

In scene 4, you zoom out to reveal what is going on outside Morgan Diamond's house. You do this by shrinking the elements that represent Morgan's house, the open window he's sitting behind, and Morgan himself.

The first and most basic change you make is to the background-color of the body element. Adding the class scene4 to the body element triggers its background to change to a gradient defined in Listing 9.14. For brevity, this listing includes only the -webkit- gradient prefix.

Listing 9.14   **Applying a Gradient to the Background (cat.css)**

```
body.scene4 {
  background: rgb(249,249,249); /* Old browsers */
  background:
    -webkit-radial-gradient(center, ellipse cover,
      rgba(249,249,249,1) 0%,
      rgba(184,198,223,1) 61%,
      rgba(135,152,181,1) 99%);
}
```

Zooming Out to a Larger Scene

The element #house, which holds the image of Morgan's mansion, has been partially visible since the beginning of the animation. However, the #house element began with a transform applied: You made it three times its normal size via the scale3d transform function.

As shown in Listing 9.15, in scene 4, you shrink the size of the #house element back down to its original size. Scene 4's CSS also moves the house 10% to the left. Because in Listing 9.2 you defined a transition on the #house element for any property changes, both of these changes—the scaling down and the repositioning—are animated.

Listing 9.15   **Zooming Out by Scaling Down (cat.css)**

```
#house.scene4 {
  width: 80%;
  min-width: 500px;
  left: 10%;
  top: 0;
  -webkit-transform: scale3d(1,1,1);
}
```

Shrinking Morgan Down as You Zoom Out

At the same time that the #house element scales down, you must also scale down Morgan to match. Listing 9.16 defines this scale-down.

The selector #cat.scene4 defines a transform that shrinks Morgan to one-third of his original size. The transform also moves Morgan slightly up and to the right, via a change to left and top. The transition you specify ensures that these changes happen over the course of 1.5 seconds.

You must also modify the #window element that Morgan is positioned inside. Previously, the #window element's size was 550 pixels wide and 564 pixels high. In scene 4, you shrink it down to 155 by 160 pixels, and you also move it a bit to the right in order to ensure that the window stays in the same place after the house element shrinks. Figure 9.4 shows the result of the zooming out.

Listing 9.16   **Scaling Down Morgan and Moving the Window (cat.css)**

```
#window.scene4 {
  width: 155px;
  height: 160px;
  -webkit-transform: translate3d(240px,-15px,0);
}
#cat.scene4 {
  -webkit-transition: all 1.5s;
  -webkit-transform: scale3d(.3,.3,.3);
  left: -112px;
  top: -150px;
}
```

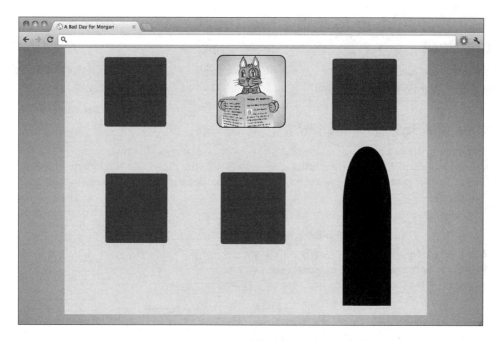

Figure 9.4   Morgan and his mansion, after the zooming out

Listing 9.17 shows the addition of scene4 classes to all the needed elements to trigger the described animations and transforms. In all cases, you delay the addition of this class by 10,100 milliseconds. This is because you first take into account the longest scene 3 delay (8,100 milliseconds for the readingPage2 animation) and also consider the duration of the longest part of scene 3 (again, the readingPage2 animation, which lasts 3 seconds total, with all its iterations). To allow all of scene 3 to complete, you'd need to wait for 8,100 + 3,000 milliseconds = 11,100 milliseconds. In this case, you allow the end of the readingPage2 animation to overlap with the start of scene 4 by 1 second, choosing a delay of 10,100 milliseconds instead.

Listing 9.17   **Triggering Scene 4 via JavaScript (cat.js)**

```
function setup(){
  // continued from Listing 9.13
  setTimeout(function () { $('body').addClass('scene4'); }, 10100);
  setTimeout(function () { $('#window').addClass('scene4'); }, 10100);
  setTimeout(function () { $('#house').addClass('scene4'); }, 10100);
  setTimeout(function () { $('#cat').addClass('scene4'); }, 10100);
}
```

Scene 5: Adding Murphy, the Toughest Cat Cop on the Beat

In scene 5 you catch the first sight of Murphy, Meow Street's feared police officer, as he walks onto the scene. What could he want?

HTML and Styling for Murphy the Police Cat

Murphy is composed of two elements that form his body—both of which are images—as outlined in Listing 9.18. These elements are animated like the pieces of a marionette in scene 6. You carefully position both his main body as well as his separate #murphyarm element in Listing 9.19.

Listing 9.18 **Murphy the Police Cat's HTML (cat.html)**

```
<div id="murphy">
  <img id="murphyarm" src="img/MurphyArm.png">
  <img src="img/MurphySansArm.png" width="300">
</div>
```

Listing 9.19 **Styling Murphy the Police Cat (cat.css)**

```
#murphy {
    position: absolute;
    top: 250px;
    left: 1650px;
    -webkit-transition:left 2s;
    z-index:2;
}

#murphyarm {
    width: 100px;
    position: absolute;
    top: 87px;
    left: 105px;
    -webkit-transform-origin: 100% 50%;
}
```

Using `transform-origin` to Align Pieces of Murphy

You previously placed the elements of Murphy the Cat in Listing 9.19. In doing so, you needed to properly align the separate images that make up Murphy's body—placing his arm in the right spot relative to the rest of Murphy's body. But now, you are going to rotate Murphy's arm in order to animate a knock on the door. In order to do this properly, you need to correctly set the `transform-origin` property on his arm.

A helpful way to determine where the location of the `transform-origin` property should be is to rotate the element manually and then modify the `transform-origin` value by editing the CSS on-the-fly with developer tools (such as Firebug or the Web Developer Toolbar in Safari and Chrome). You can keep trying values for `transform-origin` until you find one that looks good.

Figure 9.5 shows this approach. The figure shows the use of developer tools to set a rotation of 25 degrees on Murphy's arm. In Listing 9.20, you're going to define how Murphy knocks on the door—by moving from a rotation of 10 degrees in his arm to a rotation of 35 degrees—so 25 degrees is right in the middle of that. Also note in the figure that you edit the `transform-origin` value, which is currently set to `100% 90%`. This value is not the right one for what you need, as you can see in the preview of Murphy, whose arm is far further to the right than it should be. But you can keep modifying the `transform-origin` number via the developer tools until you find a value that looks correct.

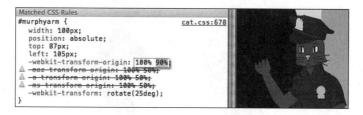

Figure 9.5   Using developer tools to find the right `transform-origin` value

Scene 6: Knocking on Morgan's Door

Scene 6 contains the keyframe animation that creates the effect of Murphy knocking on Morgan's door. You will rotate Murphy's arm back and forth between 35 degrees and 10 degrees and repeat the entire animation two times, as shown in Listing 9.20. Figure 9.6 approximates the before and after positions of each 35- and 10-degree rotation, respectively.

Listing 9.20   **The Knocking Animation (cat.css)**

```
@-webkit-keyframes knock {
  0%{ }
  10% { -webkit-transform: rotateZ(35deg); }
  20% { -webkit-transform: rotateZ(10deg); }
  30% { -webkit-transform: rotateZ(35deg); }
  50% { -webkit-transform: rotateZ(10deg); }
  60% { -webkit-transform: rotateZ(35deg); }
  70% { -webkit-transform: rotateZ(10deg); }
  80% { -webkit-transform: rotateZ(35deg); }
  100% { -webkit-transform: rotateZ(10deg); }
```

```
}
#murphyarm.scene6 {
  z-index: -2;
  -webkit-animation: knock 2s forwards 2;
}
```

Figure 9.6   Before (`rotate(35)`) and after (`rotate(10deg)`) Murphy raises his arm to knock

Just before Murphy begins knocking, Morgan folds his paper to get to the next page. And even after Murphy begins knocking, Morgan is still reading his paper. To achieve the folding animation and have it run twice, you could use `animation-iteration-count` and set it to 2. However, it would be nice to have a bit of a delay between the two folds of the paper. The `animation-delay` property applies only on the first run of the animation, not subsequent runs, so `animation-delay` won't help you here. In order to achieve what you want, you can simply call the animation twice: once on the `scene5` class and once on the `scene6` class for the `#page1` and `#page2` elements (see Listing 9.21).

Listing 9.21   **Morgan Folding His Paper (cat.css)**

```css
@-webkit-keyframes foldPage1 {
  0% { }
  50% { -webkit-transform: rotateY(74deg);}
  100% { -webkit-transform: rotateY(10deg);}
}
@-webkit-keyframes foldPage2 {
  0% { }
  50% { -webkit-transform: rotateY(-80deg);}
  100% { -webkit-transform: rotateY(-30deg);}
}


#page1.scene5,#page1.scene6 {
  -webkit-animation: foldPage1 0.8s;
}


#page2.scene5,#page2.scene6 {
  -webkit-animation: foldPage2 0.8s;
}
```

However, it is important to note that this second run of the animation does not work unless you remove the class scene5 from the elements before you add the class scene6. That is because the selector assigns the same animation to both, and the browser will conflate them into one animation unless the styles are triggered independently of each other, at different times. Listing 9.22 shows how to add scene5 and then remove it.

Listing 9.22   **Moving from Scene 5 to Scene 6 (cat.js)**

```javascript
function setup(){
  // continued from Listing 9.17
  // move murphy into view
  setTimeout(function () { $('#murphy').addClass('scene5'); }, 12100);
  setTimeout(function () { $('#page1, #page2').addClass('scene5'); }, 13100);
  setTimeout(function () { $('#page1, #page2').removeClass('scene5'); }, 14100);

  // murphy knocks
  setTimeout(function () { $('#murphyarm').addClass('scene6'); }, 15100);
  setTimeout(function () { $('#page1, #page2').addClass('scene6'); }, 15100);
  setTimeout(function () { $('#lefteye, #righteye').removeClass('scene2 scene3'); },
  ➥15100);
  setTimeout(function () { $('#lefteye, #righteye').addClass('scene6'); }, 17100);
}
```

Finally, while Murphy is knocking, Morgan slowly begins to notice. In order to express this visually, you again move Morgan's pupils, this time to the right to make him look down and toward Murphy below (see Listing 9.23). In order for this new CSS styling to be applied, you must first remove the old styles that still match Murphy's eyes. You do this via jQuery's removeClass method, as shown in Listing 9.22.

Listing 9.23   **Morgan Taking a Look at Murphy (cat.css)**

```
#lefteye.scene6, #righteye.scene6 {
  -webkit-transition: 1s;
  -webkit-transform: translate3d(2px,0,0);
}
```

Scene 7: Animating a Spinning Newspaper

In scene 7, you remove all the elements and show a newspaper. The story of Morgan Diamond's arrest is reported on the front page of the *Meow Street Journal*. Details of the case against him and his arrest for catnip-backed securities fraud, come into focus after a dizzying spin of the paper leads us in. This animation mimics the old-timey spinning newspaper animations that used to precede newsreels in theaters prior to the introduction of television in the 1950s.

Hiding the Previous Scenes

As shown in Listing 9.24, you can use the class `hide`—which simply sets `display` to none—to remove the remaining elements from the view. The triggers for adding the `hide` class—as well as adding the `scene7` class to the body and the newsreel—are driven via JavaScript (see Listing 9.25)

Listing 9.24   **Fading Out the Elements by Changing `background-color` (cat.css)**

```
.hide { display: none !important; }

body.scene7 {
  background: black;
}
```

Listing 9.25   **Triggering the `hide` Class (cat.js)**

```
function setup(){
  // setup() continued from Listing 9.22
  setTimeout(function () { $('#house').addClass('hide'); }, 21100);
  setTimeout(function () { $('#window').addClass('hide'); }, 21100);
  setTimeout(function () { $('#murphy').addClass('hide'); }, 21100);
  setTimeout(function () { $('body').addClass('scene7'); }, 21100);
  setTimeout(function () { $('#newsreel').addClass('scene7'); }, 21500);
}
```

Styling the Final Scene's Newspaper

To make the final newspaper look more realistic, you can give it a gray-to-white gradient and unevenly round the corners to make it look like it is curling upward in the top-left corner and curling backward in the bottom-right corner. Listing 9.26 provides the code for this, and Figure 9.7 shows the newspaper after the animation.

Listing 9.26   **Styling the Newspaper (cat.css)**

```
.newsprint {
  background-color: rgb(242,242,242);

  background-image:
  -webkit-gradient(radial, center top,
    200, center top,300,
    from(rgba(255, 255, 255, 0)),
    to(rgba(255, 255, 255, 0.9))),
  -webkit-gradient(linear, center top,
    right bottom,
    from(rgba(0, 0, 0, 0.15)),
    to(transparent));
}

#newsreel {
  width: 600px;
  height: 500px;
  margin: 5% auto;
  padding: 0 3%;
  display: none;

  -webkit-border-radius: 12px 100px / 100px 12px;
  -webkit-background-clip: padding-box;
}

#newsreel h1 {
  font-family: PlugNickelBlackRegular, sans-serif;
  font-size: 2em;
  padding-top: 3%;
  text-align: center;
  text-decoration: underline;
}
```

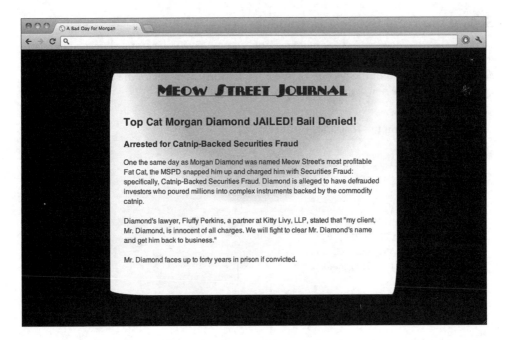

Figure 9.7   The newspaper after it finishes its `spin` animation

Spinning the Newspaper and Scaling It Up

In order to simulate the spinning newspaper that often appeared before a newsreel (see a demonstration at http://www.youtube.com/watch?v=saxwDCYVksQ), you need to rotate the newspaper many times. In Listing 9.27 you rotate it 10 times total, and thus you set the final keyframe to rotate the paper 3,600 degrees. You also want to scale up the paper to make it appear to get closer as it spins. Thus, you add a scale-up of 2 in the `60%` keyframe and `2.1` in the `100%` keyframe.

Listing 9.27   **Spinning the Newspaper (cat.css)**

```
@-webkit-keyframes spin {
/* the downside of this approach is that
  it results in quite a pixelated look :( */
  0% { }
  60% { -webkit-transform: translate3d(-100px,-200px,0) scale3d(2,2,2)
➥rotateZ(3600deg);}
  100% { -webkit-transform: translate3d(-100px,-200px,0) scale3d(2.1,2.1,2.1)
➥rotateZ(3600deg);}
}
```

Avoiding Pixelation by Scaling the Newspaper Down Initially

If you try to run the code defined in Listing 9.27, you'll notice a problem: The edges of the newspaper defined using `border-radius` looks pixelated at the end of the animation. This is because of the scaling applied.

In order to avoid this pixelation, a better approach than scaling the newspaper up is to start the newspaper scaled down and then scale it back to its original size. Since you can define the curved borders on an element of any size, you can simply increase the size of the newspaper. Listing 9.28 shows these changes. Note that another option to avoid the pixelation would be to use SVG image files, which scale up and down without any loss of image sharpness.

Listing 9.28   **A Better Approach to Enlarging the Newspaper (cat.css)**

```
@-webkit-keyframes spin {
  0% { -webkit-transform:   scale3d(.2,.2,.2) }
  60% { -webkit-transform:   scale3d(.9,.9,.9) rotateZ(3600deg);}
  100% { -webkit-transform: scale3d(1,1,1) rotateZ(3600deg);}
}
```

Support for Opera 12

There is one major wrinkle in the code for this animation: For the Opera 12 browser, which supports all the new features *except* CSS3 3D transforms—the animation will play only partially, and many of the images will be completely oversized. This is because you are relying on `scale3d` at the start. Opera 12 users will also miss out on the knock animation because you use the hardware-accelerated `rotateZ` rather than the Opera 12–supported `rotate`. But the good news is that you can leverage Modernizr to at least get the major portions of this animation working in Opera 12.

Defining Two Selectors for Each 3D Scene

The key to getting the major portions of this animation working in Opera 12 is to define two selectors for each scene that uses 3D transforms: one that includes the parent selector `.no-csstransforms3d` and one that includes the parent selector `.csstransforms3d`. This way, you take advantage of the classes that Modernizr adds to the opening HTML tag.

Listing 9.29 shows the first selector Opera 12 will use, as Modernizr appends the class `no-csstransforms3d` to the opening HTML tag. (Note that for the first time in the chapter, the code includes all the vendor prefixes.) Here, instead of using `-transform: scale3d(3,3,3)` to scale up the house element, you simply use `transform: scale(3)`, the 2D version of the same property.

> **Note:**
>
> Modernizr's check for whether or not 3D transforms are supported in a given browser is not always perfect. The engineering team at Art.sy recently wrote about their alternative approach for checking for 3D Transform support, because past browser bugs have sometimes resulted in false negatives for the 3D Transform check. Thus, one potential side effect of adjusting the code to account for unsupported browsers is that these styling hooks may get called in the event of a future browser bug that results in a false positive. To learn more, see: http://artsy.github.com/blog/2012/10/18/so-you-want-to-do-a-css3-3d-transform/.

Listing 9.29 **Using 2D Transforms Instead of 3D Transforms to Support Opera 12 (cat.css)**

```css
.no-csstransforms3d #house {
  width: 100%;
  height: 700px;
  position: absolute;
  left: 315px;
  background-image: url('../img/house.png');
  background-repeat: no-repeat;

  -webkit-transition: 2s;
  -moz-transition: 2s;
  -o-transition: 2s;
  -ms-transition: 2s;
  transition: 2s;

  -webkit-transform: scale(3);
  -moz-transform: scale(3);
  -o-transform: scale(3);
  -ms-transform: scale(3);
  transform: scale(3);

  -webkit-transform-origin: 50% 0%;
  -moz-transform-origin: 50% 0%;
  -o-transform-origin: 50% 0%;
  -ms-transform-origin: 50% 0%;
  transform-origin: 50% 0%;

  z-index: -3;
}
```

Applying Further Fallbacks for Opera 12

Listing 9.30 shows the rest of the Opera 12–specific fallbacks. In the first selector, for scene 4 on the window, rather than use `translate3d` to place an element, you use the 2D version, `translateX`. You could also simply use absolute positioning.

To shrink the house and the cat in scene 4, instead of using scale3d, you can use scale. Again, if Opera 12 didn't support 2D transforms, you could use background-size and shrink the background-image.

Finally, the knock animation will not work as written because it uses the 3D transform function rotateZ, which is hardware accelerated. Therefore, you need to create a new keyframe animation called knockOpera that uses the 2D version of the property, rotate.

Listing 9.30   **Using Modernizr-Added Class Selectors to Apply 2D Transforms Instead of 3D Transforms (cat.css)**

```css
.no-csstransforms3d #window.scene4 {
  width: 155px;
  height: 160px;
  -webkit-transform: translateX(240px);
  -moz-transform: translateX(240px);
  -o-transform: translateX(240px);
  -ms-transform: translateX(240px);
  transform: translateX(240px);
}


.no-csstransforms3d #house.scene4 {
  width: 80%;
  min-width: 500px;
  left: 10%;
  top: 0px;
  -webkit-transform: scale(1);
  -moz-transform: scale(1);
  -o-transform: scale(1);
  -ms-transform: scale(1);
  transform: scale(1);
}


.no-csstransforms3d #cat.scene4 {
  -webkit-transition: all 1.5s;
  -moz-transition: all 1.5s;
  -o-transition: all 1.5s;
  -ms-transition: all 1.5s;
  transition: all 1.5s;
  -webkit-transform: scale(.3);
  -moz-transform: scale(.3);
  -o-transform: scale(.3);
  -ms-transform: scale(.3);
  transform: scale(.3);
  left: -112px;
  top: -150px;
}
```

```
.no-csstransforms3d #murphyarm.scene6 {
  z-index: -2;
  -o-animation: knockOpera 2s forwards 2;
}
```

Summary

In this chapter, you combined transforms, transitions, keyframes, and JavaScript to create an animation that consists of many disparate elements chained together. You explored how to create a zoom-out effect by combining several scale-downs together. You also learned a few ways to provide animations and content even when browsers don't support the full range of options.

Challenge

Murphy the police cat currently walks onto the scene from offscreen. Enhance this example by creating (or finding) an image of a police car. Ensure that the wheels are separate images from the car body (or create the wheels by using a square element and a `border-radius` that is half the square's width). Then animate the police car driving up to Morgan's house, its wheels spinning as it drives.

Creating Animated Infographics

This chapter investigates how to enhance infographics by adding CSS animations. It combines the techniques used in this book to create a data visualization of the ratio of different ingredients in six different kinds of mixed drinks. You will add animations to add movement to the infographic, simulating the drinks pouring into their glasses.

What Are Infographics?

Using infographics is an increasingly popular way to present data on the web. By using infographics, you can present data that may be difficult to understand in written or tabular form in a visual way—often through illustration—in order to make the meaning and significance of the data more immediately apparent.

Image-Based Infographics

A common approach to infographics on the web has been to represent data in large, high-resolution images. These often are very tall or very wide images that the user scrolls through in order to read and take in all of the information presented.

The website Mashable has a large collection of image infographics available at http://mashable.com/follow/topics/infographics/. As just one example, the site features an infographic by MBAonline.com that describes how Amazon.com is able to keep costs low through extreme cost-cutting practices such as giving no money at all to charity (see http://mashable.com/2012/06/09/amazon-money-infographic/).

The website for *GOOD* magazine has also been a source of many compelling image-based infographics. A section of the site is entirely dedicated to infographics—see http://www.good.is/infographics. Collected on the site are a series of large images that utilize Flash to assist in zooming in, out, and panning around the image.

CSS3-Driven Infographics

Relying solely on images for infographics is a bit limiting, given all the new features available to us in HTML5 and CSS3. Back in April 2011, Paul Rouget, developer evangelist at Mozilla, issued a challenge to developers to create infographics in CSS3 and HTML5. He noted on his blog, "Most of the infographics we see are beautiful, but sooooo *static*. You can make them much more *alive* if you use the web technologies" (http://paulrouget.com/e/infographicsInHTML5/).

Paul listed three compelling side effects of using web standards to make infographics instead of relying on images: accessibility, enhanceability (via sharing the source on http://github.com), and flexible layouts that respond to mobile devices via media queries.

One response to Paul's challenge was from Jonathan Krause, who created an animated infographic with CSS3, HTML5, and jQuery. The infographic, shown in Figure 10.1, illustrates the destruction of the Amazon rainforests as of 2010 and what the projected destruction is out to 2030: http://www.jonathan-krause.de/rainforest.

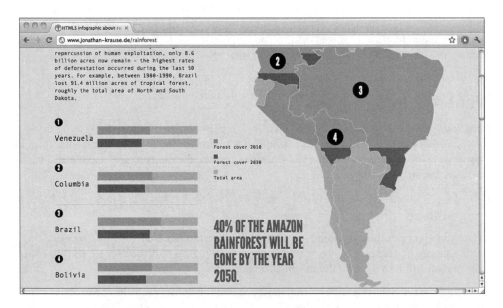

Figure 10.1   Rainforest deforestation infographic by Jonathan Krause

When you scroll down to the map, the bars to the left—which are initially empty—animate, filling up with color. You can also hover over the number presented on the map, and the relevant data for that country will be emphasized through a color change.

Animating data helps to capture the user's attention by stimulating curiosity. Rather than give users all the information at once, the information can come in progressively, with the bars filling up from the left. This elicits questions, such as When will the bars stop? and What does this represent? These questions are answered when the animation finishes and all the data is present. The simple act of adding an animation can make visitors more engaged with the data you present.

Visualizing Data for Mixed Drinks

To demonstrate how animations can be used to build infographics that make a compelling display of data, in this section you'll work with a simple data set: the makeup of common mixed drinks. Specifically, you will illustrate the ratio of ingredients in a given mixed drink. For example, a Rum & Coke is made up of two parts cola to one part rum. The inspiration for this example is drawn from the simple but useful infographic of various coffee drinks created by Lokesh Dhakar (http://lokeshdhakar.com/coffee-drinks-illustrated/).

You'll examine this breakdown across six different mixed drinks, and you'll use CSS-based graphics to visualize the ingredients and their ratio in each drink. But rather than simply illustrate and label the various parts of each drink, you will animate each ingredient "pouring" into an empty glass. Figure 10.2 shows the final state of the infographic you'll build.

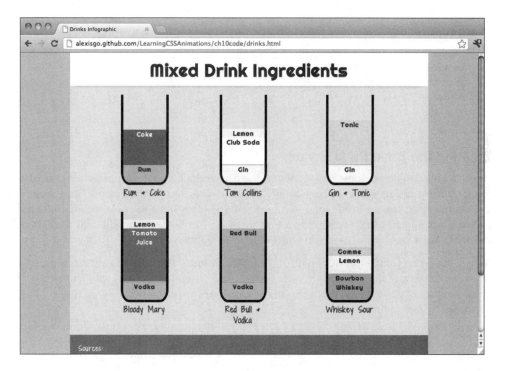

Figure 10.2   The final mixed drinks infographic

The Base HTML for the Infographic

Your infographic will consist of six glass tumblers, each with a different drink. Each drink represented in the infographic will be contained within a `section` element. Listing 10.1 provides the HTML for this example.

Listing 10.1   **Base HTML for Mixed Drinks (drinks.html)**

```
  <!-- start of file clipped ; find complete HTML at
  https://github.com/alexisgo/LearningCSSAnimations/blob/master/ch10code/drinks.html
  ➥-->
  <script src="js/modernizr.custom.57498.js"></script>
</head>
<body>
  <section id="bar">
    <h1>Mixed Drink Ingredients</h1>
    <section id="rumncoke">
      <!-- Continued in Listing 10.4 -->
    </section>
    <section id="tomcollins">
      <!-- Continued in Listing 10.12 -->
    </section>
    <section id="ginntonic"></section>
    <section id="redbullVodka"></section>
    <section id="bloodyMary"></section>
  </section>  <!-- end bar -->
</body>
```

Creating the Base Page Styles

Next, you need to define some basic styles for the page overall. You'll set a default background color, set some custom fonts, and give a bit of a `box-shadow` to the `h1` element. There is one main containing element inside the body, called `bar`. This bar has a `section` element that has a fixed size, some margin, padding, and a border radius. This bar element will hold all six of the drinks for which you are going to create CSS-based graphics (see Listing 10.2).

As with previous examples in this book, note that for brevity's sake, that the listings in this chapter include only the `-webkit-` vendor prefixes. For the complete code, with all prefixes, please see the ch10code folder on the book's GitHub page: https://github.com/alexisgo/ LearningCSSAnimations.

Listing 10.2   **Base Styles for the Drinks Infographic (drinks.css)**

```
body {
  background-color:rgb(173,216,230);
  font-family: 'Shadows Into Light Two', cursive;
}
```

```
h1 {
  font-family: 'Righteous', cursive; font-size:2.5em;
  margin: 0 -8px 8px -8px;
  text-align:center;
  background-color:white;

  -webkit-box-shadow: 0 -4px 0 12px white, 0px 1px 20px 1px black;
  box-shadow:
    0 -4px 0 12px white,
    0px 1px 20px 1px black;
}

#bar {
  background-color:rgb(233,236,236);
  width: 800px;
  height:700px;
  margin: -8px auto;
  padding:20px;
  border-radius:10px;
  position:relative;
}
```

Using Multiple `box-shadows` to Create a One-Sided Shadow

Note that you have specified *two* box-shadows in the h1 selector. The first defines a white `box-shadow`, with no blur radius (thus, it is simply a solid white outline) that has a spread of 12 pixels and is positioned 4 pixels *above* the h1 element. Next, you define a second `box-shadow`, this time a black one that has a large blur radius but a spread of only 1, that is positioned 1 pixel down from the element.

The net effect of these two shadows is that only the black shadow is shown, and only on the bottom edge of the element. This is a technique elucidated by Lea Verou in her 2011 Fronteers talk, "10 Things You Might Not Know About CSS3" (http://fronteers.nl/congres/2011/sessions/css3-secrets-lea-verou).

Utilizing Custom Web Fonts

You likely noted that Listing 10.2 uses two custom fonts. By default, you'll use the font Shadows Into Light Two, and for h1 elements, you'll use Righteous. Both fonts are open source web fonts available through Google's web fonts tool (http://google.com/webfonts). Google's tool allows you to select which web fonts you'd like to use, and then Google generates a link to a style sheet it hosts on its servers, which you place inside the head section of your HTML page, as shown in Listing 10.3.

Listing 10.3   **Linking to Google's Dynamic Style Sheet for Web Fonts (drinks.html)**

```
<head>
  <meta charset="utf-8">
  <title>Drinks Infographic</title>
  <link href='http://fonts.googleapis.com/css?family=Righteous|Shadows+Into+Light+Two'
  ➥rel='stylesheet'>
</head>
```

Base HTML for the First Drink Graphic

You begin by setting up just a single drink, a Rum & Coke. You give this `section` element the ID `rumncoke`. Inside this `section` element—and all subsequent drinks `section` elements—will be a `div` with the class `tumbler`. This `div` will contain the styles for the actual glass holding all the elements representing the drink's ingredients. Each ingredient will consist of three elements:

- A `div` element that will set the `height` and starting `position` of the ingredient
- A `p` element that will control the `background-color` and the `animation` to run
- A `strong` element to hold the drink's label

Finally, you define an `h2` element that will contain the name of the drink. Listing 10.4 shows the code to do this for a Rum & Coke.

Listing 10.4   **HTML to Set Up a Rum & Coke (drinks.html)**

```
<section id="rumncoke">
  <div class="tumbler">
    <div id="rum">
      <p>
        <strong>Rum</strong>
      </p>
    </div>
    <div id="coke">
      <p>
        <strong>Coke</strong>
      </p>
    </div>
  </div>
  <h2>Rum &amp; Coke</h2>
</section>
```

A Question of Semantics

You might wonder why you should bother having the p element surrounding strong. Why not simply have strong? You use this approach in order to avoid the need to write a custom animation to define how far up each drink ingredient should rise. This will make more sense when you get to Listing 10.9, but the choices you make in the HTML in Listing 10.1 affect what is possible later on in the chapter.

As you will see in Listing 10.7, each ingredient has a parent div element that sets the height. The inner p element has its height set to 100%. For example, the #rum div element has its height set to 40px. The p element inside #rum has its height set to 100%. If you view the computed style for this p element, you can see, in Figure 10.3, that it's set to 40px.

Setting the height in the parent div allows you, in Listing 10.9, to simply animate a change from a 0% height to a 100% height across *all* the ingredients. (Listing 10.9 shows this animation.) This saves you the trouble of writing a custom animation to change the height of each individual drink ingredient from 0 to whatever its final height needs to be (which would be, for example, 40 pixels for the rum, but 80 pixels for the Coke).

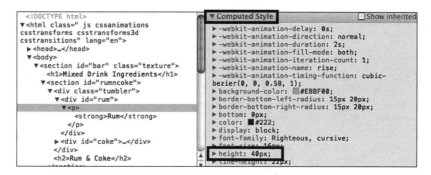

Figure 10.3   The #rum element's height is 40 pixels, and its descendent p element's height is 100%, so the p element's computed height is 40 pixels

Default Drink Styles

All the section elements nested within the outer <section id="bar"> element represent drinks, so you can style them together in a single selector, #bar section, as defined in Listing 10.5. You give the drinks a default top padding, left margin, and width and set their position to absolute.

Listing 10.5   **Setting the Default Starting Location for Each Drink (drinks.css)**

```
#bar section
{
  width: 110px;
  position: absolute;
  margin-left: 100px;
  padding-top: 20px;
}
```

You will also use CSS to define a graphic that represents the glass tumbler that holds each drink. In Listing 10.6 you define a fixed size, a thick black border on all sides except the top, and a `border-radius` on the bottom of the tumbler. You use a 20-pixel horizontal offset and a 30-pixel vertical offset to give the curve at the bottom corner a steeper slope. You also set the position to `relative` so the ingredients you nest inside this outer `.tumbler` element can be positioned relative to it. Finally, you set the overflow to `hidden` so that if any of the ingredients within overflow the tumbler, they will not be visible. Figure 10.4 shows the result of applying these styles to the very first `.tumbler` element.

Listing 10.6   **Styling the Glass Tumbler (drinks.css)**

```
.tumbler {
  width: 100px;
  height: 200px;
  border: 8px solid #336;
  border-width: 0 6px 6px 6px;
  border-color: white black black black;

  border-bottom-right-radius: 20px 30px;
  border-bottom-left-radius: 20px 30px;

  position: relative;
  overflow: hidden;
}
```

Figure 10.4   The first empty glass tumbler

Styling the Initial Ingredient

You use div elements to create the graphical representation of each ingredient in the Rum & Coke. You can begin by styling the rum. In Listing 10.7, you assign a height and an absolute position to the #rum element. You also define a background-color on the p element to give the rum its proper color.

Listing 10.7   **Setting the Ingredient's Height and Starting Location (drinks.css)**

```
#rum { height: 20%; bottom: 0; }
#rum p {  background-color: rgb(235,191,0);}
```

In Listing 10.6, you defined a border-radius for the tumbler itself. Combining the rounded corners of the tumbler with the styling of the rum in Listing 10.7 does not work exactly as you might expect. Once the rise animation runs and the #rum element is visible, its corners overlap the edges of the border-radius of the .tumbler element, as shown in Figure 10.5.

Figure 10.5   The #rum element overlapping the rounded corners of the tumbler

Modifying the z-index will not help you change this, as the overlap is occurring in the space where the tumbler element technically still is; it's simply that you've pulled in the tumbler element slightly through the use of border-radius.

In order to fix this, you can define a border-radius for the tumbler's very first div element—and *only* for its very first div element. To do so, you can use the nth-of-type pseudo-class, and you specify that it select only the first div contained in the element .tumbler, as outlined in Listing 10.8. You are targeting the first div because it represents the first ingredient, which always sits at the bottom of the tumbler glass. Adding this code will result in the rum (and all subsequent first ingredients) appearing rounded at the bottom corners and fitting nicely within the .tumbler element (see Figure 10.6).

Listing 10.8   **Setting the Ingredient's Height and Starting Location (drinks.css)**

```
.tumbler div:nth-of-type(1) p {
  border-bottom-right-radius: 15px 20px;
  border-bottom-left-radius: 15px 20px;
}
```

Figure 10.6   The #rum element no longer overlapping the rounded corners of the tumbler

Animating the Ingredients Being Poured In

To make this infographic more dynamic than the typical static image-based infographic, you will add an animation to each ingredient. You will approximate the illustration of each ingredient in the drink being "poured in" by making the liquid rise up from the bottom of the glass.

The animation will consist of increasing the height from 0% to 100%, which will give the appearance of the liquid rising up toward the top. This animation is assigned to every p element that is nested inside a div element that is itself nested in an element in the class tumbler. This is more simply expressed in the selector .tumbler div strong, as shown in Listing 10.9. In this listing, you also set the ingredient's font to the open source web font Righteous.

The most important part of Listing 10.9 is the value you set for the animation-fill-mode property. In the animation shorthand, you set animation-fill-mode to the value both. Recall from Chapter 4, "Keyframe Animations," that animation-fill-mode defines what happens to the element being animated either before or after the animation is running. Setting animation-fill-mode to the both keyword applies the style of the first keyframe (in this case, a height of 0) to the period before the animation runs, and it also applies the styles of the final keyframe (a height of 100%) to the element when the animation has finished executing.

Listing 10.9   **Making the Ingredients Rise (drinks.css)**

```
@-webkit-keyframes rise {
  0% { height: 0;}
  100% { height: 100%; }
}

.tumbler div p {
  font-family: 'Righteous', cursive;
  width: 100%;
  height: 100%;
  margin: 0 auto;
  position: absolute;
  bottom: 0;
  text-align: center;
  -webkit-animation: rise 2s both ease-out;
}
```

Why Use Keyframes Here?

The rise animation you have defined via keyframes is a simple one that could also be achieved through a transition. So why use keyframes here? You use keyframes in this case for two reasons. First, they allow you to trigger animations by using timing, via the animation-delay property. If you used transitions, you would need to rely on JavaScript to trigger the ingredients rising in a staggered fashion. Second, using keyframes allows you to apply these animation delays across the different ingredients while still reusing a single, shared animation.

Styling the Remaining Ingredient

Now that you've set up the animation to make the drink ingredients rise, you can complete the Rum & Coke drink by styling the second and final ingredient, the cola, in Listing 10.10. In the #coke selector, you assign the height and the initial position of the cola. Because the rum is 20% high and 0% from the bottom of the containing .tumbler div element (as defined in Listing 10.7), you position the cola as bottom: 20%. The animation-fill-mode: both, defined earlier, in Listing 10.9, ensures that the initial height of the element before it animates is 0%.

In order to ensure that the animation of the cola ingredient rising up animates after the rum rises, you set an animation-delay here on the p element's selector. Because you have not previously defined an animation-delay, by default none of the ingredients have a delay. By setting one here, you are differentiating the cola element from the rum element and causing its animation to run only after 2 seconds, which is the amount of time the rum animation takes to complete.

Listing 10.10   **Styling the Coke and Delaying Its Animation (drinks.css)**

```
#coke {
  height: 40%;
  bottom: 20%;
}
#coke p {
  background-color: rgb(151,95,55);
  color: white;
  -webkit-animation-delay: 3s;
}
```

Fading in the Ingredients Labels

Right now, the Rum & Coke's ingredients labels are visible immediately and rise along with the ingredients. You can modify the CSS to utilize a second animation that will fade in the text of the label after the ingredients have finished rising. As with the rise animation (defined in Listing 10.9), you can use keyframes not because they are the most efficient but because you can utilize different animation-delays on different elements while still reusing a single, shared animation.

In Listing 10.11, in the first keyframe of the ingredientFadeIn animation, you set the text color to transparent. In the .tumbler div p strong selector, you have specified, via the animation shorthand property, that animation-fill-mode should be set to both. Because animation-fill-mode is set to both, the text label for the ingredient will be invisible to the viewer when the animation begins (and before that). In the 100% keyframe, you do not set any property at all, nor do you set the color property again. This causes the relevant strong element to reset back to its original color—whatever that might have been. The Rum & Coke with all its ingredients visible is displayed in Figure 10.7.

Listing 10.11   **Fading in the Ingredient Names (drinks.css)**

```
@-webkit-keyframes ingredientFadeIn {
  0% { color: transparent;}
  100% { }
}
.tumbler div p strong {
  font-size: 0.9em;
  -webkit-animation: ingredientFadeIn 1s 2s both;
}

#coke p strong {
  -webkit-animation-delay: 5s;
}
```

Figure 10.7   A Rum & Coke with labeled ingredients

Adding a Second Drink

Now you'll repeat the process just described to define a second drink: a Tom Collins. Like the Rum & Coke, the Tom Collins consists of a containing section element, a div for each ingredient, and a p and a strong element inside the div that represents each ingredient. The drink is rounded off by an h2 element that calls out the name of this drink (see Listing 10.12).

Listing 10.12   **HTML for the Tom Collins (drinks.html)**

```
<section id="tomcollins">
  <div class="tumbler">
    <div id="tcGin">
      <p><strong>Gin</strong></p>
    </div>
    <div id="tcClubSoda">
      <p><strong>Club Soda</strong></p>
    </div>
    <div id="tcLemon">
      <p><strong>Lemon</strong></p>
    </div>
  </div>
  <h2>Tom Collins</h2>
</section>
```

Base Styles for the Second Drink

In Listing 10.13, you define the basic styles for the drink and all its ingredients. You position this drink 250 pixels to the left of the containing #bar element (which is the containing block). The first ingredient, gin, is positioned at the bottom of the glass tumbler. Since it will make up two parts of the drink, you set its size to 20%. In the p element, you set both a top border color and a background-color.

Next, you set up the initial position, height, background-color, and animation-delay for the second ingredient, club soda. To make the club soda begin rising only after the gin has completed the rise animation, you wait 2 seconds before the rise animation runs on the #tcClubSoda's p element.

To make the text label for the club soda appear only after the club soda has appeared, you delay the animation by 4 seconds before running it. This 4-second delay includes the 2 seconds that the rise animation takes on the #tcClubSoda element and the 2-second animation delay applied to the #tcClubSoda element.

Listing 10.13   **CSS for Tom Collins Ingredients (drinks.css)**

```
#tomcollins { left: 250px; }
#tcGin {
  bottom: 0;
  height: 20%;
}
#tcGin p {
```

```
  border-top: 2px solid rgba(0,0,0,.3);
  background-color: rgb(231,255,255);
}


#tcClubSoda {
  bottom: 21%;
  height: 30%;
}


#tcClubSoda p {
  background-color: white;
  -webkit-animation-delay: 2s;
}
#tcClubSoda p strong {
  -webkit-animation-delay: 4s;
}
```

Delaying the Pouring of a Third Ingredient

Listing 10.14 defines the animation delay required to ensure that the third and final ingredient in the Tom Collins, the lemon juice, animates at the right time. Here you follow the same pattern outlined in Listings 10.10 and 10.13. Rather than delay the `rise` animation by only 2 seconds, though, you delay it by 4 seconds. This ensures that the lemon juice rises only after both the gin and club soda ingredients have been animated.

Listing 10.14   Delaying the Animation of the Lemon Juice (drinks.css)

```
#tcLemon { bottom: 51%; height: 10%;}
#tcLemon p {
  background-color: yellow;
  -webkit-animation-delay: 4s;
}
```

Similarly, in order to make the Lemon text appear only after the lemon's p element has risen into view, in Listing 10.15 you increase the delay of the `ingredientFadeIn` animation. Recall from Listing 10.10 that all elements that match the selector `.tumbler div p strong` will play the `ingredientFadeIn` animation, and this includes the `strong` element inside `#tcLemon`. You set the animation delay to 6 seconds. This 6 seconds includes the 4-second delay before the `#tcLemon` p element is visible and the 2 seconds the `rise` animation takes to run.

Listing 10.15   Delaying the Display of the Lemon Juice Label (drinks.css)

```
#tcLemon p strong {
  -webkit-animation-delay: 6s;
}
```

Adding the Remaining Drinks

The HTML and CSS for the remaining drinks follow the same basic pattern outlined above for the Rum & Coke and the Tom Collins drinks. You can find the complete code for the remaining four drinks on GitHub, at https://github.com/alexisgo/LearningCSSAnimations/tree/master/ch10code.

Citing Data Sources

Our final step is to ensure that you have provided links to the sources of all the data. You will add this information in its own section, called #sources, where you will build up an unordered list containing all the links to the relevant Wikipedia page where you obtained the information about the ratio of ingredients in a given drink. The #sources element is given a specific size and position, and the links are styled to be white. Listing 10.16 shows the HTML, and Listing 10.17 shows the CSS. Figure 10.8 shows a close-up of the resulting graphic.

Listing 10.16   **HTML for the Infographic's Citations (drinks.html)**

```
<section id="sources">
  <strong>Sources:</strong>
  <ul>
    <li>
      <a href="http://en.wikipedia.org/wiki/Cuba_Libre">
        http://en.wikipedia.org/wiki/Cuba_Libre (Rum &amp; Coke)
      </a>
    </li>
  <!-- excluding additional list items and links for brevity -->
  </ul>
</section>
```

Listing 10.17   **CSS for the Infographic's Citations (drinks.css)**

```
#sources {
  background-color: gray;
  top: 650px;
  /* need the !important to override
  the '#bar section' selector */
  width: 800px !important;
  margin-left: -20px !important;
  padding: 20px;
  color: white;
}

#sources a {
  color:white;
}
```

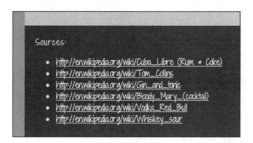

Figure 10.8   The infographic's sources `section`

Supporting Older Browsers with Modernizr

When considering fallbacks for infographics, your initial inclination may be to take a screenshot of the resulting graphic built through CSS3 and simply present this large static image as a fallback. But you actually don't even need to do this, given how you have built this example.

The only new HTML5 or CSS3 feature used in this example that older browsers won't safely ignore is the new HTML5 semantic elements. But because you are using Modernizr, which includes the html5Shim, any of the new elements that older browsers don't recognize will still be able to be styled. You can see in Figure 10.9 that, although it is imperfect, the graphic still renders even in Internet Explorer 6. The animation won't play, but you still see all your elements, simply with fewer graphic enhancements: You don't have rounded corners or a slight box shadow on the `h1`, but you can see the drinks and all their ingredients and still glean the main content from the infographic.

Figure 10.9   The drinks infographic rendered in Internet Explorer 6

Additional Resources

For further reading on using CSS3 for infographics, I recommend the following examples and resources:

- Why You Should Build Your Infographics in HTML5 and CSS3 from Paul Rouget: http://paulrouget.com/e/infographicsInHTML5/

- CSS3 infographic of top 4 GOP candidate Google search trends from January 2012: http://existdissolve.com/2012/01/css3-infographic/

- The JavaScript library D3.js: http://d3js.org

Summary

In this chapter, you combined CSS3 effects with CSS animations to make a more compelling infographic than one made from a large, static image. You defined two main animations to be shared across all the elements of the page: one to make the levels of ingredients rise and one to fade in text labels. You used keyframes to declare specific, per-element delays to the animations, even when multiple elements share a single animation.

Challenge

While you've already added the major liquid ingredients in each of these common mixed drinks, you haven't added the garnishes that typically accompany them. As a challenge for this chapter, enhance the drinks infographic to include garnishes. For example, use CSS and CSS3 effects to draw a celery stick for the Bloody Mary or a lime slice for the Rum & Coke.

Once you have created graphics for these garnishes, use CSS animations to add some movement to the garnishes. You could make the celery stick sway back and forth in the Bloody Mary or emulate a squeeze to the lime slice into the Rum & Coke.

Building Interactive Infographics

A natural enhancement to infographics on the web is the addition of interactivity through a language such as JavaScript or a library such as jQuery. In this chapter, you will make some simple additions to the infographic from Chapter 10, "Creating Animated Infographics," enhancing it with the details of the drink recipes, using a combination of CSS animations and jQuery.

One thing that is missing from the example in Chapter 10 is a written description of the drink ingredients. For example, you *visually* demonstrated that a Rum & Coke is composed of one part rum and two parts cola, but you did not detail this in text anywhere on the page. In this chapter, you will amend that. You will add the information to the HTML such that it is viewable via a screen reader, but you will use CSS to initially hide it. You'll then use CSS animations to reveal the information in response to a user's click.

Creating an Element to Hold the Drink Recipes

To display the complete recipe for each drink, you will make use of a new `section` element to which you'll give the class `recipes`. The `recipes` element will contain a series of `ul` elements outlining the ingredient list for each drink presented. A `strong` element will contain the name of the drink. Each `li` element will contain an ingredient, except for the final one, which will link to the Wikipedia page for the mixed drink.

You need to make sure the order of the ingredients in the glass tumblers matches the order in the HTML of the recipe page. This is because you will later use the `nth-of-type()` pseudo-class (see Listing 11.8) to match clicked drinks to their relevant recipes.

Listing 11.1 shows the first two of the `ul` elements containing recipes; this listing omits the final four for brevity and because they follow the same pattern outlined in the first two `ul` elements. The complete HTML can be found on the book's GitHub page, at https://github.com/alexisgo/LearningCSSAnimations/. You can also view a demo of the webpage you are building in this chapter at http://alexisgo.github.com/LearningCSSAnimations/ch11code/drinks.html.

Listing 11.1   **Adding the HTML for the Recipes of Each Drink (drinks.html)**

```html
<section class="recipes">
  <h3>Rum &amp; Coke</h3>
  <ul>
    <li>One Part Rum</li>
    <li>Two Parts Coke</li>
    <li>Garnish with Lemon or Lime</li>
    <li><a href="http://en.wikipedia.org/wiki/Cuba_Libre">Complete Recipe at
    ✻Wikipedia</a></li>
  </ul>
  <h3>Tom Collins</h3>
  <ul>
    <li>Two Parts Gin</li>
    <li>Four Parts Club Soda</li>
    <li>One Part Lemon Juice</li>
    <li><a href="http://en.wikipedia.org/wiki/Tom_Collins">Complete Recipe at
    ✻Wikipedia</a></li>
  </ul>
</section>
```

Styling the Drink Recipes

Next, in Listing 11.2, you outline the basic styles for the `recipes` element: its `width` and starting position. You begin with the `recipes` element positioned offscreen to the right, at `-300px`. You set the `z-index` to 2 to ensure that when you move the `recipes` element into view, it overlaps the drink elements. You also set up a `transition` for the `right` and the `top` property so that once you update these values to move the `recipes` element onscreen, this change is animated.

Finally, you give the `recipes` element a gradient background. Figure 11.1 shows the resulting recipe page.

Listing 11.2 and the other listings throughout this chapter use only the `-webkit-` syntax for brevity. You can find the final code, with all prefixes, at http://github.com/alexisgo/LearningCSSAnimations/.

Listing 11.2   **Styling the `recipes` Element (recipes.css)**

```css
.recipes {
  width: 250px;
  position: absolute;
  top: 60px;
  right: -300px;
  z-index: 2;
  -webkit-transition: right 1s, top 1s;

  background: #e3c997;
```

```
/* Gradient code generated by colorzilla.com;
Complete list of vendor prefixes defined in the
recipes.css file at:
http://github.com/alexisgo/LearningCSSAnimations */
background: -webkit-radial-gradient(center, ellipse cover,  #e3c997 67%,#dcbd87
*87%,#cda567 100%);
background: radial-gradient(ellipse at center,  #e3c997 67%,#dcbd87 87%,#cda567
*100%);
}
```

Figure 11.1   The recipes element, which holds the drink recipes

Hiding the Ingredients by Default

Unless a drink has been clicked on, you do not want to display the recipe for it. Therefore, you must define the default styles for all the recipes—which are each contained inside a ul element—to be invisible.

In Listing 11.3, you set the display property of ul elements inside the recipes element to be none. You use display:none on the ul element rather than opacity:0 because if you used the latter, when you click from one drink to another, while the recipe won't be visible, the height of the recipes element will be enlarged to contain the text of all the ul elements.

Listing 11.3   **CSS to Initially Hide the Recipe's ul Element (recipes.css)**

```
.recipes ul {
  margin-top: 0;
  padding: 0 10px;
  display: none;
}
```

In Listing 11.4, you set the styles for the h3 elements and the li elements inside the recipes element. You set the display type for the h3 elements to none initially, and you set the initial opacity of all li elements inside the recipes element to 0.

Listing 11.4 **CSS to Initially Hide the `h3` and `li` Elements (recipes.css)**

```css
.recipes h3 {
  padding: 10px 0;
  margin: 0 20px;
  display: none;
}

.recipes ul li {
  opacity: 0;
}
```

Unveiling the Recipe Page

Next, you will define how the recipe page should look when it is made visible. You do this by defining the CSS for a class called `visible`. You can use jQuery to both set up the event handlers and add the class `visible` to the appropriate elements when those event handlers are called. But before you get into the jQuery, let's examine the CSS that will make the recipe page visible.

Sliding in the Recipe Page

In Listing 11.5, you specify that once the class `visible` has been applied, the location of the `recipes` element moves from its initial location offscreen to 20 pixels from the right edge of the window. You also add a basic `box-shadow` to the element to make it look like it is resting over the drinks.

Recall that in Listing 11.2 you set up a transition on changes to the `right` property:

```css
-webkit-transition: right 1s;
```

Because you previously set this transition, the change to the `right` property will be animated, causing the `recipes` element to slide in from the right. Figure 11.2 illustrates the recipe page sliding in when the visible class has been applied. Note that you are using jQuery to apply the visible class, and this jQuery code is defined later on, in Listing 11.7.

You also want to reveal the text that the recipe contains, which includes the drink title in the h3 element and the ingredient list stored in the ul element. Recall from Listing 11.3 that these ul and h3 elements are initially set to `display:none`. In Listing 11.5, you change the ul and h3 elements' `display` type to `block` when the `visible` class is present.

Listing 11.5 **Bringing the Recipe into View (recipes.css)**

```css
.recipes.visible {
  right: 20px;
  -webkit-box-shadow: -2px 2px 5px rgba(0,0,0,0.3);
  box-shadow: -2px 2px 5px rgba(0,0,0,0.3);
```

```
}

.recipes ul.visible,
.recipes h3.visible {
  display: block;
}
```

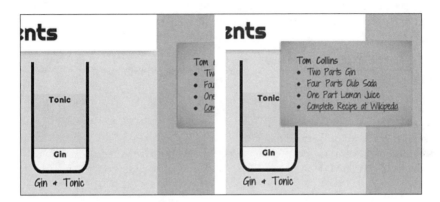

Figure 11.2   Sliding in the recipe page

Making the Recipe Visible When the User Clicks a Drink

In order to use the styles defined on the `visible` class (refer to Listing 11.5), you must add this class to your code. To unveil a recipe in response to a user clicking on the relevant drink, you must add the `visible` class programmatically. When a drink's name or any portion of the drink itself is clicked, the recipe page will slide in from the right, as explained previously.

To achieve this, you can use jQuery. To begin, in Listing 11.6 you define a function called `setup` that is called as soon as the entire page has loaded (`$(document.ready(setup))`).

Listing 11.6   **The Setup Method (drinks.js)**

```
$(document).ready(setup);

function setup() {
  // continued in Listing 11.
}
```

Next, you build on the `setup` function begun in Listing 11.6 in order to set up code that will run in response to the user clicking on one of the drink labels (defined as h2 elements—see the file drinks.html or Listing 10.4 in Chapter 10). You do so by using jQuery's `on()` method, which allows you to define what code should be run in response to some specific user action on a given element (or elements).

In Listing 11.7, you use on() to bind the click event of each h2 element within the containing #bar element to an anonymous function. The code in this anonymous function will be called when any of the drink h2 elements are clicked. The new code you are adding to the setup function appears in boldface in Listing 11.7.

In the anonymous function, you call two additional functions: resetClasses and revealRecipe. resetClasses, defined a bit later, in Listing 11.9, clears out any previously visible recipes when you switch from one drink to another. revealRecipe, defined in Listing 11.8, triggers the animation that brings in the recipe page.

Listing 11.7   **The Basic h2 Click Handler (drinks.js)**

```
$(document).ready(setup);


function setup() {
  // if we click on a drink's title
  $('#bar h2').on('click', function() {
    resetClasses($(this));
    revealRecipe($(this));
  });
}
```

Determining the Recipe for the Selected Drink

Next, you will define the function revealRecipe, which displays the appropriate recipe in response to a drink's h2 element being clicked. To accomplish this, you will leverage the fact that the order of the section elements that make up the drinks matches the order of the ul elements containing the recipe text in the recipes element. You can determine the index of the selected drink and then use that index number to display the corresponding recipe by making the ul:nth-of-type(index) element visible.

Revealing the Recipe Page When Drink Titles Are Clicked

The first thing you do in the revealRecipe function is determine which drink was clicked on. In Listing 11.8 you use two jQuery methods, closest() and index(), to determine which drink was clicked on and, thus, which recipe to display.

closest('section') begins at the current element (the h2 that has been clicked), and then searches up through the DOM for the first instance of a section element. Because every drink h2 element is contained within a section element, calling closest in this way returns the containing drink element.

The closest method indicates which section drink element you're on, but you also need to know the *index* of this element. You need to know this so that you can use the index number to match your drink section element with its corresponding recipe. For example, Gin and Tonic is the second drink section element, so you need to reveal the second ul element inside recipes.

You accomplish this by calling the index method on the results of closest('section'). Because you need to know where the selected drink is in relation to the other section elements that contain drinks, you can pass the selector '#bar section' (defined in the drinks.css code in Chapter 10 and used again here) to the index method. When you pass this selector to the index method, the method returns the position of the closest('section') element relative to all the other section elements contained within #bar.

You then use this drinkIndex value to determine which ul in the recipes element to make visible—which you accomplish by adding the class visible to the correct ul element by passing the drinkIndex value to the selector '.recipes ul:nth-of-type(drinkIndex) '.

Listing 11.8 **The revealRecipe Function (drinks.js)**

```
function revealRecipe($elem) {
  var drinkIndex = $elem.closest('section').index('#bar section') + 1;
  $('.recipes ul:nth-of-type(' + drinkIndex + ')').addClass('visible');
  $('.recipes h3:nth-of-type(' + drinkIndex + ')').addClass('visible');
}
```

Selecting the Correct Index

One important thing to note about the jQuery index method is that it is *zero based*. In other words, the first matched element has an index of 0. So if you click the first drink, Rum & Coke, $(this).closest('section').index('#bar section') returns 0 as the index. If you click on Gin & Tonic, the index returned is 2. This is typical behavior of indexes in programming. The problem in this case, however, is that you want to match the index returned with the correct ul element in the recipes element, and you do so by using the nth-of-type pseudo-class.

The nth-of-type pseudo-class is *not* zero based. To style the first li element in a list using nth-of-type, you must style li:nth-of-type(1). Trying to select li:nth-of-type(0) returns null.

For example, compare the console output for the following two lines of code:

```
console.log("nth(0) " + $('.recipes li:nth-of-type(0)').html());
console.log("nth(1) " + $('.recipes li:nth-of-type(1)').html());
```

Figure 11.3 shows the results of this code As you can see, nth-of-type(0) returns null, and nth-of-type(1) returns the first drink recipe.

Figure 11.3 nth-of-type(0) returns null

> **Alternate Approaches to Revealing the Correct Recipe**
>
> You might wonder why you don't give each drink an `id` and each recipe in the `recipes` ele-ment an `id` and then set up a click handler and appropriate CSS selector for each. You could indeed take that approach. The downside of that approach, though, is that it involves sub-stantially more code. The approach you've taken instead, which is to determine the index of the drink clicked, allows you to match that index to the index of the appropriate recipe in the `recipes` element and then utilize the `nth-of-type` pseudo-class in order to make the cor-rect recipe visible. This approach reduces the amount of CSS customization and the amount of code overall that you need to write to achieve the effect you want.

Hiding an Old Recipe When a New Drink Is Clicked

When a new drink is clicked, you don't want the recipe from the previous drink to still be displayed. In order to hide the recipe of the last drink clicked, on the next click, you must remove all visible classes. You accomplish this via the function `resetClasses`.

Listing 11.9 defines the function `resetClasses`. The first thing you do in this function is make the `recipes` element visible by adding the class `visible` to the element. This is accomplished via jQuery's `addClass()` method.

Next, you remove any previous instances of `class="visible"` on `ul` elements nested in the `recipes` element. This is to clear out earlier recipes when clicking from recipe to recipe. Without this line, previous recipe text would remain visible.

Listing 11.9   **The `resetClasses` Function (drinks.js)**

```
function resetClasses($elem) {
  //removes ALL classes from the elems that match
  // these jQuery selectors
  $('.recipes ul, .recipes h3, .recipes ul li').removeClass();
  $('.recipes').removeClass('row2');
  $('.recipes').addClass('visible');


}
```

Adjusting the `recipes` Element Placement for the Second Row of Drinks

For the Bloody Mary, Red Bull & Vodka, and Whiskey Sour drinks, the position of the `recipes` element is a bit high. In order to lower the placement of the `recipes` element for these three drinks, you can once again use the `nth-of-type` pseudo-class. In Listing 11.10, you add a few lines to the `resetClasses` function (the added code appears in bold) in order to specify that any drink with an index of 4 or greater will have the class `row2` applied to it. This `row2` class (defined in Listing 11.11) will change the location of the `recipes` element to be closer to the drinks in the second row.

Listing 11.10   **Adding the `row2` Class to Drinks in the Second Row (drinks.js)**

```
function resetClasses($elem) {
  //removes ALL classes from the elems that match
  // these jQuery selectors
  $('.recipes ul, .recipes h3, .recipes ul li').removeClass();
  $('.recipes').removeClass('row2');
  $('.recipes').addClass('visible');

  // which drink I'm on
  var drinkIndex = $elem.closest('section').index('#bar section') + 1;
  if (drinkIndex >= 4) {
    $('.recipes').addClass('row2');
  }
}
```

In Listing 11.11, you set the value of `top` to `350px` for the recipe page when both the `visible` and `row2` classes have been applied. In this code listing, you also modify the transition previously defined in the `.recipes` selector to define an additional transition for changes to the `top` property, which will ensure that changes to `top` are animated.

Listing 11.11   **Styling the `recipes` Element for Row 2 Drinks (recipes.css)**

```
.recipes.visible.row2 {
  top: 350px;
}
.recipes {
  // we are updating the code previously defined in Listing 11.2
  -webkit-transition: right 1s, top 1s;
}
```

Fading in the Recipe Text

Currently, when you click away from one drink h2 element and onto another, the recipe text changes instantly. You will now define an animation to fade the text in instead. You will use this animation when you change which drink recipe you are viewing. In Listing 11.12 you set up a keyframe animation called `fadeTextIn` that changes the opacity from 0 to 1. You apply this simple keyframe with `animation-fill-mode` set to `forwards`, in the `.recipes ul.visible li` selector. This ensures that the changes to opacity are preserved past the end of the animation.

Listing 11.12   **Setting Up the `li` Elements to Fade In (recipes.css)**

```
@-webkit-keyframes fadeTextIn {
  0% { opacity: 0; }
  100% { opacity: 1; }
}
```

```
.recipes ul.visible li {
  /* forwards ensures that we preserve the end state of opacity 1 */
  -webkit-animation: fadeTextIn 1.5s forwards;
}
```

There's one problem with the code defined in Listing 11.12: It relies on a CSS animation to change the opacity to 1 for the li elements of the selected drink recipe. This is fine for browsers that support CSS animations, but for those that don't, when you click a drink, the recipe page will appear, but the li elements will not, as their opacity will still be set to 0.

To fix this, you can use Modernizr and create a new selector to handle browsers that do not support CSS animations. In Listing 11.13, you prepend .cssanimations to the existing selector .recipes ul.visible li. This ensures that you set up the keyframe animation fade-TextIn only if the browser supports it. You also add a new selector (which appears in bold, to distinguish it from the existing code), .no-cssanimations .recipes ul.visible li. In this selector, which is for browsers that don't support CSS animations, you manually change the li element's opacity back to 1 so that the recipe page's text is visible.

Listing 11.13   **Setting Up the li Elements to Fade In (recipes.css)**

```
.cssanimations .recipes ul.visible li {
  -webkit-animation: fadeTextIn 1.5s forwards;
  -moz-animation: fadeTextIn 1.5s forwards;
  -o-animation: fadeTextIn 1.5s forwards;
  animation: fadeTextIn 1.5s forwards;
}

.no-cssanimations .recipes ul.visible li {
  opacity:1;
}
```

Highlighting the Selected Ingredient

In addition to allowing the user to click the h2 drink title elements, you should allow the user to click on the drink ingredients to also reveal the recipe details. Any time one particular ingredient is clicked, you will highlight that ingredient on the recipe page by adding text-shadow to it. But rather than add the text-shadow all at once, you'll slowly add it through a keyframe animation.

Animating Changes to the Selected Ingredient

Listing 11.14 defines an animation to change the text-shadow property on the li in the recipes element for the ingredient div that is currently selected. The glow animation begins with no `text-shadow` applied to the `li`. Then, from 0% through 50% of the animation, you apply four different `text-shadow` properties, one to the bottom right of the element, one to the bottom left, one to the top left, and one to the top right. This creates a smoky glow around the element. You let that effect remain for 10% of the animation's duration by making the 60% keyframe empty (thus preserving the prior effect from keyframe 50% to 60%). Then, from 60% to 100% of the animation, the `text-shadow` shrinks to just a single `text-shadow` at the bottom right of the `li`'s text.

Because the `.recipes ul.visible li` selector previously had an animation set (the `fadeInText` animation), if, in the `.recipes ul li.highlight` selector you simply set up the glow animation, you'll overwrite the `fadeInText` animation. Thus, you must instead specify both. Figure 11.4 approximates the effect of this animation.

Listing 11.14   **Highlighting the Selected Ingredient (recipes.css)**

```
@-webkit-keyframes glow {
  0% {}
  50% {  text-shadow: 2px 2px 10px gray,
         -2px -2px 10px gray,
         -2px 2px 10px gray,
         2px -2px 10px gray; }
  60% {}
  100% { text-shadow: 1px 1px 10px black;}
}

.recipes ul li.highlight {
  -webkit-animation: fadeTextIn 1.5s both, glow 2s forwards 0.5s;
}
```

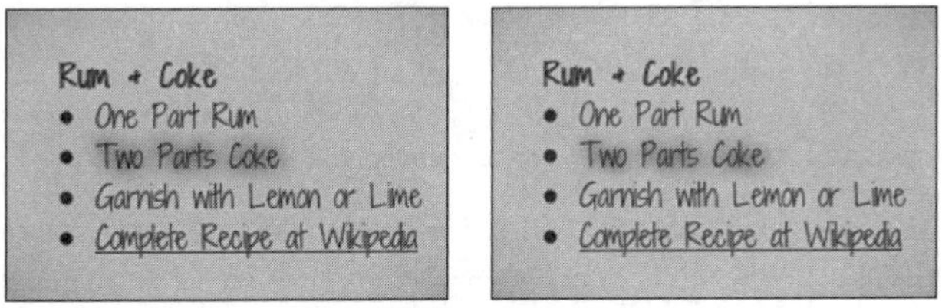

Figure 11.4   A pulsing shadow effect for highlighted ingredients

Triggering the Ingredient Highlight via jQuery

In Listing 11.15, you set up yet another jQuery click handler to also reveal the recipe page upon clicking an individual drink ingredient.

As you did in Listing 11.7, when setting up the code to respond to clicks on the `h2` drink elements, you first call the functions `resetClasses` and `revealRecipe` (defined in

Listings 11.9 and 11.8, respectively). As a reminder, the `resetClasses` function adds the visible class to the parent `recipes` element and removes any other prior instances of the class visible on `ul`. The `revealRecipe` handles unveiling the recipe page.

Listing 11.15   **Making the Selected Ingredient's Parent Drink Visible (drinks.js)**

```
$('.tumbler div').on('click', function() {
  resetClasses($(this));
  revealRecipe($(this));


  // continued in Listing 11.16
}
```

Now that you have ensured that the correct recipe is displayed, you need to determine which ingredient was clicked, so you can add a class called `highlight` to that ingredient.

In Listing 11.16 you determine which ingredient to add the `glow` animation to by matching the index of the clicked ingredient `div` with the `li` of the `recipes` element. The `glow` animation is added to that `li` element by applying the class `highlight` to it.

Listing 11.16   **Highlighting the Selected Ingredient (recipes.css)**

```
$('#bar section .tumbler div').on('click', function() {
  // continued from Listing 11.15

  //add one since nth-of-type(1) is the first elem; nth-of-type(0) is null
  var ingredientIndex = $(this).index() + 1;

  // find the right ingredient element
  var elem = '.recipes '
    + 'li:nth-of-type('
    + ingredientIndex + ')';

  // add highlight class to the right ingredient in the paper
  $(elem).addClass('highlight');
});
```

Ensuring Compatibility in Older Browsers

Currently, when you click an ingredient, the `text-shadow` is added by the `glow` keyframe animation. For browsers that don't support CSS animations, this animation does not run, and the `text-shadow` is never added. To amend this, you can use Modernizr to add the `text-shadow` without an animation when ingredients are clicked in browsers that do not support CSS animation.

In Listing 11.17, you first amend an existing selector by simply prepending the class selector `.cssanimations` in front of it. This addition is displayed in bold. Doing this ensures that after an ingredient is clicked, you set up the CSS animations only if the browser actually supports them.

The next selector (which is all new code and thus is all in bold) is for browsers that do *not* support CSS animations. While you could simply explicitly set text-shadow here, that's not an ideal approach because some of the browsers (or versions of browsers) that don't support CSS animations also do not support text-shadow (for example, Internet Explorer 9). Thus, instead of adding text-shadow here, you make the highlighted li element bold instead.

Listing 11.17   **Adding text-shadow on Highlighted Ingredients in All Browsers (recipes.css)**

```
.cssanimations .recipes ul li.highlight {
  -webkit-animation: fadeTextIn 1.5s both, glow 2s forwards 0.5s;
  -moz-animation: fadeTextIn 1.5s both, glow 2s forwards 0.5s;
  -o-animation: fadeTextIn 1.5s both, glow 2s forwards 0.5s;
  animation: fadeTextIn 1.5s both, glow 2s forwards 0.5s;
}


.no-cssanimations .recipes ul li.highlight {
  font-weight:bold;
}
```

Changing the Cursor

The final tweak you will make to this example is to make it obvious which parts of the info-graphic are clickable. Currently, because neither the h2 drink labels nor the ingredients are link elements, the cursor is a simple black arrow when you hover over them.

In order to make it obvious that the h2 drink elements and the ingredients are clickable, you can change the cursor to a pointer for these elements. You do so by setting cursor: pointer on each one, as outlined in Listing 11.18. The new lines added to the drinks.css file are high-lighted in bold in Listing 11.18.

Listing 11.18   **Changing the Drink h2 and Ingredients Cursor to Pointers (drinks.css)**

```
#bar section h2 {
  font-size:1.1em;
  margin:5px 0;
  text-align:center;
  cursor:pointer;
}
.tumbler div {
  width:100px;
  position:absolute;
  cursor: pointer;
}
```

> **Additional Resources**
>
> To see how others are using CSS3 and JavaScript to build interactive infographics, I recommend exploring the following examples:
>
> - HTML/CSS infographic of NASA's Mars Rover *Curiosity* landing: http://mars.jpl.nasa.gov/msl/multimedia/interactives/edlcuriosity/index-2.html
> - 8 Interactive Infographics Created with HTML, CSS and Javascript from Designmodo: http://designmodo.com/interactive-infographics/
> - Jamie Brightmore's Interactive infographic about Dribbble: http://lab.4muladesign.com/dribbble/

Summary

In this chapter, you enhanced the infographic you created in Chapter 10 by adding HTML that contains the recipe text for each drink. You also made the infographic interactive by making some of the elements of the infographic clickable. You made these elements clickable through the use of jQuery and then animated changes to elements with CSS animations in response to user clicks.

Challenge

The challenge from Chapter 10 was to enrich the drinks in the infographic to include garnishes such as a celery stick for the Bloody Mary or a lime slice for a Rum & Coke and to animate them. For this chapter's challenge, make the animations to the garnishes you added in the previous chapter triggered by clicks rather than played when the page loads.

If you didn't add garnishes yet, do so now and then have them animate when a user clicks on them. Make the celery stick stir the Bloody Mary when it is clicked. And make a lime slice appear to get squeezed when clicked (via a scale transform, for example).

Index

E

Z

THE MANCHESTER COLLEGE
COLLEGE LIBRARIES
ASHTON OLD ROAD
MANCHESTER
M11 2WH